An
Accident *of* Hope

An
Accident *of* Hope

The Therapy
Tapes of
Anne Sexton

Dawn M. Skorczewski

Routledge
Taylor & Francis Group
New York   London

Routledge
Taylor & Francis Group
711 Third Avenue
New York, NY 10017

Routledge
Taylor & Francis Group
27 Church Road
Hove, East Sussex BN3 2FA

© 2012 by Taylor & Francis Group, LLC
Routledge is an imprint of Taylor & Francis Group, an Informa business

Printed in the United States of America on acid-free paper
Version Date: 2011912

International Standard Book Number: 978-0-415-88746-5 (Hardback) 978-0-415-88747-2 (Paperback)

Library of Congress Cataloging-in-Publication Data

Skorczewski, Dawn.
    An accident of hope : the therapy tapes of Anne Sexton / Dawn M. Skorczewski.
       p. cm.
    Includes bibliographical references and index.
    ISBN 978-0-415-88746-5 (hardcover : alk. paper) -- ISBN
    978-0-415-88747-2 (pbk. : alk. paper) -- ISBN 978-0-203-83398-8 (e-book :
    acid-free paper)
    1. Sexton, Anne, 1928-1974--Criticism and interpretation. I. Sexton, Anne,
    1928-1974. II. Title.

    PS3537.E915Z876 2012
    811'.54--dc22   2011034294

Visit the Taylor & Francis Web site at
http://www.taylorandfrancis.com

and the Routledge Web site at
http://www.routledgementalhealth.com

Contents

Acknowledgments

My deepest gratitude to my writing partner, Wendy Walters, who has encouraged and guided me through every step of the long process from idea to book. Her advice and enthusiasm have carried me through many difficult periods. Thanks too, to my dear friend and walking partner, Ellen Rome, a voracious intellectual who can be trusted for honesty, insight, and genuine curiosity.

Linda Gray Sexton was first an inspiration to me as a writer. In the process of writing this book, she has become a valuable colleague and friend. She answered many questions about her mother and also approved of the excerpts to be published from the tapes. Our work together has brought me great joy and made me feel that in many ways the creative spirit of Anne Sexton is still very much alive.

Adrian Jones, author of an unpublished comprehensive study of Anne Sexton's poetry and therapy tapes, was a valued collaborator in this project. I know much more now than I did before I met Adrian, and this book has become a much more thorough study thanks to his research and advice. His study of Sexton's therapy will add much to my own when it appears in print.

I thank the endlessly patient and helpful staff of the Schlesinger Library for their invaluable assistance over the many years I have been listening to the tapes. I would also like to express my appreciation to the staff at the Harry Ransom Humanities Research Center in Austin, Texas, for cheerfully hunting down manuscripts and tapes. I owe a deep intellectual and personal debt to the late Diane Wood Middlebrook, who listened to all of the tapes and made a rough transcript of them, wrote a wonderful biography of Sexton, and attempted to assist me in the archival research in the last days of her battle with a terminal illness.

Kristopher Spring served as an insightful editor from the start, and I owe him credit for his vision and support. Danielle Berger and Jose Zelaya were fabulous copyeditors. Waite Warden provided sage editorial assistance and encouragement that kept me going from across the ocean during my sabbatical year.

Many thoughtful and generous friends, writers, and clinicians read portions of the manuscript and offered invaluable advice:

Deborah Britzman, Cara Crandall, Helen Epstein, Ellen Helman, Lynne Layton, Terri Maltzberger, Anna Ornstein, Matthew Parfitt, Ellen Pinsky, Lowell Rubin, Paula Salvio, and Martin Silverman.

Special gratitude to Ann Rea for traveling to the Austin archives with me and sharing my excitement in the final hours of research.

Thanks to Stijn Van Heule and Gert Beulens for inviting me to present portions of my manuscript in Ghent, Belgium. Stef Craps was especially helpful as he led me to consider aspects of trauma that had eluded my attention.

Joelle, Tess, Barbara, and Joseph Skorczewski have cheered me on for as long as I remember and they ask great questions. Emily Rome offered daily advice and encouragement, not to mention a fabulous triathlon partnership. And because of Leni Herzog, I would still not trade my state with kings.

Buzzy Jackson oversaw process and product with her infectious exuberance and keen intelligence. I especially appreciate her advice about titles, drafts and "just pressing send."

Finally, my most sincere and immense gratitude to Lewis Kirshner, who tirelessly read drafts, listened to half-formed ideas, and offered the kind of support, wisdom, and hope that could never be called an accident. This book would not be what it is without his suggestions and encouragement and vision. I dedicate it to him with all my love.

All of the poems that appear in this book, in full or in excerpt, appear in *The Complete Poems* (Sexton, 1999): "Briar Rose" (pp. 290–294); "Christmas Eve" (pp. 139–140); "Flee on Your Donkey" (pp. 97–105); "For John, Who Begs Me Not to Enquire Further" (pp. 34–35); "Housewife" (p. 77); "Little Girl, My Stringbean, My Lovely Woman" (pp. 145–148); "Menstruation at Forty" (pp. 137–138); "The Moss of His Skin" (pp. 26–27); "Old Dwarf Heart" (pp. 54–55); "Said the Poet to the Analyst" (pp. 12–13); "Self in 1958" (pp. 155–156); "Wanting to Die" (pp. 142–144); "The Wedding Night" (pp. 144–145); "You, Dr. Martin" (pp. 3–4); and "Young" (pp. 51–52). All appear courtesy of Houghton Mifflin.

Introduction

And if I tried
to give you something else,
something outside of myself,
you would not know
that the worst of anyone
can be, finally,
an accident of hope.

—"For John, Who Begs Me Not to Enquire Further"

In the poem cited above, Anne Sexton suggests that the damaged head—the psyche in need of psychiatric intervention—lies at the origin of creativity. Published in her first book, *To Bedlam and Part Way Back* (1960), "For John …" offers her most direct response to John Holmes, her first poetry teacher and earliest critic. Holmes had advised Sexton not to use her own experience as the subject of her poems. Sexton's poetic reply begins with an insistent reference to the source of her inspiration: "I tapped my own head/a cracked bowl," and it ends with an affirmation: "the worst of anyone/can be, finally/ an accident of hope." It is no accident that she claims "the worst of anyone" can offer "hope." After all, it was at her "worst," in a psychiatric hospital, with psychiatrist Dr. Martin Orne's encouragement, that Anne Sexton began her poetic career. Fewer than 10 years later, she achieved what had seemed an impossible "hope" a decade before; she won the Pulitzer Prize.

Anne Sexton wrote her first published poems in a mental institution. In the summer of 1956, at the age of 28, she experienced a postpartum depression that left her unable to care for herself or her two young children. She was admitted to Westwood Lodge, a neuropsychiatric mental hospital in Westwood, Massachusetts. There she met Dr. Martin Orne, who was just finishing his psychiatric training when he was assigned to Sexton's case. Orne was the son of Martha Brunner-Orne, Sexton's first psychiatrist, whom she'd seen for postpartum depression after the birth of her first daughter, Linda, in 1953. Orne was immediately effective with Sexton, who chose to see him two to three times per week until he left Boston in 1964. With Orne's encouragement, Sexton began to draw from personal experience to craft what became known as "confessional poems" about depression, suicide, women's bodies, family secrets, love affairs, war, God, and the complexities of human relationships. Her first volume, *To Bedlam and Part Way Back*, was published in 1960, just three years after she met Orne. By the end of the eight-year period of her treatment with him, she had received fellowships from Antioch and Bread Loaf to attend writers' conferences, been awarded a Bunting Fellowship, a traveling fellowship from the American Academy of Arts and Letters, and two Ford Foundation Fellowships. She had published two volumes of poetry, both nominated for the National Book Award, and received the Levinson Award from *Poetry* magazine. She had also written much of *Live or Die*, her third book, which would be awarded the Pulitzer Prize.

Martin Orne, just 29, was an ambitious resident psychiatrist who was also pursuing a Ph.D. in psychology when he met 28-year-old Anne Sexton. Born in Vienna, Orne was the son of a surgeon and a psychiatrist who left Austria with their son in 1938 to move to the United States. Orne received his bachelor's degree and doctorate from Harvard University and a medical degree from Tufts University. From the time he was an undergraduate, he published papers on the role of memory in hypnosis, research that questioned the validity of patients' memories that emerged when they were in trance. For most of the eight years he saw Anne Sexton for therapy, he conducted research in memory studies for four branches of the U.S. military: the Army, Marines, Air Force, and Navy. In later years, Orne was to become known as an expert on false memory syndrome. He also served as an expert witness on cases such as that of Patty Hearst, who was kidnapped and accused of assisting her captors in a bank robbery; Orne proclaimed her innocent.

When he was a graduate student and psychiatric resident, Orne's colleagues considered him a bit of a maverick because of his interest in hypnosis. And yet, in many ways, Orne embodied the psychiatric scene in Boston in the late 1950s and early 1960s. At the Massachusetts Mental Health Center, where he took his psychiatric residency, Freudian theory and ego psychology were embraced by his supervisors; most were also practicing psychoanalysts. Massachusetts Mental was a place in which doctors were thought to see the truth while it still remained obscure to their patients. In classic analytic style, questions from patients were very often met with silence to allow the unconscious meanings of the questions to emerge. It was also a cultural and psychiatric climate in which women's identities were thought to be found in attachment to marriage and children, and in which women's roles as sexual objects for men remained largely uncontested.

But Massachusetts Mental was also home to Orne's mentor, Elvin Semrad, a revered supervisor and clinician who was a training analyst at the Boston Psychoanalytic Society and Institute. Semrad had established a reputation for his folksy, empathic connection to patients and his reverence for the wisdom to be gathered from the details of people's lives. Orne clearly learned from his mentor about the value of his patients' stories and their pain, and he added his own conviction that patients who had found something productive to do with their lives fared better in treatment than those who did not. It is nonetheless extraordinary that in this cultural climate, in a mental ward in a Boston suburban mental institution, a psychiatrist's encouragement could help a young mother become an internationally published poet in scarcely two years. To this day, Sexton's poems are popular with women and men of all ages and educational backgrounds, including but not limited to readers who struggle with mental health issues.

Anne Gray Harvey Sexton was born in 1928, the youngest of three daughters in a wealthy suburban Boston family in Wellesley, Massachusetts. Sexton's father, Ralph, owned a wool business and her mother, Mary Gray Staples Harvey, educated at Wellesley, was the only child in a prestigious family that included journalists and politicians. Her mother's uncle was a former governor of Maine. The Harveys enjoyed an active social life and had their daughters when they were still in their 20s. As the youngest and most rambunctious child, Anne was often pronounced too clumsy and sloppily dressed to join in the family's social activities. When she did attend the family's formal dinners, she was regularly criticized by her father, who once left the table claiming that her acne was making him physically ill.

Sexton's great aunt, "Nana" Dingley, lived with the Harveys until Anne was 13. Nana was to provide Anne's only memories of loving physical contact. Nana offered afternoon cuddling sessions and back rubs, providing an especially intimate relationship compared to the formality and unavailability of Anne's parents. While Anne was asked to appear in formal dress for dinner, and to "put on the show" for her parents' friends during social events, she remembered no loving contact from them. In fact, she later described embarrassing examinations of her genitals by her mother (she had a cyst when she was five), and enemas that were painful as well as humiliating. Her father, whose personality changed completely when he was drunk, once beat Anne with a riding crop because she had stolen her sister's birthday money. His ambivalence toward Anne became loathing and ridicule in the evening, after cocktails, when he often made disgusted remarks about Anne's appearance or lewd sexual remarks about Anne and her sister Jane. Later, Sexton was to speculate about whether she had been sexually abused by Nana or her father, a question which returned in her therapy sessions dozens of times and which is the subject of many of her poems (as well as her Broadway play *Mercy Street*).

Sexton became a social butterfly once she entered adolescence, enjoying her role as the leader of a group of girlfriends. She began to write poetry to boys, the first of whom was her high school boyfriend, Jack McCarthy, who later reported that Anne's father traveled to his home to beg him to marry his daughter when Anne was only 16. During her senior year in high school Sexton published poems in the school paper, but when her mother accused her of plagiarizing Sara Teasdale, she stopped writing poetry. After high school, in 1947, Sexton attended finishing school at the Garland School in Boston. She became engaged and began planning a big wedding. However, in 1948, Sexton met and fell in love with Alfred Muller Sexton II, nicknamed Kayo. In August of the same year, afraid that she was pregnant, Sexton and Kayo took the advice of Anne's mother and eloped to North Carolina. She got her period before they crossed the state line, but the two were crazy about each other, and married anyway.

Anne and Kayo went to Colgate (where he was pre-med). She learned to cook, and attended many parties at his fraternity house, becoming the house mascot. Kayo left Colgate after a year, claiming that he was wasting his parents' money; he soon obtained a job in Ralph Harvey's wool business. The young couple lived with both parents alternately until Kayo was shipped overseas with the naval reserves. In the fall of 1952, Sexton joined him in San Francisco, where his ship was being overhauled. She almost immediately became pregnant, electing to return to Boston to stay at her parents' home for the remainder of her pregnancy. Their first daughter, Linda Gray Sexton, was born on July 21, 1953. Shortly thereafter, the Sextons bought a house in Newton Lower Falls, Massachusetts, and Sexton was forced to take on the responsibilities of motherhood and housekeeping on her own for the first time. Kayo's work as a traveling salesman in Anne's father's business kept him away from the house for a week at a time. Their second daughter, Joyce Ladd, was born August 4, 1955.

If daily life on her own with a two-year-old was not easy, it became unmanageable when the Sextons' second daughter, Joy, was born. In the summer of 1955, as Joy neared the age of one, 28-year-old Sexton began to feel overwhelmed by the responsibilities of motherhood. Alone in the house with two children, she became paranoid, depressed, and suicidal. She heard voices, fell into apparent trances, and twirled her hair into knots. She could not care adequately for either of her daughters, nor could she function as a wife to her husband Kayo. Frightened by the thought that she might kill herself and her children, she was subsequently admitted to Westwood Lodge. At Westwood, she met the youthful resident psychiatrist, Dr. Martin Orne. Almost as soon as they began to work together, Sexton chose him as her new therapist; they were to meet at least two or three times a week for the next eight years.

Sexton told Orne that the only thing for which she had a talent was prostitution, because she knew how to make men feel sexually powerful. Orne argued that her diagnostic tests revealed that she was actually very creative. He suggested that she might want to write about her experiences so that she could help others who suffered from similar problems to feel less alone (Middlebrook, 1991, p. 42). With Orne's encouragement, and after watching a PBS special in which Harvard professor and literary critic I. A. Richards explained how to write a sonnet, Sexton began to write poems again, poems that Orne proclaimed as "wonderful." Over the next six months, fueled by his encouragement, she brought him more than 60 completed poems, and, as she later told an interviewer, she knew she had "finally found something to do with [her] life!" (p. 43). In the fall of 1957, Sexton enrolled in a poetry workshop at the Boston Center for Adult Education, where she met the poet Maxine Kumin, her other most important interlocutor. As Sexton's closest friend, Kumin sat on the other end of the telephone wire writing poems in silence as Sexton wrote hers. They whistled when either wanted to try out a line. Kumin was later to argue that writing poetry enabled Sexton to endure her illness and extend her life for as long as she did (Sexton, 1999, p. iv).

From the start, it was clear to Orne that Sexton was unable to remember much from one session to the next. From his point of view, Sexton's "memory trouble" proved the biggest obstacle to her progress. To address this problem, he eventually suggested (at the end of 1960) that they tape her sessions so that she might listen to what they discussed and reflect upon it in between sessions. Orne believed that transcribing the sessions would help Sexton "understand what she was doing" (Middlebrook, 1991, p. 44). Faithfully transcribing each tape, Sexton often arrived at a session prepared to discuss what had transpired in the previous hour. She commented that she often only "heard" his part of the dialogue when she wrote it down. On several occasions, she told Orne that she was grateful for the tapes, and that she hoped one day that they could help someone else. Their mutual commitment to the taping process, which intensified in the

final months of the treatment, produced the data upon which this
book is based.

Medical professionals take a vow of confidentiality when it comes
to conversations between themselves and their patients. It was a
shock, therefore, when it was revealed that Orne had delivered the
tapes of his therapy sessions with Anne Sexton to her biographer,
Diane Wood Middlebrook, for her to use in writing *Anne Sexton: A
Biography* (1991). Hundreds of pages in newspapers, popular maga-
zines, and professional journals were devoted to the controversy.*
Although Orne reported that Sexton had offered the tapes to him as
a resource for patients who struggled with depression and bipolar disorder, and for those seeking to heal themselves through creative work,
the fact was that she had signed no legal agreement, and therefore
never gave Orne explicit permission to release the tapes.

In the flurry of editorials and articles published after the release
of the tapes was announced, many health professionals argued that
Sexton's psychiatrist violated the essential privacy of the therapeutic relationship by releasing the tapes. Some speculated that other
patients might be harmed by Orne's negligence. Others noted that the
dead do not have the same rights as the living. People from the literary
community contended that Sexton made a professional life out of the
kind of self-exposure that many patients fear, and that she would have
been thrilled to see that she and Dr. Orne had made it to the front
pages of the *New York Times*. Sexton's daughter Linda wrote to the
New York Times to defend Orne, and Orne himself entered the fray,
submitting that he suggested taping the sessions so that Sexton could
transcribe and therefore remember what she said from one therapeutic
hour to the next.

Perhaps because of the controversy surrounding the tapes, no
scholars have thus far followed Sexton's biographer into the archives
to listen to the recorded therapy sessions and published an account of
what they say. When I chose to do so and was granted access by Linda
Gray Sexton, Sexton's literary executor, I was amazed to discover that
these remarkable tapes far exceed what Sexton described when she

---

* Adrian Jones (2010) offers a thorough review of the responses to the release of the
  tapes.

offered them to Orne as a resource for others. The sessions do offer material that could be useful to patients who struggle with depression and bipolar disorder, as well as for patients seeking to heal themselves through creative work. They provide a vivid portrait of a woman's transformation from a high school-educated, depressed housewife into a nationally recognized public intellectual. But they also contain a firsthand account of at least one version of how psychotherapeutic practice shaped people's lives in the late 1950s and early 1960s. When considered in relation to Sexton's work, the tapes have the potential to transform our understanding of Anne Sexton as a woman poet struggling to establish her identity at a time when American culture left little room for women to become powerful poets and scholars in their own right.

The unique material of the tapes allows Sexton to speak for herself, 10 years before her death by suicide in 1974. In choosing to listen to the tapes and report on what I heard, I was aware that some readers might accuse me of voyeurism. Who wouldn't want to be invited into the private life of a famous controversial woman poet who was known to have had numerous affairs with men and women, including other famous poets? And yet, my reasons for listening had little to do with the details of Sexton's private life, although I was indeed curious to discover whether I would agree with Middlebrook and Orne that Anne Sexton had never been sexually abused. The results of my listening for this issue were inconclusive, although I present my version of the issue in Chapter 2.

My primary motivation was to figure out how Sexton's life as a patient in intensive psychotherapy, with a psychiatrist trained in a hospital known for its psychoanalytic approach to mental anguish, might help us understand her life as a famous poet. How did Sexton's therapy relate to her rise to fame as a woman who wrote about the most intimate matters? How did the private subjects of her poems relate to what she discussed in therapy, where she so often spoke about these subjects? Did these conversations shape not only her personal development but her mode of self-expression in her poetic *oeuvre*? In each chapter I consider the ways in which poetry, therapy, and the cultural climate inform and disturb one another.

Three years of audiotaped therapy sessions exist in the Schlesinger Library at Harvard University. This book explores only the last six months of tapes, when Sexton knew that Orne would soon be leaving Boston to accept a research position in Philadelphia. Of the 300 tapes in the collection, these are by far the most interesting. In her final months of therapy, Sexton discussed themes that were prominent throughout the treatment, while attempting to draw conclusions about what it all meant, so that she might take some lessons from their work into the future. But she also broke down as she struggled to imagine a life without her beloved Dr. Martin.

In the pages that follow, I invite readers to "listen in" on large segments of the final tapes, recorded in the months from November 1963 to April 1964. Her conversations with Orne about politics, domestic life, sex, violence, mental illness, motherhood, poetry, politics, and suicide provide fascinating perspectives on what it meant to be a woman, poet, wife, mother, and psychiatric patient in the early 1960s. The earlier tapes, which I do not study here, offer a picture of a very sick woman becoming well as she crafted poems, studied the art of poetry, and made connections with academics and writers that would last throughout her lifetime. The final tapes show something slightly different: an already successful poet who is struggling to maintain confidence in herself although she will soon lose her most important interlocutor, her beloved psychiatrist.

The experience of listening to the tapes cannot be fully represented. Some of them are barely audible, while others are interrupted by music, newscasts, and the sounds of children playing. It is immediately apparent that technology has come a long way since 1960. At times, Sexton and Orne sit in silence. Sometimes the tape of the session ends and music that had been previously recorded on the tape plays. Orne apparently reused tapes on which he had recorded music and television programs, and these would emerge at times, providing a kind of background to the session. As a historical note, Walter Cronkite's voice is audible on one tape, and an ad that describes secretaries as "floozies" can be heard on another. Classical music is also common, and it is clear that sometimes Sexton herself taped over painful sessions with what she told Orne was "beautiful music."

The tapes recorded toward the end of 1963, at which point this book begins, are of a better quality than many of those recorded before that time. Perhaps Orne had purchased new equipment. Sexton's voice sounds stronger, as does Orne's, and both are more audible. Orne's Viennese accent does not seem any weaker over the years, although Sexton's Boston Brahmin tones do seem more modulated. Most of the words on the tapes can be heard perfectly well, complete with Sexton's exclamatory "Oh, Dr. Orne!" and Orne's protracted "mmhmmm's." Some tapes feature the long silences of Sexton's trances, the dissociated states she entered when angry or upset, presumably in an attempt to manage her feelings. We can hear Orne's soothing voice as he attempted to coax her back to consciousness, and the flare of his anger when she refused to do so, even though the appointment had come to an end and another patient was waiting outside.

To listen to the tapes is also to hear the sounds of smoking, sounds that are not as common in our time as they were in Sexton's. It was not unusual for Sexton to ask Orne for a light or to offer him one. Sexton's long inhalations and slow exhalations punctuate many of her sentences. Orne's pipe catches fire at one point, although he soon extinguished it. On another occasion, she remarks that he has dumped tobacco down his shirt. During a session after he had left Boston, Orne apparently switched to cigarettes, because Sexton exclaimed that she was smoking his cigarette! If I could have found a way to signify the sounds of smoking in the sessions I cite, I would have done so, for it performs a rhythmic background to their hours.

Living in Anne Sexton's head for hours every day, and in Martin Orne's somewhat as well, I sometimes felt as if I'd joined the cast of the TV series *Mad Men*. There were discussions of a smart blue pantsuit she wore to see Dr. Tartakoff, and the lipstick Orne had never seen her without. Dozens of strands of pearls were broken on the floor of Orne's office; she twisted them while she spoke. Cocktail parties and cocktail hours abounded in their suburban neighborhood, sometimes completed by dancing into the wee hours of the morning. Many days were spent in darkness in her room, however, as depression kept her away from everyone, enraging her husband Kayo, who traveled for work and did housework as well. Her depressions also kept her from enjoying her children. She told Orne she was never, for example, awake when they went to school, because sleeping pills kept her unconscious into the later hours of the morning.

Sometimes the gossip in the sessions was fascinating. Sexton and Orne talked about other doctors a lot, particularly the psychoanalysts that her friends saw and what they said and did. Sexton met many doctors in her social circle as well, and could report on one who seemed to want to seduce her, or another who sounded like a buffoon. Other writers and patients also entered the sessions, for she was consulted for referrals and advice. When patients of other doctors sought Sexton's council, she spoke to Orne about advising them with pleasure, although she protested that she hardly knew why they sought her out for help. Nonetheless, she was proud of her ability to offer guidance to others in distress. "See, I'm just like you," Sexton exclaimed more than once, assuring Orne that she knew "all the right things to say."

When young poets wanted her to read their work, Sexton almost always agreed, but she did not refrain from sharing her opinions of them with Orne. She always sounded like an expert who knew exactly how much talent each poet had, and she frequently remarked that people wanted to become famous poets without devoting themselves to the task as assiduously as she herself did. She often commented that she was working on a poem, although she only sometimes discussed her poetry. As will become clear, I believe this is because Orne discouraged her from doing so. When she did, however, she seemed to feel so much better that it made me question Orne's decision about this important issue.

After each session was recorded, Sexton either took the tape home and played it, transcribing it in her notebook, or listened in an office across from Orne's. She wrote detailed transcripts of the sessions, and often studied old notebooks to see what she could learn from them. Many sessions began with her quoting from the transcript of the previous session, often exclaiming, "You were right! I was so stubborn, but you were right!" Orne used the tapes with other patients as well, although he always insisted that he did so only when it was indicated as important for the treatment. Orne claimed that he used the tapes infrequently, but Sexton once remarked that she saw many patients transcribing in the office near the waiting room before her own session, and once Orne accidentally gave her another patient's tape to listen to instead of her own. Sexton admitted that she did indeed listen to the other woman's tape, because she would "do anything to know [Orne]!" Sexton liked it that Orne's practice was quite unconventional, and she appreciated this fact, as well as his tendency to allow her to exceed the 50-minute hour (particularly during the early years of treatment, when Sexton's tendency to decompensate at the end of an hour was frequent).

Most critics who discuss Sexton's mental illness note that in her time there was not an existing diagnosis for bipolar illness with borderline features in the terms we understand it today. It is difficult to imagine how she, her family, and Orne himself tolerated Sexton's dark depressions, her self-absorption in the face of the emotional and physical needs of her daughters, and her almost constant demand for all the attention in a room. Sexton speaks on the tapes about slapping and hitting her daughter, and inviting both of her daughters to explore her body as well as to give her daily back rubs. When Linda was 14, long after Sexton's treatment with Orne had come to an end, Anne made morning visits to her daughter's room to masturbate against her daughter's body. Although she thought that Linda was asleep, Linda was profoundly affected by this betrayal, and later wrote about it in her two memoirs. In small and sometimes significant ways, Anne Sexton proclaimed herself an exception, demanding to be treated as if she were a child. At the same time, however, she poured out love for her family, performing her own role as mother in a perplexing paradox that Linda Gray Sexton explores in *Searching for Mercy Street: My Journey Back to My Mother, Anne Sexton* and *Half in Love: Surviving the Legacy of Suicide.*

Throughout the three years of recorded tapes, I listened to Anne Sexton attempting to come to terms with her illness and speculate about leaving it behind forever. She asks Orne to help her be honest about her feelings, although she admits that it feels almost impossible to do so at times. In her therapy as in her poetry, Sexton never left the subject of truth telling far behind. Beginning with the epigraph to her first volume, *To Bedlam and Part Way Back,* she identified writing poetry as a struggle toward and away from self-disclosure. Taken from a letter from Goethe to Schopenhauer, the passage asserts, "It is the courage to make a clean breast of it in the face of every question that makes the philosopher…. But most of us carry in our heart the Jocasta who begs Oedipus for God's sake not to inquire further" (Sexton, 1981, p. 2). Throughout her career, Sexton would remain preoccupied with the conflict between making a clean breast of it and not inquiring further, of exploring her early experiences and current conflicts and remembering what she had discovered. She would repeatedly enter and explore the murky waters of the incestuous material that Jocasta begs remain undisturbed.

Nowhere are these issues of disclosure and concealment more apparent than in her therapeutic conversations with Dr. Orne, conversations that were recorded precisely because of her tendency to forget most of what she said in her sessions. When Sexton transcribed each session before the next took place, she showed her determination to understand exactly what she was revealing to her therapist as she "made a clean breast of it." As she wrote in a letter to an aspiring poet in 1960, Sexton believed that

> writers … must try *not* to avoid knowing what is happening. Everyone has somewhere the ability to mask the events of pain and sorrow, call it shock…. But the creative person must not use this mechanism any more than they have to in order to keep breathing…. Hurt must be examined like a plague. (Sexton & Ames, 1977, p. 145)

Given Orne's and Sexton's interests in the theoretical bases of clinical work, it should not be surprising to readers that each chapter of this book considers their therapy sessions in terms of a clinical concept that has been contested and redefined in the half century after Sexton's treatment with Orne. Sexton and Orne worked together at a time when Michael Balint, Melanie Klein, Heinz Kohut, and D. W. Winnicott were not accepted by analysts in the United States, although most were in Europe (with the exception of Kohut). Orne might or might not have known of these theorists, but his practice certainly included traditional Freudian terms such as *transference* and *narcissism*. Sexton herself also read classical psychoanalytic literature, especially Freud and Erikson. Often she mentioned an idea from one of her readings to Orne, reminding him of a concept such as resistance, for example, to explain behavior that he found curious.

As I listened in to the final months of Sexton's therapy, I also considered the poems that Sexton wrote contemporaneously, which speak aptly to our own era even as they gesture backward to tell us something about the years in which they were composed. Often the poems tell us something about Sexton's relationship to Orne that we might not understand from merely listening to the tapes. Occasionally, they offer a way of understanding Sexton and the period of American history in which she lived and I wrote. Most frequently, the poems complement the sessions, and the sessions the poems, offering reciprocal interpretations of Sexton's life and work that could not be made without the two together.

The first five chapters of *An Accident of Hope* focus intently on the two-month period from November to December 1963, a period from which 18 tapes exist in the archive. These tapes offer a day-to-day and week-to-week impression of Sexton's therapy, as well as an opportunity to consider its relationship to the poetry she wrote during those two months. The final chapters move quickly from February to April 1964, as only eight recordings exist from this period. But the few tapes that we do have from February to April provide a picture of Sexton's struggle to keep herself together as Orne prepared to leave Boston, a struggle that led her to self-destructive patterns of drinking but also to write some of her most famous poems.

The subjects of poetry and therapy were intertwined for Sexton from the start. Chapter 1 considers Sexton's insistence that she and Orne cocreated her poetic identity, a claim Orne sharply denied. Their different views on this question invite us to consider contemporary versus classical theories of the analyst's participation in the treatment. Sexton's search for the roots of her mental problems often led her to examine painful and even traumatic childhood memories. Chapter 2 considers trauma theory from 1960 to the present to understand why both Sexton and her husband seemed spurred to marital violence in the aftermath of the Kennedy assassination. Chapter 3 explores a poem that arose from a therapeutic impasse. In a two-part conversation focused on disruption and repair, Sexton framed a new understanding of her relationship to Orne and to her own illness, a reframing most evident when considered in relation to the poem. Chapter 4 returns to the topic of domestic violence in Sexton's life, as it uses Ferenczi's concept of a "confusion of tongues" to speculate about Orne's effect on his patient's developing sense of a woman's identity outside the domestic frame of wife and mother in mid-December 1963. Chapter 5, the final tape of 1963, considers Orne's pattern of accusing Sexton of needing to feel special, as if this tendency were itself a disease, an accusation that she questioned in a poem and within a session. My discussion of this issue suggests that Orne and Sexton both, as Sexton put it, "wanted to be great." By his suppression of his own narcissism and his pejorative analysis of Sexton's, Orne pathologized what might be identified as the creative drive for recognition that was shared by doctor and patient.

Once Sexton knew Orne was most certainly leaving Boston, fewer recorded tapes made it into the archive. Perhaps Sexton destroyed these or they were lost, but the absence does seem to reflect her personal loss of coherence and determination in the face of Orne's departure. In Chapter 6, Oedipal themes, prominent in Sexton's therapy and poetry, come to the fore as she described her desire to track down a Wellesley physician she had once dated, and her trip to the same town to buy sexy black lingerie to show to her husband. Sexton's ability to move from desiring an illicit affair to engaging in what Orne called "healthy conventional sex" with Kayo signifies a developmental accomplishment. She seems to have learned to use Orne and her husband to meet her needs to feel loved. As she and Orne discuss her objects of desire, they visit Oedipal theory even as they foreshadow a wave of literature on the Oedipus complex that was still to come. Chapter 7 shows an often inebriated Sexton attempting to assimilate Orne's forthcoming move to Philadelphia as Orne himself appears to be stuck in a denial of the significance or even the reality of his departure. The chapter and the sessions it reviews revisit almost all of the central concepts that organized the entire treatment and reconsiders Sexton's role in her own healing process.

In the epilogue, I briefly quote from four tapes that Linda Gray Sexton removed from restricted access in the Sexton archive at the Harry Ransom Center in Austin, Texas, just as I was completing the manuscript of the book. I asked Linda to remove the restriction when I learned of their existence from scholar Adrian Jones, who has studied the tapes as part of his unpublished dissertation, "Resistance,

Rejection, Reparation: Anne Sexton and the Poetry of Therapy." The tapes show Sexton and Orne attempting to negotiate what was to become an "untenable" relationship between Sexton and Dr. Frederick Duhl, the new therapist Sexton saw as Orne's successor for five years. Duhl violated the boundaries of the therapeutic relationship by engaging in a sexual affair with Sexton that represented an eventual disaster for her. Looking into the future together, Sexton and Orne explore a serious boundary problem of therapists having sexual relations with their patients that was eventually to become more widely recognized and taken more seriously in psychoanalytic treatments in the years to come, including Sexton's own. I cite a few of the letters that Duhl wrote Sexton during the same period to give the reader a glimpse of what was to be Sexton's experience of therapy with this man once Orne had left Boston.

Throughout this book, I question the ways in which the expertise of a psychiatrist can limit or expand his patient's understanding of herself, her potential, and her world. I consider what the consequences of particular theoretical techniques and decisions might have been in the life of Anne Sexton, and how those consequences could be seen in Sexton's life and work. I also consider the ways in which a creative patient can influence her doctor or even an entire profession. In placing the discourses of therapy and poetry beside each other, I ask my readers to think with me about these two ways of assimilating life experience as creative arts, though Sexton insisted that psychiatry was one of the lesser of those.*

---

* Orne reported that Sexton considered "psychotherapy [as] really one of the 'minor arts'" (Hughes, 1991, p. 21).

1

"You, I, We Created the Poet"

November 1963*

Sexton: My poems are my accomplishment.
Orne: No. You are your accomplishment.[†]

(November 7, 1963)

The fall of 1963 was an important time for Anne Sexton. With a travel grant from the American Academy of Arts and Letters, she set off for Europe in September, accompanied by her friend Sandy Robart. In the first weeks, they toured Paris and Belgium, following in the footsteps of her Aunt Nana's European tour decades before, with Nana's letters in tow. Even when their car was broken into in Brussels, and their luggage stolen (including Nana's letters), Sexton remained upbeat. But once they arrived in Italy in October, she began to unravel. She found it very difficult to be so far away from the two men in her life, Kayo and Orne. Worse yet, she had received a letter from Maxine Kumin in which Kumin told her that Kayo was hoping her trip to Europe would sever her ties with Orne and end therapy:

> Anne, the reason he wants you to stay is that he thinks this year abroad will break your dependence on Orne and make it possible for you to quit treatment, or at least treatment with Orne. He has big hostility about him, calls him kook, etc., all of which you know very well but I didn't.

---

[*] An earlier version of this chapter appeared in the *Journal of the American Psychoanalytic Association*, *58*(3), 2010, pp. 421–444.

[†] All citations of Sexton's November 1963 to April 1964 therapy tapes are courtesy of the Schlesinger Library, Harvard University, and may not be used for any other purpose.

When I said not kook Kayo, he said please, that's my defense. Don't mess it up.[*]

Perhaps as a result of reading the letter, Sexton's journey through Europe soon dissolved as she experienced familiar chaotic feelings.[†] She flirted with Louis, a German-speaking Yugoslavian man she had met in Rome, and had an affair with him in Capri. She later told Orne that Louis had flirted with several women in Capri, but chose Anne after she asked him if she could write down his story of being a prisoner of war in World War II. Concerned that she had become pregnant, she began making long calls to Orne in Boston in a desperate attempt to stabilize herself. By late October, unable to keep herself together any longer, she returned to Boston with what Orne, drawing from Erik Erikson, told her was a "leaky ego."

Ashamed of her regression but eager to continue her work with Orne, Sexton resumed therapy in what seemed to be a further deterioration of her mental state. She became increasingly depressed as she neared her 35th birthday, November 9. Kayo had planned a big cocktail party for her birthday, which she did not want to attend. In fact, she could barely function. On November 7, she told Orne how suicidal she was, describing her birthday as "an ax hanging over me," insistent that she would "like to bleed all over [her] books." He told Sexton, "There's one rule in psychotherapy; you've got to have a patient" (Middlebrook, 1991, p. 209). She was admitted to Westwood Lodge after the appointment. When Orne phoned Kayo to tell him he was sending Anne to Westwood, Kayo demanded to speak to her. Presumably fearing that Kayo would talk her out of it, Orne told him that there was not time. Kayo was enraged.

Two weeks later, having been released from Westwood with Kayo's help, Sexton learned in a session that Orne was considering a move to another state. His announcement marks the beginning of the final six months of Sexton's twice weekly therapy with him. I shall cite exchanges from three sessions in the first of these six months, November 1963. In all three sessions, Sexton asserts that her poetry

---

[*] Maxine Kumin to Anne Sexton, October 8, 1963 (HRC restricted collection).

[†] In a December session, Orne suggested that Maxine's letter precipitated Sexton's decline. Sexton agreed that Kayo's determination to end her therapy was extremely upsetting to her.

is a sign of her progress in treatment, and Orne reminds her that her poetry is just a part of who she is.

The epigraph at the start of this chapter captures the essence of Sexton's conversations with Orne about the value of her therapy. In various ways, Sexton wanted Orne to acknowledge the fact that she had made herself into a poet with his help. Could she ground herself in her poetic accomplishments? Did her creative accomplishments point to aspects of her psychiatric progress that might otherwise have been overlooked? Sexton returned to these questions many times, asserting her achievements and seeming to look for affirmation from her psychiatrist. As is captured in his forceful "no" in the epigraph, Orne persistently responded in much the same way: The poetry is not as important as the person.

It is tempting to conclude that in deflecting attention from Sexton's poetry to her innate value as a human being, Orne contradicted his efforts to help her get better. After all, Sexton met Orne when she felt worthless; together, they had crafted her now brilliant career. But his decision to push Sexton toward a broader acceptance of herself as a person first, while still acknowledging her many talents, tells us something about his therapeutic technique. Orne trained as a psychiatrist in an environment dominated by Freudian conflict theory, rather rigid in its assumptions during the period. He would have learned to be an objective observer who helped patients correct defensive distortions of external and internal reality. Mental health came from being able to, as he once told Sexton, "keep reality straight."* Orne's responses to Sexton's queries about her value as a poet suggest that a patient as ill as Sexton gets better as she learns to distinguish between opposites: her defensive masks and the emotional realities they obscure. In keeping with theories of therapeutic action circulating at the time of the treatment, Orne urged Sexton to avoid the trap of intellectual discussions, which might conceal her "real" affect, with its accompanying memories from the past.†

---

* Segal (2006) offers an excellent overview of psychoanalysis as a search for truth about the patient.

† Dr. John T. Maltzberger, personal communication, June 17, 2009. Maltzberger trained as a resident with Orne at Massachusetts Mental in the late 1950s and early 1960s.

Sexton's exchanges with Orne about the value of her poetry and her poetry itself assert her very different theory of the relationships between doctors, patients, and the products of therapy for both patients and psychiatrists. Long before the term *analytic third* became commonplace in psychoanalytic discourse, Sexton's conversations with Orne and her poems reflect a vision of a psychiatrist and mental patient working together to construct something larger than the two people involved—a third thing, beyond the already existing "you" and "I." Given her depression, agoraphobia, and suicidal preoccupations, Sexton's desire to have Orne affirm the value of her poetry seems to have reflected her need to build a sense of identity that could fill the vast emptiness she experienced every day. If she had written published, much celebrated poetry, she could not be as worthless as she imagined; this is what she wanted her doctor to acknowledge. She also had cultural reasons to seek recognition as a public figure. Emerging as a significant American poet just as women writers were beginning to receive attention from places like the Radcliffe Institute, Sexton was exposed to new perspectives on women's identities and realities. These perspectives challenged established notions of "reality" and "woman" that dominated the psychoanalytic world of the early 1960s.

As we listen to these November 1963 tapes, it becomes clear that while Orne invokes binary oppositions that reflect psychoanalytic concepts and discourses popular in his time, Sexton's theory of therapeutic change has more in common with research about coconstruction and intersubjectivity in psychoanalysis and human development that became popular long after her death. Her vision of therapy as an architectural project, a cocreative construction, contrasts with Orne's apparent view of therapy as an archeological uncovering, a removal of distortions of reality (Jimenez, 2008, p. 590). Most strikingly, their contrasting views of identity—for Orne, as already there, if distorted, and for Sexton as emergent—speak volumes about the power of the creative imagination to challenge existing structures of thought, even structures designed to define the psyche itself.

November 14, 1963: "I Mean, We Can Really Talk!"

When Kayo picked Sexton up from Westwood Lodge, he told her he wanted her to seek an outside consultation immediately. He doubted that she and Orne were making progress in therapy given her abrupt premature return from Europe and her almost immediate descent into a state in which she required hospitalization. In a previous session, Sexton commented to Orne that Kayo was jealous of their relationship, but Orne defended Kayo, saying that there was no reason not to consult another physician to assess their progress from a more objective point of view. This did not please Sexton, who often seemed to split her alliances between her husband and Orne. Despite Kayo's insistence, Sexton did not sever her relationship with Orne; instead, she continued with Orne and asked Kayo to enter therapy (which he did).

In this November 14 session, Sexton began by defending her work with Orne. When Orne asked why she was reluctant to see another doctor, she protested. In the next five minutes, she and Orne discussed what doctor she might consult, including whether she should return to Dr. Riggs, a doctor she had seen the previous summer when Orne was away. Sexton explained her desire to remain with Orne:

> *Sexton:* I feel like I want to continue treatment with you. Not just because I am transferred to you…. I think that our relationship, even though it is stormy, is really pretty good. I like to talk to you. I feel like I can. As much as I can talk to anyone. I mean really talk. You can use a lot of words.
>
> *Orne:* Mmhmmm.
>
> *Sexton:* And I think the tapes are very … I listen to them and it's a different thing. In the first place I really hear you. Much more than I hear you here. Then again I hear me too, as much as I can bear to. Oh, I keep looking for some kind of magical thing. If there were just some …
>
> *Orne:* Some? What?
>
> *Sexton:* Well, I'd like to say to you do you think I will ever get well, and you'd say what do you mean by well.
>
> *Orne:* Mmhmmm.
>
> *Sexton:* But you know what I am talking about. And then when Kayo says, "Well, you know, he's spent seven years and he hasn't done much

for you." That's pretty stupid. I haven't done much. But then I want to list for him some of the gains. Because when I go back and when I have to list that childhood and my own attitudes when I began therapy then I see that it takes a long time …

[Two-minute exchange about which doctor]

Sexton: I'd like to say, why, this one's impressed with my writing, why aren't you? You know? I did it all for you.

Orne: I am impressed with *your* writing.

Sexton: What does that mean?

Orne: My interest is you, and I am impressed with your accomplishment.

Sexton: Would you be just as impressed if I'd never been anthologized and never awarded? No, because you know that you're not a judge.

Orne: Probably not because I am not a judge.

Sexton: And neither would probably someone else.

Orne: No, that's not true. I think in an area where I was competent to judge I would not need anyone else's statement. Because some people I am very impressed with …

Sexton: Of course you know my history so well and you know me so well that what I write in a poem you already knew.

Orne: It's not the issue. You don't understand it. You see, if you say am I impressed with your work, yes, it's very impressive. But you keep wanting me to be more interested in your poems than in you.

Sexton: Well, they are my accomplishment.

Orne: No, you are your accomplishment.

Sexton: Well, I haven't done very well, let's face it.

Orne: But this isn't, you know first of all …

Sexton: But in this area I did accomplish something. And in another. I don't know it may get shaky, because right now they're at a pretty good age. But I hope that I've grown enough to catch up with Linda's maturity when that arrives. But I have done that. That's just a fact. Once I said I don't want the children, I can't be a mother, I don't want them. Now I have the children. And I'm a pretty good … I am their mother. Not very good, but I am their mother.

Orne: And let me be very clear so there is no question between us. I view
this [being a mother] as just as significant an accomplishment.

Sexton: I do too.

Orne: Even though [the children are] not anthologized. But, you know,
that one I can judge.

Sexton: Yeah. Oh, I understand. Well, if I hadn't been I couldn't have
stood myself any longer.

Orne: And you see when I say Dr. Riggs was impressed with your
poetry, what I am saying is that it is fine that a therapist
be interested in your work. It is not fine that he be more
interested in your work than in you…. I want to keep reality
straight for you.

Orne spoke in dichotomous terms in this excerpt, distinguishing between Sexton's creative self and what she produced. On the
one hand, there was Sexton's personal "you," the patient Orne saw
in front of him. On the other hand, there were her poetic achievements, which could, with the wrong emphasis, obscure who she was.
He provided the example of Dr. Riggs (whom Sexton had seen when
Orne was away) as a psychiatrist who became distracted by the fact
that Sexton was a famous poet.* Orne knew that Sexton sometimes
viewed her poetry as her *only* accomplishment. Many times in the
years of recorded sessions, Sexton proclaimed that she did what she
needed to—written her poems—and she was now ready to die. Orne
always countered with statements about how the poetry was not her
value, instructing her that she needed to learn to distinguish between
her worth as a human being and her abilities as a poet. He was especially adamant about this in 1963, the year of Sylvia Plath's death, for
Sexton had, earlier that year, expressed her jealousy that Sylvia "[died]
perfect" (Middlebrook, 1991, p. 216).

We must admire Orne's efforts to prevent Sexton from killing herself and leaving her poetry for posterity. But we should also acknowledge that Orne's position on who she was and what would harm her
or make her feel better was historically situated. Orne and Sexton
worked together at a time when the social context for women's realities

---

* At another point in this session, Sexton talked about a student she had sent to Riggs
for a consultation. The student told Sexton that her book was displayed on his desk.

was largely domestic, and the professional climate in Boston offered its own very particular meanings for women's accomplishments. Orne spoke with certainty about the value of Sexton as mother in this excerpt at the same time that he denied his ability to judge her poetic achievements. He was neither parent nor mother, and yet he told Sexton that he felt he had some expertise in the mothering arena but not in that of judging poetry. Indirectly, Orne placed a higher value on Sexton as a mother than on her identity as a prominent American poet. Sexton eagerly agreed with her assessment of the importance of her maternal role, but she seemed less convinced of his explanation of why he could not speak of her poetic achievements. It was as if the "reality" Orne wanted to "keep straight" for her included a vision of poetry as less important than she believed it was.

The pedagogical climate of Massachusetts Mental, the psychoanalytically informed hospital in which Orne was training as a resident in psychiatry when he saw Sexton, would have offered very particular meanings for his ways of understanding reality. This climate is aptly captured in Erik Erikson's "Reality and Actuality" address to the American Psychoanalytic Association in December 1961, in which he concludes that "the psychoanalytic method, then, by its very design attempts to further man's [sic] adjustment by helping him to perceive facts and motives 'as they are,' that is, as they appear to the rational eye" (1962, p. 453). Orne's comments to Sexton suggest that his was the "rational eye" in the treatment room. He openly stated that he had a much better conception of reality than Sexton, and he saw it as part of his job to help her to understand his version of the way things are. It may be true that Sexton sometimes distorted facts and mistook her own projections as real. In this particular example, however, it is hard to differentiate between Orne's stance as an expert interpreter of the world and his efforts to help Sexton correct an obvious distortion of facts or events.

Most significantly here, Orne distinguished between Sexton as a human being seeking mental health and her public persona as a poet. Often in the tapes, he told Sexton to value herself first and foremost as a human being, not a person defined by prescribed social roles. Urging Sexton to value the "you," rather than the "what," Orne appeared to offer Sexton a perspective on her inherent worth as a human being. But he also revealed his entrenchment in a then commonsense

Cartesian view of the inner world of a unified human subject, a subject apart from the external circumstances or context in which she lived. Feminist psychoanalyst Adrienne Harris, writing 40 years after Orne worked with Sexton, notes, "We have saddled ourselves with a metapsychology that is both overly moralizing and unrealistically Cartesian." She argues that there remains "a split between the socially emergent and the personally authentic, a split that the constructivist perspective seeks to heal and critique" (1996, p. 551). Although innumerable "constructivist" writers have challenged Cartesian conceptions of reality in the past 50 years, Harris's summary offers two important points. First, she identifies a psychoanalytic metapsychology as one that moralizes and rigidly categorizes. Second, she identifies the work of constructivist approaches to subjectivity as healing the "split between the socially emergent and personally authentic." Orne clearly subscribes to this split in the above exchange, when he says that Sexton's poetry is not what he values about her. His emphasis on "*your* writing," and Sexton's question "What does that mean?" draw an important distinction between their ways of seeing the world. Orne cannot see the socially emergent poet Sexton as continuous with her "real" self; Sexton does not appear to make this distinction between "I" and "writer of poetry" so readily.

In fact, Sexton's repeated request that Orne acknowledge her poetry as *their* creation mingles "socially emergent" and "personally authentic" self-states. Perhaps Sexton felt that her personally authentic self, a product of childhood trauma and mental anguish, would best be augmented by, rather than differentiated from, the self that she and Orne were fashioning together.* Sexton spoke in threes: her relationship to Orne, the possibility that she might one day be "cured," and the fact that she is a nationally recognized poet. These three positions, the "we" of Orne and Sexton together, the "I" of the mentally ill woman, and the "you" of Orne as the first audience for her poems, constituted a repeating theme for Sexton in the tapes. Sexton felt ill much of the time, turned to Orne and poetry to help her out of illness, and

---

* Sexton discussed emotional and physical abuse by both parents, and speculated that she might have been sexually molested by her father and her great aunt Dingley, who lived with the family until she was institutionalized when Anne was 14 (see Middlebrook, 1991, pp. 41–66).

mused about the effects of their exchanges on herself and Orne, separately and together. Although we can see the value in Orne's efforts to help Sexton solidify a coherent identity, Sexton's representations of the doctor-patient relationship emphasize the shared creation of identities in the therapeutic setting: the "we" that can make a new self that is not the "you" but also not the preexistent "I." Sexton did not work to stabilize or reveal an already present identity, but to create a new one to supplement or even supplant the void she experiences in everyday life.

However we read what Sexton says in the session with Orne, we must acknowledge that her poetry offered an important feminist challenge to the Cartesian view of the human subject at the advent of the women's movement in the United States. Sexton's representations of doctor-patient relationships poignantly reflect her more fluid theory of subjectivity and mental health. In her first published volume, *To Bedlam and Part Way Back* (1960), Sexton stages a number of dialogues between the therapist and patient, dialogues in which the "you" and the "I" play pivotal roles in the making of the poetic object. The very first poem in the volume, "You, Dr. Martin," is addressed to a psychiatrist who happens to have Orne's first name:

> You, Doctor Martin, walk
> from breakfast to madness. Late August,
> I speed through the antiseptic tunnel
> where the moving dead still talk
> of pushing their bones against the thrust
> of cure. And I am queen of this summer hotel
> or the laughing bee on a stalk.

As Dr. Martin walks from the sensible world of his breakfast "to madness," he traverses the clear boundary between the inside and the outside worlds. The "I," in contrast, moves between observation and participation in a world that rapidly shifts from "tunnel" to "hotel" to "stalk." Beginning with long hospital hallways as tunnels, the speaker turns the hospital into a "summer hotel," a temporary dwelling place, and then into a "stalk," a part of a living plant, which we presume is outside. The image of the speaker as "laughing" Queen Bee is undoubtedly feminine, with its incumbent suggestion of generativity.

We may associate the speaker's queenly role with power, but the surrounding images remind us that her power extends only to the walls of the hospital. The other mental patients act as "moving dead," oxymoronic live corpses struggling to return to life by "pushing" against "the thrust/of cure." The images evoke both sexuality and death. Note that the "thrusting" and "pushing" occur simultaneously; the movement is from death to life. Each party here is active, in procreation as well as potential conflict.

If the speaker-patient-poet plays a fluid role, addressing one world as she makes an art form of the other, the doctor being addressed walks a seemingly straight line from the real to the unreal, a division emphasized in the trochaic staccato of "breakfast" and "madness." Once the doctor enters the hospital, he becomes "god of our block." However, ironically, the speaker proclaims her attachment to the doctor, and her adoration of him: "Of course I love you." She depicts the psychiatrist as a "god," but she also undercuts his divinity in images that assert his temporality; "you lean above the plastic sky/god of our block." Doctor Martin (*not* Doctor Orne) is the god of a plastic world, a small space of land, a "block." He "leans" from above, looking down at the patients as if he were always, inevitably above them, even as he bends toward them.

The "I" does not cast herself as a helpless victim in juxtaposition to the image of the doctor. Instead, she emphasizes her power, in lines in which the "I" figures prominently:

> I am queen of all my sins
> forgotten. Am I still lost?
> Once I was beautiful. Now I am myself,
> Counting this row and that row of moccasins
> Waiting on the silent shelf.

The speaker moves away from an identification as a beautiful woman toward one of a "queen[ly]" mental patient who writes poetry. Questioning if she is still "lost," perhaps because of her "sins/forgotten," the speaker does not seem to think so. She makes a number of first-person assertions: "I am queen/I was beautiful/Now I am myself." When she asserts that she is now her own self, a self who "counts" and "waits," she points to the boundaries of her situation even as she gestures beyond it, to a time after the waiting might end. She also repeats the verb "to be": I am/I was/I am. Cataloguing the loss of oneself in the service of another, the speaker reminds us that she uses language to describe and perhaps transform experience.

Note the contrast between the mask, "I was beautiful," and what it concealed: "Now I am myself." The self is a mental patient, but she is clearly also a maker of poems. She leaves behind a seemingly false, socially fabricated self as she embraces a self with multiple possibilities. The "beautiful" self belongs to a world that places value on appearances. The speaker's new self appears to enjoy words more. The final image of the poem, the "silent shelf," leaves the reader with a sense of potential; there might be more words, more images to come to this world. The "I" has not died, but merely stopped speaking. There is a power in her silence. A poem that begins with a "you" ends with an image, not the "I" only, but the creative "I," who makes images, and who clearly will make more. The "silent shelf" is not an empty vessel, moreover, as Sexton often described herself, but instead a place of potential meanings, a marker for ideas or images to come. And the "moccasins," or "mock-a-sins," that sit on the silent shelf aptly demonstrate the power of the imagination to turn the paralyzed patient into a maker of new meanings, one who makes a mockery of her sins.

November 19, 1963: The Announcement

At the beginning of the next session, Sexton mused about a fight with her husband over whether she should find a new therapist. As she staunchly defended their work together, she clearly did not know that she was describing a treatment that would soon become a part of her past: "I feel so connected to you. No one else could connect us—what I say to you is only between you and me—no one else could believe in its value: not your mother, not my husband, not anyone. I do believe in you … just us." After this comment, Sexton suggested that Kayo did not love her, and Orne disagreed, arguing that Kayo felt "ashamed and lost." Sexton, who had begun the session in a voluble mood, proclaiming the injustice of Kayo's request that she see another therapist, became much less talkative, falling into an incoherent state, mumbling and moaning. She clearly felt threatened by her husband's visits to other psychiatrists, and was almost inaudible as she lamented her situation.

After several attempts to coax her back from her whispers about how "doctors lie," Orne made an unusual comment: He said that he needed to tell her something important. As he led up to revealing the truth that he needs to tell—that there was a chance that he would leave Boston in September—Sexton emerged from the trance. The ensuing exchange ended the conversation about whether Sexton should find a new therapist and her tendency to polarize the men in her life: doctor versus husband. She repeated a phrase several times: "Just tell me. Just say it." Once she registered Orne's news, Sexton says, "Thank you for telling me," and Orne replied, "If I don't go you'll have wasted a lot of emotion." Just before Sexton left the session, she and Orne had the following exchange:

> *Sexton:* I'm only sorry how much of my life is tied up with yours—
> you are [attached to me] too—it's an odd kind of transfer-
> ence. I'm not in love with you; you are not a father figure.
> What is this attachment that I can't let you go? No one
> else will do with you what we did; we have seven years of
> past and it would not be normal. I would want to continue
> to see you.
>
> *Orne:* And there is a chance that I would not go.

It is poignant that Sexton articulated her deep ties to Orne in this exchange while he did not respond in kind. It is difficult to determine the reason for his silence. Perhaps he was not sure that he would be leaving, but it is also possible that he found Sexton's outpouring unsettling for his own reasons.

When Sexton said "doctors lie," she perhaps alluded to what was happening between them. As she bared her soul, Orne backed off into a statement about the fact that his departure might or might not occur. In a sense, Orne did not admit that he was in a meaningful relationship with Sexton, a relationship between two parties. His quick movement into "reality" took him away from that relationship. Orne might well have been "lying" behind his own theory here, a theory that placed human connection in a lesser role to the realities of time and space. Would Orne leave? He did not know. But he should have known that Sexton was speaking the truth as she stated her attachment to him, and his to her.

Sexton's direct statement about Orne's impact on her, and her need for him, was expressed in terms of the "we," rather than on the two of them individually. The "we" holds the power of their working relationship, a power that Orne has over Sexton, but also one that she had over him, for he could not create what they had with anyone else. Orne's failure to acknowledge his own role in the therapeutic relationship, a relationship that led to Sexton's establishment of herself as a powerful poet, ostensibly offered Sexton all the credit for her self-transformation. But it also pointed to a theory of identity formation as a process of differentiation that had its roots in classical psychoanalytic theory, which is profoundly patriarchal.

Jessica Benjamin (1988) points out that for Freud, "union, merger, and self-other harmony" were considered "regressive opposites to differentiation and self-other distinction," while "merging was a dangerous form of undifferentiation" (pp. 46–47). In his theory, Freud placed connection in conflict with the growth of the healthy ego. In keeping with Freud's theory, Orne said very little on the tapes about their joint accomplishments, as if he feared that to do so would be to become too identified with his patient. It would appear that he wanted to give Sexton her due credit, but his refusal to recognize or own his own role in the creation of Sexton's poetic persona may well have been a product of his socialization as a male therapist as well. In theory and in cultural practice, to be a man in Orne's time required a sharp differentiation of self from other and a repudiation of deep interconnectedness; deep connection could result in a loss of identity.

Although many theories of the coconstructed therapeutic relationship might facilitate our understanding of what Sexton might have been imagining with Orne, contemporary theories of human development articulate the work of cocreation in a way that is remarkably similar to the above excerpt. E. Z. Tronick, a researcher in the field of infant mental health, establishes that a mother and child together create something beyond what either of them was capable of before their interaction, without the other person's input:

Briefly, in the mother-infant interaction, each partner communicates their affective evaluation of the state of what is going on in the interaction ... a dyadic state of consciousness emerges, [which] increases the coherence of the infant's state of consciousness and expands the infant's (and the partner's) state of consciousness.... An experiential effect of the achievement of a dyadic state of consciousness is that it leads to feeling larger than oneself. Cocreative processes produce unique forms of being together, not only in the mother-infant relationship, but in all relationships. (2003, pp. 474–475)

Tronick's theory emphasizes a few elements of human relatedness that might escape our notice. Unlike earlier developmental theorists, who imagined that children mirrored what they saw in their parents' faces, Tronick argues that infants and parents *each* communicate to each other a sense of "what is going on in the interaction." A new state, a dyadic state of consciousness, emerges from the interaction, which increases the coherence of not only the infant's state of consciousness, but of both parties' states of consciousness. This new state leads to a "larger than oneself" feeling for both. Tronick argues further that cocreative processes are not unique to infant-parent exchanges, but exist in all relationships.

Sexton's comment to Orne just after he announces that he may end their work together suggests that Sexton's theory of the therapeutic interaction bears much in common with Tronick's developmental model. She emphasizes her attachment to Orne as an interdependence, rather than a dependency: "I'm only sorry how much of my life is tied up with yours—you are too." When she says "you are too," Sexton begins to consider Orne's attachment to her. She underlines their cocreated relationship. She also underlines the fact that she and Orne are a uniquely creative dyad ("no one else will do ..."). Sexton may identify their attachment as a "cannot let you go" relationship because Orne helps her to nurture the creativity that she had shown as a child, but which had not received her parents' praise. But perhaps too, Sexton recognizes that she and Orne were a uniquely qualified couple, able to make together what she herself had not seen how to create in the past. Sexton knows that Orne will see other patients in Philadelphia. She reminds him and herself of their unique bond, although Orne does not seem to pick up on the value of the relationship in his response.

Tronick is careful to emphasize that the direction of a mutually created dialogic exchange is not predetermined, but emerges in the interaction:

> When two individuals mutually engage in a communicative exchange, how they will be together, their dynamics and direction are unknown and only emerge from their mutual regulation. Thus, while we can look at an exchange that has taken place and make a narrative account of it, we must realize that there was no narrative or blueprint structuring the exchange before or even as it was happening. Seeing this difference— that what has happened can be narrated, but what is happening cannot be narrated—and holding on to the distinction has critical implications for understanding what goes on in relationships, including the therapeutic relationship. (p. 476)

Orne's attachment to "preexisting narratives" seems, at least at times, to have influenced his responses to Sexton's assertions about her poetry. He predictably diffuses Sexton's enthusiasm about the value of her poetry by turning it back toward her, as a person capable of many things. What he does not focus on, which Sexton values again and again, is what Tronick might term the mutually beneficial, cocreative aspects of their bond, a bond without a predetermined outcome or plot. Orne also does not seem to make a distinction between what is happening and what has happened; instead, he acts as if the action of the therapy relates only to Sexton's mental state and to her past history.

Sexton, in contrast, seems to understand the unknown direction of therapeutic exchanges differently. She articulates her sense of the emergence of meaning through interaction most fully in her poetry, where actual dialogues between therapists and patients take place. As she recreates a therapeutic dialogue in a poem, Sexton reflects on the experience and invites us into it at the same time. In keeping with Tronick, she illustrates how the past *and* the future hover in the dialogue between patient and therapist in a present moment. In "Said the Poet to the Analyst," also published in her first volume, the speaker-poet points out the differences between the two professions:

My business is words. Words are like labels,
or coins, or better, like swarming bees.
I confess I am only broken by the sources of things;
as if words were counted like dead bees in the attic,
unbuckled from their yellow eyes and their dry wings.
I must always forget how one word is able to pick
out another, to manner another, until I have got
something I might have said ... but did not.
Your business is watching my words. But I
admit nothing. I work with my best, for instance,
when I can write my praise for a nickel machine,
that one night in Nevada: telling how the magic jackpot
came clacking three bells out, over the lucky screen.
But if you should say this is something it is not,
then I grow weak, remembering how my hands felt funny
and ridiculous and crowded with all
the believing money.

This speaker compares poetry and analysis as professional occupations in these lines, with emphasis on the work of the poet. In order to do her work with words, the poet needs to forget how they work together to make new meanings beyond her control. She must leave the analytical self, that which seeks the real "sources of things," aside, so that she can arrive at something new, something she "might have said ... but did not." The image is of a past event that might have had a meaning, but in the present moment of the poem it becomes a metaphor that evokes many meanings simultaneously.

Until the last four lines of the poem, the speaker identifies the writing of poetry with the work of imagination, work involving possibilities and choices about what to say and when, a world in which one thing can be three (or more): "Words are like labels,/or coins, or better, like swarming bees." The "labels" and "coins" evoke the definitions of words, with their particular linguistic values, but the image of "swarming bees" expands their possibility far beyond the realm of definitions and numbers. Swarming bees can suggest a world of sound and action, of potentially stinging danger as well as life-affirming motion. The images swirl together and shift in rapid succession.

Just as she did in "You Dr. Martin," the speaker here casts herself in a land of bees, but this time she raises them from the dead, using their sounds to make meaning. The analytical frame of mind hovers, threatening to "unbuckle" their "yellow eyes" from "their dry wings."

Although the speaker's powers of creation reverberate in stanza one, the second stanza reveals how heavily she relies on the presence of the analyst to witness her creative efforts. He helps her sustain her side of the dialogue in silent affirmation: "Your business is watching my words." The analyst does his job well in silence, but if he turns to negate her, if he "should say this is something that it is not," he has the power to send the speaker into a "ridiculous" and "crowded" world of faith in "money." The poet's power speaks best when she can "write [her] praise," while the analyst's power comes from his ability to say "no," to confront denial (the "something that it is not"), and, we might infer, to insist on reality. For this speaker, the analyst's denials interrupt or at least censor the production of the imagination; they silence the dialogue. The speaker feels strong, even "best," when working with words, but the analyst can tear her from this state by insisting on what is. As in "Dr. Martin," the psychiatrist's role in this poem remains locked in a world of yes and no, while the poet seeks to find her way into some other reality. But the speaker needs the doctor if she is to make meaning, even if the meaning she seeks goes beyond his understanding of what it could be.

If we imagine this poem to tell us something about Sexton's representation of her relationship to Orne, we see the conflict that was evident in the sessions cited above. The poet-speaker works with her words until she has "got something." This third thing, created by the poet, but witnessed by the listening and watching analyst, holds potential, but only if the condition imagined by the speaker is not fulfilled. If the analyst does not say that "it is something that it is not," the poem lives; if he does, the speaker ends up in a world that does not make sense, is "crowded" with others, and is based solely on exchange as the currency of relationships "filled with all the believing money." The poet speaker works against the moneyed world with her images. The analyst as audience acts as fellow creator; his assent allows the poet's creation. But his capacity to deny the validity of the creation can return the words to the pedestrian realm of commerce and goods for sale.

The "believing money" also conjures up the opposite of belief—the speaker's doubt. What if the poet is not what she seems? What if her praise exists only in the world of the "nickel machine," a pretend world in which she seeks a jackpot that will never come to her? The poem seems to await the response of the "analyst" to make sure that its artistic value is intact. As we know from Orne's silences in the sessions, that affirmation would not come to Sexton in the real world of moment-to-moment interaction; in the world of the imagination, only, it remains possible, even into the futures of her readers.

November 21, 1963

In the next recorded session, November 21, 1963, Sexton began to process Orne's departure by remembering their first days together:

> *Sexton:* I remember the first time I met you, you giving me the Rorschach test, I liked you…. Funny that you don't care about me as a poet. But you created me as a poet. You cared about me, then you, I, we created the poet.
>
> *Orne:* Anyone you formed a relationship with would see way beyond the poet.

Here Sexton again turned to the creation of her poetic self as a mutual creation; she and Orne together created the poet. And Orne, predictably, attempts to focus on the reality that exists "way beyond the poet." He almost suggests that the poet is in the way of what is worth seeing about Sexton. And yet, it is what Orne does not say that interests me most here. Why does he devalue their mutually created success? Why does he seek to avoid any acknowledgment of his role in the therapeutic process?

Professionally trained in therapeutic technique in the 1950s, Orne would surely have learned to consider the relationship between himself and his patient as manifestations of the patient's own mental states, unconscious fantasies, and neurotic conflicts, not as material for mutual exploration. In a paper originally presented at the 20th Congress of the International Psychoanalytical Association,

Paris, July–August 1957, Ralph Greenson summarized the analyst's main tasks:

> [The analyst] must be able to use interpretations, the making of the unconscious conscious, as his most effective and final lever in influencing his patient. Neither his erudition, his sympathy, his instinctual needs nor his ideals may supplant his knowledge of the unconscious and his awareness that the patient requires insight given by a trustworthy conveyor of understanding and not gratification or punishment.... The analyst's interpretations are the decisive and ultimate instruments, used in an atmosphere of compassionate neutrality which enables the patient, communicating via free association, to recapitulate his infantile neurosis. The analyst's goal is to provide insight to the patient so that he may himself resolve his neurotic conflicts—thus effecting permanent changes in his ego, id, and superego, and thereby extending the power and the sovereignty of his ego. (1958, pp. 200–201)

To an analytically trained professional in 1963, Sexton's inquiry into the power of her relationship with Orne might have been interpreted as evidence of her desire for "gratification." Orne's interpretations would most likely, in contrast, be seen as "instruments," and his negation of her gesture toward discussing their bond would be seen as evidence of "compassionate neutrality." Conventional neutrality at that time would not, surely, involve an analyst's reflections on his own contributions to the patient's growth. In fact, Greenson warns that "personal preferences are a hindrance and tend to obscure our insights and limit our objectivity and require our constant self-observation and self-analysis. We work to help our patients and not to obtain followers, disciples, converts, or accomplices" (p. 201).

For Sexton, however, Orne was a very important kind of accomplice, a cocreator of her life's most prominent work. Her representation of her work with Orne as mutually constructed bears some important similarities to ways of thinking about the therapeutic relationship that emerged well after her death. In the poems cited above, the therapeutic dialogue authorizes its speaker as creator, but the listening analyst is the necessary witness-participant in the conversation.* It was not until well after this time that a considerable number of theorists of the therapist's role in the psychotherapeutic process began to emphasize the ways in which the therapist partici-pates in the patient's constructions of illness, healing, and indeed what it means to live a human life. Although we might consider numerous writers on this subject, Lewis Aron (1990) aptly sum-marizes the emerging notion of a two-person model, in which each participant in the therapeutic relationship contributes to the making of psychoanalytic meanings about the patient:

> The implication of a two-person psychology is that who the analyst is, not only how he or she works, but his or her very character, makes a real difference for the analysand. It affects not only the therapeutic alliance or the so-called "real relationship," but the nature of the transference itself. From the perspective of a two-person psychology, the impact of the analyst needs to be examined systematically as an intrinsic part of the transference. (p. 477)

Aron emphasizes the impact of the analyst's individuality on the patient's healing process. The movement toward a focus on the rela-tionship and away from the inner world as the center of psychoana-lytic work leads to a new understanding of the analyst's role in the therapeutic interaction. Infant researchers Beebe and Lachmann (1998) articulate this shift, which, though commonplace now, would have been a departure from standard technique for most practicing analysts in the late 1950s and early 1960s:

> Psychoanalysis has tended to privilege inner state as the focus of inquiry. Freud (1923/1957) argued that perceptions of what goes on in the envi-ronment are never as important as those arising from within … instead, we suggest that the inner and the outer worlds are coconstructed … dyadic process may (re-)organize both inner and relational processes, and reciprocally … changes in self-regulation in either partner may alter the interactive process. (p. 481)

---

* See Poland (2000) and Stern (2009) for further discussions of the analyst as witness-participant in the therapeutic process.

In contrast to a world in which the analyst focuses on the patient's inner state, Beebe and Lachmann define mutually created, coconstructed worlds. Like Sexton, who notes the "I," "you," and "we" of the therapeutic dialogue, Beebe and Lachmann emphasize that the healing process involves two creative partners. They cite the potential for a reorganization of the inner world of the patient and her relational processes. The emphasis on one partner's influence over the other extends to the patient's influence on the analyst as well. In the years since they published their study, critics have raised questions about the role of the internal relationship in maintaining a sense of equilibrium even in the presence of another. But the clear need for an emphasis on the power of a relationship to change both the patient's and the therapist's inner worlds remains.

Sexton wrote one of her better known poems in the weeks in which she attended these therapy sessions in November 1963: "Menstruation at Forty." Drawing its real-life content from the pregnancy scare Sexton had as a result of an affair she had in Italy in October, the poem appears at first glance to have little to do with the dialogue about the relationships between poetry and identity that I have reconstructed in the pages above. But it does address Sexton's personal dilemmas at the time, dilemmas that animated both her work and her therapy: What are the consequences of my childhood experiences? What kind of mother am I? Should I take my own life? Of what use is my poetry? What is a woman's worth? And if we look closely, we can hypothesize that it also provides a thought about the role of poetry in the healing process, a subject Orne deliberately chose not to explore. In remaining silent on these issues, Orne sent a silent message to Sexton about what was important and unimportant in her experience.

The speaker begins with thoughts of motherhood and suicide surrounding the realization that she is not pregnant:

> I was thinking of a son.
> The womb is not a clock
> nor a bell tolling,
> but in the eleventh month of its life
> I feel the November
> of the body as well as of the calendar.

In two days it will be my birthday
and as always the earth is done with its harvest.
This time I hunt for death,
the night I lean toward,
the night I want.
Well then—
speak of it!
It was in the womb all along.

These lines about not becoming a mother were written at a time when we know that Sexton's analyst adamantly praised her role as a mother. Although the speaker mourns the loss of the son she might have had, she also mourns the loss of a part of herself, her youth. The images of autumn evoke a time without procreative potential, but the active verbs in these lines tell us that the speaker "thinks," "feels," "hunts," "leans," and "wants." The speaker asserts her agency even as she moves toward an evocation of her own death. At the end of the first stanza, she suddenly addresses herself in the third person, as if ordering a revelation that part of her wants to avoid. The speaker "leans toward" and "wants" "the night" of her own death, but a new voice proclaims, "Well then/speak of it!" We cannot help but think that the new voice knows something about the talking cure. This invented interlocutor, though not named an analyst, plays a very similar role of witnessing her experience as the analyst does in the "Said the Poet to the Analyst."

As soon as she introduces the second voice, which orders "speak of it," Sexton illustrates her capacity to make life and take it in her poetry, a creative capacity that perhaps helps her to fight the urge to kill herself. The voice that responds to the command "speak of it!" moves her toward imagining the Slavic son or daughter she might have had. Thus, a poem that begins as a monologue steeped in death moves toward a dialogue in which the speaker conjures up and even begins to mourn the son she would have "possessed before all women." She kills the son she has invented, and then mourns him. The internalized "other" who demands that Sexton "speak of it" illustrates how the art creativity is a product of a dialogue; in this instance, the speaker who drifted toward the call of suicide in stanza one then conjures up a story to satisfy the demands of the second voice. The telling sends her away from death and into the life of the creative imagination.

Turning the actual experience into a poetic one, Sexton gains some control over the powerful emotions that might, in the world of the poet, move her toward an untimely death. If we think in real terms, the "it" that was "in the womb all along" is actually just an image, an invention, for Sexton herself did not know if she had been pregnant. But in the world of the poem, an opportunity to be a mother and the urge to kill oneself are both representations that can be manipulated and transformed. The final incantation, "calling you mine, calling you mine," identifies the speaker as one who names and then owns experiences. See how powerfully the "I" for Sexton lives in the world of the poem, a world in which being a poet is deeply tied to speaking to a rapt, even demanding, listener.

When the controversy about the release of the tapes emerged in the pages of the *New York Times*, Martin Orne granted an interview in which he explained how he remembered his responses to Sexton's poetry in the therapeutic sessions:

> "She brought all of her poems to me," he acknowledged, "but I never commented. All I said was, 'They're very interesting. They should help people.' I was very careful about that…. I did not discuss her poems with her as a source of insight into psychological problems, because if that had been done, she would have rationalized all kinds of things…. And I believed it was very important that she owned the poetry…. I couldn't not listen to her 'You, Dr. Martin.' But I went out of my way not to discuss poetry." (Hughes, 1991, p. 21)

I have tried to show that for Sexton, "owning" poetry involved a real life witness; it was neither a possession nor a solitary endeavor. Like swarming bees, money in a magical slot machine, or a fantasy child, poetry offered a fuller way of being, an orientation to a world of possibility rather than depression and defeat. Orne denied that the poetry could provide "insight into psychological problems," but it is clear today, in reading the poems against the sessions, that Sexton's poetry provides ways of considering the psychologies of both the patient and her doctor, as well as the ways in which her doctor's understanding of what psychology is (and is not) shaped his patient's worldview.

2
DID ANNE SEXTON KILL JOHN F. KENNEDY?

Late November 1963

Trauma survivors live not with memories of the past, but with an event that could and did not proceed through to its completion, and therefore … continues into the present.

—**Laub and Auerhahn (1993, p. 288)**

Adults who have been sexually abused as children are only too willing to believe that the nightmarish memories that begin to flood their waking thoughts are not real. It is a most heartfelt wish to be convinced that what they begin to perceive as a traumatically overwhelming past is merely a fantasy of their own creation.

—**Davies and Frawley (1992, p. 32)**

On November 23, 1963, barely a week after Dr. Martin Orne told Sexton that he might leave Boston, President John F. Kennedy was assassinated. Kennedy's death plunged the Sextons into more marital turmoil than they had known. There were violent arguments that ended in Kayo striking Sexton, arguments in which Sexton urged her husband to "go ahead and finish the job." As she began to explore the chaos in her home in her therapy sessions, Sexton acknowledged that she seemed to seek punishment from her husband. In her associations, she linked this behavior to both her earliest history and to the possibility of Orne's departure. These three traumas—on the national level, in her domestic life, and in the transference to Orne—contributed to the volatile environment in Sexton's home. They also produced a series of responses from Dr. Orne that tell us something about how trauma was heard and interpreted in the early 1960s.

In the clinical repertoire of Martin Orne, as for many psychiatrists of his time, the language that we are familiar with today for thinking about and treating the symptoms of trauma and its aftermath was in its earliest stages of development. Since the 1890s, the majority of the literature on trauma considered the internal *conflicts and fantasies* stimulated by an external event, with an emphasis on the fact that these conflicts and fantasies were possibly quite different from "reality." With few exceptions, it was not until the late 1970s, in the wake of the testimonies of war veterans, holocaust survivors, and the women's movement, that attention was drawn to identifying and treating the posttraumatic experiences of patients as veridical in their own right. As Orne listened to Sexton's posttraumatic somatic symptoms, witnessed her dramatic acting out in her personal life, and read the explicit representations of trauma and its aftermath in her poetry, he attempted to help her understand these as internal responses to external realities. For Sexton, in 1963, a more personally attentive and empathic therapeutic language that could address her posttraumatic experiences was still waiting to be heard.

A product of his psychiatric training and cultural milieu, Orne did not identify the overwhelming nature of Sexton's responses to the trauma of the Kennedy assassination, the traumatic memories it evoked from the past, and the prospect of his own eventual departure. Although they discussed each of these issues, Orne's emphasis was on gaining control of them and moving on. He encouraged Sexton to behave like a rational adult who had some power over her unconscious need to repeat the violence from her past, while she alternated between trying to please him and reliving the traumas of her childhood. As he sought to help her understand and then control her internal world, Orne maintained a focus on trauma as an intrapsychic event. Sexton, however, suggested that she experienced the effects of trauma on a somatic level, as well as on a completely disorganizing mental level. Understanding the violence in her marriage was for Sexton more complex than gaining control of inner demons. Orne may have insisted that her inner world was "not a volcano that erupts," but Sexton, in actions, words, and poetry, conveyed experiences that exceeded her ability to master them.

November 30, 1963, is the first recorded session after Kennedy's death. A very rich hour, it crystallizes much of the material in the December tapes that follow: arguments at home, Sexton's own traumatic history (which may have involved sexual abuse), her anxiety about Orne's departure, and Orne's efforts to persuade Sexton that she actively pursued violent arguments to gain some relief from her anxiety. For her part, Sexton focused her attention on a terrible battle that she and Kayo had the night before, which culminated in his choking her as she screamed in encouragement. Orne attempted to convince Sexton that she instigated the argument to serve her own purposes, while Sexton insisted that the argument was caused by Kayo's revelation that he had strangled a prisoner of war when he was in Korea, a fact that made her fear for her own life.

Sexton's and Orne's very different ways of understanding traumatic experiences, which persisted throughout the treatment, became particularly evident as they spoke about her argument with Kayo. The boundaries between the temporal realms of past and present and the separation of psychic and external reality remained firm for Orne, but from his point of view they were not always well differentiated for Sexton. For the most part, Orne carefully acknowledged the genetic origins in early life that influenced and perhaps determined Sexton's adult behavior. Yet his main interventions were designed to redirect her attention from the past to her power to manage the violence in her present life. Orne interpreted her responsibility for eliciting anger and violence from important men in her life, including himself and her husband. As he urged Sexton to take ownership of her role in the violence she described (and feared), he underplayed its roots both in her earliest history and in its traumatic repetition at home with Kayo and in the transference with him. We might say that Orne himself was caught up in the reenactment in the treatment and tone deaf to what we might hear today as the reverberations of early trauma in his patient's life.

Although the subject of Sexton's and Kayo's traumatic histories became the focus of much of the session, it began and ended with a discussion of the death of President Kennedy. Like most Americans, Sexton spent the end of November 1963 glued to the television, grief-stricken and obsessed with images of Kennedy's death and funeral.

Her husband Kayo, however, was furious and anxious. Sexton reported that when he heard the news of the assassination, Kayo entered her study with a terrible look on his face, a look that seemed to blame her for Kennedy's death. Sexton commented that it was as if Kayo believed she had killed Kennedy so that he could become a national hero. When she had voted for Kennedy, she told Orne, it was "the first time she voted for an idea instead of an income." Kayo, who would not vote for Kennedy under any circumstances, accused her of wanting to give all of their money away: "He said you are voting against all your money. You will lose everything if you vote for that bastard." She was angry that he seemed to blame her for Kennedy's death, but Sexton also realized that Kayo was concerned that her strong feelings about the assassination could send her back into the suicidal depression that had led to her hospitalization in early November.

For both Anne and Kayo, the national trauma of the Kennedy assassination raised questions about episodes of violence in their own pasts, which bore most heavily on the violent arguments in their home. Kayo was in the process of finding a new therapist (at Sexton's request), as his former therapist, Dr. Liederman, had moved away the previous summer. Perhaps spurred by the Kennedy assassination, Kayo suddenly felt free to talk about a horrendous incident that he had spoken about with Dr. Liederman, an incident that occurred while he was serving with the Marines during the Korean War. He told Anne that he had killed a captured prisoner with his bare hands. Revealed and relived in the aftermath of the Kennedy assassination, Kayo's discussion of his own traumatic experience threatened to displace Sexton as the mentally unstable person in their house. It also prompted Sexton to turn her husband's violent potential against herself.

Although the argument was the focus of most of the session, Sexton provided a quick summary of her visit to Dr. Helen Tartakoff, the psychiatrist that she and Kayo were both seeing as a consultant in order to find a therapist for Kayo and to ascertain the efficacy of Sexton's treatment with Orne (which Kayo believed was useless). When Sexton left Westwood Lodge in November, she agreed to Kayo's request that she seek an outside opinion about her work with Orne, but she insisted that he also see a therapist. Thus, for different reasons, they each visited Dr. Tartakoff. Sexton told Orne that she left

Tartakoff's office wondering if she was important enough for the new doctor. She had noticed the extensive library that served as Tartakoff's office waiting room and confided in Orne her wish to have her own book included there. She even gave a copy of her two published books to Tartakoff, which Orne later interpreted as a gesture to impress her and become a special patient.

Sexton did not deny that she wanted her poetry to mean something to this woman and to all the prominent psychoanalysts she met. She was particularly interested in seeming to be a serious artist to an analyst who clearly valued books at least as much as she herself did. She told Orne that she did not want to be seen as "some little housewife." The fact that Sexton began her session with this detail tells us once again that she was looking for affirmation of her value as a poet, an affirmation Orne made it a point not to provide. Perhaps Sexton felt that recognition of who she was in the world would be stabilizing in the face of the shameful story she was about to tell about her current experiences as a housewife.

When Orne remained silent during her report of the consultation with Tartakoff, Sexton moved on to recount the drama of the previous day. She had allowed Kayo time and space to talk to his mother and his sister in the playroom in the afternoon, so that he could tell them about his memories of having killed someone while he was in Korea. She was proud of herself for having offered Kayo his privacy, because, she admitted, she really wanted to listen at the keyhole. After his mother and sister had left, during their usual cocktail hour before dinner, Kayo finally told Sexton about the incident:

> He did sit and describe this incident to me. I mean he wanted to. And I asked him in particular about it and how he felt and I was reassuring in a way. I wanted to hear. And then I sat very coldly, told him about me and my father and Nana and later he told me I'd told him this three times and I said to him "maybe I did but I don't remember."

Thus, in response to his revelation that he had strangled a prisoner of war while he was guarding him on a small boat off the Korean coast, Sexton told Kayo about a traumatic memory of her own—one that she visited many times in her therapy with Orne. She remembered, or thought she remembered, her father coming into her room with a bottle, lying next to her in bed, touching her private parts, and kissing her on the lips. She also thought that her Aunt Nana, who lived with the family, might have witnessed the event and expressed disgust at Anne's behavior.

Although she had barely spoken about it with her husband, the memory did recur in the treatment, differing slightly in its details, particularly the age Sexton was when it occurred and whether the scene was witnessed by her aunt (Middlebrook, 1991, pp. 56–57). Nana lived with Anne's family until she was admitted to a mental institution when Anne was 13, and their cuddling together was Anne's only memory of receiving loving touch as a child. But Nana became almost unrecognizable before she was taken to the psychiatric hospital, seeming especially angry at Anne, whom she had seen kissing a boy. Anne thought she remembered Nana trying to choke her and saying, "You're not Anne!" This incident often overlapped in Anne's mind with memories of her father standing naked in the guest room holding a drink in his hand, or of him visiting her room to kiss her on the mouth and touch her genitals. Most disturbing to her was the fact that she felt that she had appreciated the physical attention from her father, if not the sexual contact. Anne was to explore whether these memories were true in many therapy sessions, in more than a dozen poems, and in her unpublished Broadway play *Mercy Street*. She would also return to the Nana/Daddy/Anne triangle in many of her discussions of her identity in relation to issues of gender and sexuality. Was she a lesbian? A prude? A flirt?

Years later, when Orne discussed Sexton's memories of sexual abuse with her biographer, he warned that false memories were common for people like Sexton, and he assured Diane Middlebrook that he did not believe Sexton was in fact abused, "because it wasn't the father's style when he was drinking." Despite his disbelief, he reported, "I dealt with it in therapy as a real event, because there were times that it was real to her.… If you ask me either as a psychiatrist or scientist, however, I would have to say that I am virtually certain that it never occurred" (p. 58). Orne's disbelief was perhaps silently held, but it is hard to imagine that someone as sensitive to him as Sexton would not have detected that. It is telling that Orne emphasized his two credentials as an expert as he provided Middlebrook with his opinion. Perhaps he did not realize that those schooled in psychiatry and science also participated in the silencing of victims of sexual violence in the era in which he treated Sexton (Herman, 1992; Skorczewski, 1996).

Middlebrook concurs with Orne's assessment of Sexton's memories, offering further evidence that Sexton might have been making up a story to explain her feelings. Tracing Sexton's early interest in Freud's studies of hysterical patients (such as Anna O.), Middlebrook speculates that Sexton "sounds suspiciously like updated versions of Freud and Breuer's *Studies on Hysteria*" (p. 55). She also expresses doubt about the incestuous scene that Sexton presented as a memory to Orne as early as 1958, less than two years into the treatment. The memory, "recalled several times in trance at widely spaced intervals … cannot be established historically." She cites Sexton's fear that she perhaps invented a trauma to attach to her symptoms, which Orne, to his credit, responded to by asserting that Sexton's father was "communicating something" to her when he was drunk. Ultimately, however, Middlebrook decides, in agreement with Orne, that "it seems reasonable to allow her narratives in trance during psychotherapy were not reports of actual events but explanatory fictions" (pp. 57–58).

Middlebrook does describe the genital examinations and enemas that Sexton's mother regularly subjected her to as a child. She also states with certainty that Ralph Harvey made explicit sexual comments about his daughters when he was drunk. In fact, she argues that Sexton's "physical boundaries were repeatedly trespassed by the adults in her family in ways that disturbed her emotional life from girlhood onward" (pp. 57–59). Having established that Sexton was indeed a survivor of some kind of sexual violation, both verbal and physical, she then quotes an excerpt from a 1961 therapy session:

> *Orne:* When your father was drinking he was communicating something to you.
> *Sexton:* Disgust.
> *Orne:* Or attraction.
> *Sexton:* Sitting beside Daddy, his saying I can't eat when she's at the dinner table—I thought pimples were a sign of things inside that were showing.
> *Orne:* Your feelings about him?

Although Orne began here by attributing the sexual boundary violation to Sexton's father, who must have been "communicating something" when he was drunk, he does not follow his patient's association to the word *disgust*. Instead, he first attributes the desire to Sexton's father, but then turns the subject back to Anne's desire for her father in a traditional Freudian interpretation of the daughter's wish to replace her mother and marry her father. It seems obvious that Sexton's comment expresses the shame she must have felt at being told she was so disgusting that she spoiled her father's appetite, but Orne's theoretical lens does not allow them to discuss that in the session.

Taken together, the testimonies of Orne and Middlebrook about the veracity of Sexton's memories of sexual abuse offer a picture of a patient who was prone to storytelling, fond of seeing herself in relation to other patients with different disorders from her own, and vulnerable to exhibiting psychoanalytic symptoms that might impress her doctor. They do not do much to establish how we might interpret Sexton's life and work differently if we were to assume that her story might have been true. As I listened, I at first found myself in agreement with these powerful interpreters of Sexton, who knew her more intimately in person and in print than almost anyone. They form another kind of parental couple, one that is most influential in Sexton scholarship, joined in their certainty that Sexton was not sexually abused, despite the evidence to the contrary. But when I listened to one of the final tapes in the Schlesinger collection, recorded in late April 1964, I heard Sexton ask Orne if she *had* to tell her new therapist about "that other thing, that *might* have happened." Attentive to her uneasy, almost embarrassed tone, I found myself questioning what her uncertain voice was really saying. She did not seem proud of the possibility that she had been sexually abused. In fact, she wanted Orne to tell Duhl (her new doctor) about that for her.

Most certainly, Orne did not understand Sexton's behavior as we might today—typical for a survivor of sexual abuse. Jodie Davies' summary of the clinical picture of a "typical" survivor argues that the patient has within her a frozen, enraged, and helpless child:

In the patient who has been sexually abused, the child aspect of the self
representation, along with that of the abusing other and their complex
system of emotional connection and exchange, is cordoned off and isolated from the rest of the personality. It remains virtually frozen in time,
the images unmodulated by any others of a different, perhaps gentler
nature. These images become the embodiment of the murderous rage
and pernicious self-loathing that drive the child in his or her relationship with others. In their intensity they fuel the psychotic-level terrors
of annihilation and world destruction that so infuse the patient's internal experience. The child cannot grow. Her anger and self-hatred go
untempered, therefore unintegrated. Her world is a world of betrayal,
terror, and continued emotional flooding…. Her mind is a constant
state of upheaval and confusion. When, as a child, she turned to those
around her for a way out, she was confronted either with threats and
further abuse or with neglect and formidable denial. The child is incapable of expecting anything different from the analyst. She experiences
herself as terrified, completely alone, and helpless. (Davies & Frawley,
1992, pp. 25–26)

Davies' summary speaks to numerous issues that Sexton raised in
the years she saw Orne and in the poems she wrote from the beginning
of her career until its end. She often told Orne that she had a trapped
child within her, a child who knew far more than she, and she begged
to be hypnotized to let "Elizabeth," or the "little bitch" (as her father
once named her when he was drunk), speak (Orne refused, fearing
that she would develop multiple personalities). She wrote many poems
representing father-daughter incest, in which the daughter is described
as frozen, numb, dissociated, sleepless, frightened, confused, isolated,
and in constant danger. These poems represent stuck or frozen girls
who have a severed or weak mother-daughter bond, a domineering
father, and a daughter whose needs are subordinate to his.

"The Moss of His Skin," one of Sexton's earliest representations of a father-daughter "marriage," cites as its epigraph from the
Psychoanalysis and Psychoanalytic Review, which explains that "daughters in Saudi Arabia were buried with their fathers as a sacrifice to
the goddesses of the tribes." The poem offers a grotesque image of

the father accompanied by a dissociated daughter who "falls out of herself" as she lies beside her dead father:

> I held my breath
> and daddy was there,
> his thumbs, his fat skull,
> his teeth, his hair growing
> like a field or a shawl.
> I lay by the moss
> of his skin until
> it grew strange. My sisters
> will never know that I fall
> out of myself and pretend
> that Allah will not see
> how I hold my daddy
> like an old stone tree.

Here we see images of a dissociated daughter who clutches the "stone tree" of her father while she pretends she is invisible. She must keep their relationship a secret, holding her breath while lying next to his "strange skin." These images would become more pronounced in other poems, perhaps culminating in "Briar Rose," a rewritten version of Sleeping Beauty, in which Briar Rose is an insomniac who can only sleep with the help of drugs, and never with the prince, from whom she feels estranged. She experiences states of numbness and suicidal wishes: "You could lie her in a grave and she'd never call back hello there." Briar Rose feels tainted, marred, and inanimate: "an awful package." She does not remain fully in her body, and mentally she distances herself from what her body may be feeling. She also invites the reader to revictimize her: "This trance girl is yours to do with." The poem ends in a chilling image:

> Daddy?
> That's another kind of prison.
> It's not the prince at all,
> but my father
> drunkeningly bends over my bed,

circling the abyss like a shark,
my father thick upon me
like some sleeping jellyfish.

The image suggests that the father's body is on top of the daughter's, smothering her. The tactile impression is slimy, like semen might seem to a child. The father is a predatory invertebrate, and the daughter is its prey. Although this is perhaps Sexton's most explicit representation of father-daughter incest, she was to offer many others in the years after she worked with Orne. She was also to sexually abuse her own daughter, a possible repetition of her own story, which had disastrous consequences.

Given his training in a psychoanalytically oriented residency program, it should be no surprise that Orne did not seem to know much about the lasting effects of sexual abuse. Freud had identified sexual trauma as a real etiological event in causing neuroses in the 1890s, but he suggested that it was a fantasy for most of his patients only a few years later. His focus shifted from historical truth to psychic fantasy, and this orientation remained in place until well into the 1970s. Bennett Simon's (1992) review of the psychoanalytic literature on child sexual abuse before the 1980s concludes that "although the effects of sexual abuse are often serious and enduring—denial, rage, protection of the guilty perpetrator, extreme guilt and shame, some form of dissociation, or at the least a fluctuating disbelief in what had actually happened—there was an almost complete absence of literature on treatment issues, and no consensus about what was curative" (pp. 959–960). Simon notes especially the prevalence of abuse, the difficulty in recognizing countertransference issues, and the lack of consensus regarding treatment. Orne could not have known his own blind spots, but he certainly moved away from the discussion of the possibility of Sexton's abuse rather quickly in this session.

Perhaps taking her cue from Orne, Sexton did not focus much on her past in this session, but she did explain that she offered Kayo the example of her own traumatic experience because she had often doubted that her experiences were true, just as he doubted his, and she wished to make it easier for him to express his own feelings so that he would know he was not alone. From listening to the tape, it sounds as if the Kennedy assassination had heightened Sexton's already present feeling that something was terribly wrong. She had, after all, returned prematurely from Europe late in October, and she had entered the mental hospital less than a week after her return to Boston. She had also just learned that Orne might be leaving Boston.

It would make sense, then, that given Kayo's revelation of yet another disturbing fact, she would be vulnerable to reliving her own posttraumatic memories. Kayo appeared to think that Sexton was once again turning the focus on herself, and proceeded to end the conversation so that he could get the dinner on the table and then busy himself with household chores after dinner. Sexton told Orne, "Of course I felt rejected." Perhaps because Sexton and Kayo each felt abandoned by the other, a violent argument broke out soon after dinner:

> *Sexton:* Kayo and I started to have a horrible fight. He was furious. And
> of course I don't remember I really black out the whole thing.
> And to just simply say he beat me up is to so oversimplify
> the thing. The thing should be recorded for anyone to know
> what happens. Because I am horrible and I am hysterical and
> I am hitting myself. I say, "Don't stop hitting me," and I am
> hitting myself. "Go on!" I say to him. Then I know the worst
> part is when I say, "Go on you're a killer! Go on, just finish
> the job. Come on kill me!" … But he didn't kill me, I don't
> know why. But it was terrible.
>
> *Orne:* Mmhmmm.

Sexton's tone as she told Orne about the argument was forceful and self-critical. She characterized herself as a screaming hysterical woman, and emphasized her role in escalating the violence. Although she did not sound as if she were looking for sympathy from Orne, she received nothing more than a mmhmmm. She continued to talk when Orne responded in this way, apparently awaiting a genuine comment or question. She described the terrible argument as very physical, and suggested that Kayo was ready to choke her to death but stopped himself. When he stopped, she hit herself repeatedly, leaving marks that were visible the next day. Even when it seemed that she was inviting Orne to comment on these events, he remained silent. From the tone of his mmhmmm's, it seemed as if the dramatic physical battle in Sexton's sound-proofed bedroom was no surprise to him.

During the argument, Sexton reported, the phone rang. It was Kayo's former psychiatrist, Dr. Liederman, whom Sexton had tracked down at his Florida home earlier in the evening. She had wanted to ascertain whether Kayo had told him of his memory of murdering someone and whether the doctor thought it was true. Liederman insisted on speaking with Kayo, but he did indirectly confirm the memory's validity. He also listened as Sexton complained that he had left Kayo the previous summer when he moved away. Liederman urged Sexton to pursue her anger with Orne.

Sexton clearly gave Orne an opportunity to connect her anger at Liederman to his own revelation that he might leave Boston, but Orne did not pursue any of these details. It is worth noting that in Sexton's first description of the battle with Kayo she took responsibility for hitting herself and goading Kayo into killing her. At the same time, she insisted that her husband was violent, and that it would be hard for her to live with a man who had the hands of a cold-blooded murderer. She also, perhaps most importantly, raised two painful experiences that entered her consciousness as she thought about the argument: her memories of sexual abuse and her feelings about Orne's possible departure.

Orne did not comment on the relationships between Sexton's associations as she recounted the story, nor did he empathize with her emotional or physical pain. He remained focused on the argument and Sexton's persistent fear of her husband's violence. Although he seemed to be listening to every detail of the story, Orne's tone suggested that he did not share Sexton's conclusion from the story—that Kayo was a murderer who could, if provoked, murder her. In fact, he appeared to retreat entirely from Sexton's terror into an identification with the perpetrator of the physical violence: Kayo.

Orne signaled that he was more interested in Kayo's experience than Sexton's, as he asked for explicit details of what Kayo had actually done:

Orne: What happened with him? What did he do?

Sexton: They were bringing prisoners down and they tied their hands and they muffled them and they stuck one on Kayo's boat and they said, "Here take care of this gook." I asked Kayo not to refer to this person anymore as a gook. I couldn't stand it. When the prisoner began to yell, Kayo tried to restrain him, the prisoner fought back, and the only thing he could think of was kill him, shut him up. He was in terror. So he did.... Then he said he saw in the light of the day that he was just a kid and I said, "Did you look at his face?" and he said no. So I guess that's what really happened ... but the trouble is I've really always known that he is just.

Orne: He's just?

Sexton: Well, so capable of this.

Orne: Is he? You mix up two things.

Sexton: Mmm. I forgive him. Look, he didn't know what he was doing. Maybe the guy had to have been killed....

Orne: It doesn't sound like aggressive killing. Sounds like fear.

Sexton: Yeah it was fear.

Orne: Kayo himself was a panicky kid. How old was he?

Sexton: Not too young. He was older than most people, 24 maybe. Not a young kid. We'd been married.

Orne: He wasn't exactly a seasoned combat man.

Sexton: No, this was really his only combat. And he didn't know what to do. I am really not blaming him.

Orne: That's not really what I am talking about. It's that you interpret it as violence but it is not really violent type behavior.

Sexton: If you saw him violent you'd understand it is so close to it.

Orne: You mix up two things.

Sexton: How can I look at his hands and not think that they killed someone? With his own hands he choked someone till there was no more air. Someone with their hands tied.

Orne: Mmmmm. Why do you dwell on this?

Sexton: Because so many times he has almost killed me. I can't help it you know what I am like ... for my own reasons because so many times he has almost killed me ... and then when he stops I start hitting myself.

Orne: I said you use him to serve a purpose.

Orne twice repeated that Sexton "mixes up two things." He seemed to mean that Sexton mixed up Kayo's past with their present struggles. He minimized Kayo's capacities as a killer and wondered why Sexton insisted on "dwelling on this." First, he decided that Kayo was a "fearful kid." Then, when Sexton agreed with him but added that he was in fact married and in his mid-20s at the time, Orne changed his approach. Although Kayo killed a prisoner of war who had his hands tied behind his back, for Orne, strangely, this was "really not a violent type behavior." Attributing Kayo's behavior to fear, Orne clearly could not accept Sexton's theory that the story of Kayo's having murdered a man in Korea should be connected to his tendency to hit Sexton when they argued. As we have seen, she had already admitted her own tendency to instigate and then escalate the argument, but she also admitted that she was terrified by Kayo's capacity to become physically violent during their arguments.

Orne's responses to Sexton suggest an emphasis on separating different kinds of violence to help Sexton sort through the argument from an apparently "objective" point of view, with Orne as the voice of "reality," while Sexton was prone to distortions. It should not be surprising that Orne did not address domestic violence as a threat to Sexton's life, although she insisted that Kayo had almost killed her in the past. Domestic violence, like war trauma and sexual abuse, was not an issue to be discussed and explored in professional offices in 1963. In most cases, these events simply did not exist for professionals as problems worthy of therapeutic attention in their own right. In 1960, not one article on domestic violence had been catalogued in the psychoanalytic archives. The first wave of the women's movement was just beginning, and domestic abuse had barely been addressed as a national issue. Connections between women's experiences of abuse and battery had not been explored, and it was even acceptable to blame a woman for her role in inviting the violence she experienced. Women were regularly accused of "asking for" sexual assault, for example, and domestic disturbances reported to the police often received little attention from the authorities, except for efforts to "calm down" a couple who were reported to the police (Goldner et al., 1990).

Just as sexual abuse was almost invisible as a cultural reality in 1963, the traumatic effects of wartime experiences on combatants and their families were largely unaddressed until the very end of the 1960s. To locate the first articles on the new diagnosis of posttraumatic stress disorder, we must look to the literature of the late 1970s (van der Kolk & van der Hart, 1995; Westerlund, 1986). Kayo's posttraumatic symptoms—most notably his rage, which could easily be accessed by Sexton—dovetailed with her own, but they would most likely not have been on Orne's mind as he spoke with her about their fighting. Orne urged Sexton to separate different kinds of violence to help her find her part in the argument, but he failed to do so himself. Sexton's story involved a father fondling his daughter in her own bedroom, while Kayo's was a story of an adult soldier killing a younger soldier in a wartime situation. Given what transpired in the Sextons' bedroom, we might hypothesize that in Anne Sexton's mind, she was identified with Kayo's young victim. She suggested that even if she did provoke Kayo's violence, she was also in danger of being strangled in her own home. Orne seemed to dismiss this possibility out of hand. In doing so, he not only denied the reality of Sexton's experience as if it were an exaggeration, but he also curiously refrained from acknowledging the reality that Kayo did kill someone, and not on a battlefield; he had not been assigned to kill the prisoner of war but to guard him. He also neglected the differences in power in the examples: Kayo was a man who killed a boy; Sexton was a child who thought she had been fondled by an adult male, her father.

Today, we know from Vietnam veterans that the trauma of perpetrators of violence has a different effect from that of victims. We also know that survivors of sexual abuse have their own posttraumatic symptoms, including the depression, disorientation, self-blame, suicidal ideation, and vulnerability to further abuse that Sexton described (Herman, 1992). Orne did not deny that Sexton's experience had real effects, but he did not spend much time exploring them, nor did he comment on how a history of abuse might relate to the effect of her husband's traumatic story on her.

A second reason Orne might not have wanted Sexton to see herself as a victim of Kayo, but to see her own role in the argument, reverberated in his repetition of the words "you mix up." Despite the fact that Sexton acknowledged what she did to exacerbate the fighting, Orne placed the emphasis on what he saw as the reality of the situation. At Massachusetts Mental Health Center, where Orne finished his residency training in August 1960, and where he continued to work until 1964, the clinical climate was dominated by the thinking of its director, the prominent Boston Psychoanalytic Society and Institute training and supervising analyst Dr. Elwin Semrad. Semrad was known for his great respect for patients, and his ability to induce the most ill to describe their painful memories. He was lauded for his insistence on the importance of truly listening to patients' pain, yet he also emphasized the importance of helping patients identify their distortions of reality if they were to get better:

> Semrad taught that patients suffered from the denial of reality and self-imposed isolation that followed from their attempts to avoid the experience and knowledge of unbearable grief and pain.…. His repertoire of interventions ranged from a gentle explication of the pain and grief that a fuller knowing and feeling might bring to a more stark and forceful confrontation of what was being avoided.…. He placed great therapeutic value on the patient's coming to recognize and know The Truth. Although he could be sensitive to patients' needs for support in facing this truth, his therapeutic intent was tactfully but firmly to let them know it. (Levine, 2002, p. 310)

Orne most certainly steered Sexton back to "The Truth" of his version of the interaction with Kayo in this excerpt. As their conversation continued, he made his idea of what the truth was clear:

> *Orne:* You use him. The violence is not just his. Not even primarily his … it is not a volcano that erupts.

Orne did not contradict Sexton's admission of her part in the violence, but he also did not suggest that it was a two-person construction. Sexton's emphasis was on her interaction with her husband, and how their joint dynamic spurred her toward more violence. Orne went so far as to suggest that the violence was primarily Sexton's. In a 1964 article entitled "Assisting Psychotic Patients to Recompensate," Semrad asserts that "to go along with the idea that the patient is not responsible for his illness robs him of the continuity of his life" (p. 366). He further warns against "the physician's being satisfied with the patient's success, for when this happens, the patient feels the doctor is not really interested in him" (p. 366). Perhaps these remarks, which were clearly intended to be helpful to suffering patients, reflect the climate of thinking among Orne's teachers at Massachusetts Mental. Certainly we can see Orne implementing both principles in this hour, as he first remained silent when Sexton discussed wanting acknowledgment of her work, and then told her that she basically "controlled" the violence with her husband.

Orne's investment in helping Sexton take charge of her ability to spur men to violence became more explicit as the hour progressed. Sexton returned to the subject of sexual abuse. She told Orne that Kayo brought it up again after the violence ended between them, telling Sexton that "after all my [Kayo's] story is normal." Sexton's story, he told her, made him think disturbingly of their own daughter, Linda. Sexton seemed to understand that incest and murder occupied different social spheres for Kayo, and she encouraged him to end the conversation. Kayo was at first empathic, offering his wife "some of the things you [Orne] would have said, like it was really your father's fault." Despite Kayo's sympathy, Sexton then suggested that maybe her story was more than abnormal; perhaps it was untrue:

> *Sexton:* But the trouble is that I am not so sure this is true. I made up a story and it is awfully real. I am acting it out all over the place.
>
> *Orne:* Maybe, but I don't know. It is something that happened between you and them.
>
> *Sexton:* I will say I don't remember her [Nana] choking me it seems like I just have a feeling. Maybe it is what is it called? A screen memory. I don't know but it is a memory.
>
> *Orne:* I think it is kind of important that you understand your use of Kayo's violence.
>
> *Sexton:* I use him to punish me. If my story is true, it does not make me feel very much like a princess.
>
> *Orne:* Whether it is true or not it doesn't make you feel very much like a princess. But what were you using the fight for? Oh, to get punished. Also the positive ... to get ... relief.
>
> *Sexton:* That is a horrible way to think about it. But it does work.
>
> *Orne:* It is a question of understanding that it is not a volcano that erupts. You basically control it. What I am trying to point out is that ... you can evoke real anger and do.... If you can

do it [evoke anger] with me. And hopefully this would be
difficult....

Sexton: Then think what I could do with him.

Orne: Given the rage. You see your great fear of Kayo—and this is the
awful thing that you've got to gain control of—is your fear of
what you do to bring this out and if you can gain control of it
you have nothing to be afraid of.

Orne remained focused on Sexton's rage in this exchange, and her
ability to enrage the men she was closest to, although Sexton offered him
an opportunity to help her make sense of the role of abuse in her acting
out with her husband. She used a Freudian term, a "screen memory,"
to depict her recollection of Nana strangling her, which she thought
might have happened in response to her father's sexual advances. Orne
did not pick up on her discussion of what might or might not have happened, acknowledging that it "didn't make [her] feel like a princess" but
then, in the next breath, returning to what he feels she "really needs to
understand," which is "her role in Kayo's violence." His response suggested that whatever happened in her house she had provoked it.

Orne's insistence on Sexton's capacity to elicit men's anger was
not located in relationship to her stories of betrayal and loss. As he
separated her past from her present, he moved away from his patient
and into a prescription for her behavior. We might return to Freud's
"Remembering, Repeating, and Working-Through" (1914) for a
glimpse of the theory that Orne could have had in mind as he focused
on Sexton's need to take charge of her actions. Freud notes that the
analyst must be prepared for "a struggle with his patient to keep in the
psychical sphere all the impulses which the patient would like to direct
into the motor sphere" (p. 153). The successful analyst, for Freud, celebrates it as a "triumph for the treatment" when the patient remembers
what she once would have "discharged in action," or acted out.

Although she knew that she did encourage Kayo to kill her, Sexton
also knew that she did not want him to do so. Her tone was pleading
with Orne—could he help her to stop this, she asked? At the same
time, she offered Orne another question: "Did it really happen?" Orne
suggested that *something* happened but he did not pursue the question
of truth as significant to the question of interpersonal violence. It is

important to note that because psychoanalytic attention focused on fantasy and hysteria for more than half a century, "a broader inquiry into the effects of sexual abuse" was prohibited (Herman, 1992, p. 973). As a result, Orne would have read textbooks like the one Bennett Simon (1992) cites in his comprehensive study, in which a reference to "incest" is coded as "see under Oedipus." In three words, reality is relegated to fantasy, which increases any ambivalence that the patient might already possess:

> Virtually from the beginning of what we can call psychoanalysis (Freud's work in the early 1890s), there have been unsolved problems about the role of actual external trauma in producing neurosis (and later in the field, in producing psychosis). Also, like the defense victims of incest frequently learn to adopt, psychoanalysis has both known and not known, simultaneously or oscillatingly, about the role of actual incest and the trauma inflicted by an adult. One can see this split evidenced in Fenichel's textbook (1945) and in Brenner's (1955) textbook by looking under "incest" and being referred to the Oedipus complex ... key terms such as "seduction" and "trauma" have proven distressingly elastic. (p. 962)

We can see how Orne "knows" and "does not know" if Sexton was abused by her father in the above excerpt. Orne was likely to have read portions of Brenner's textbook when he was a medical student or a young resident. But whether or not he actually encountered the texts that Simon describes, the point is that Orne practiced in a climate in which sexual violence was unreported, misunderstood, relegated to fantasy, blamed on the victim, and simply ignored. And his professional identities—as a psychiatrist and researcher into hypnosis and memory—made him even more suspicious of early memories of abuse such as the ones Sexton described.

Were she reporting these events three decades later, Sexton might have received a different response from her therapist. By the late 1980s, clinicians would know that "the conflict between the will to deny horrible events and the will to proclaim them aloud is the central dialectic of psychological trauma" (Herman, 1992, p. 973). Sexton might have been comforted to know that many sexual abuse survivors have difficulties distinguishing fact from fantasy, and that their difficulties can be exacerbated by clinicians who have doubts about what is fact and what is fantasy in the patient's account. Sexton might have been helped to identify her self-destructive behavior, somatic disturbances, diminished self-esteem, difficulties in interpersonal relationships, and problems regarding sexuality as classic symptoms of posttraumatic stress occurring after experiences of early abuse (Alpert, 1991). Finally, she might have learned that personal control—for both victims and perpetrators—is a central issue in domestic violence, and that domestic violence assumes a predictable pattern from escalation to denouement, which victims come to expect as a "normal" pattern (Umberson et al., 1998, p. 444).

Without access to what we know today as the common features of posttraumatic stress disorder, Sexton and Orne each tended to blame Sexton for her symptoms, as if somehow gaining control of her unconscious affects would resolve them. Just as Kayo suggested with a glare that she had assassinated the president, Orne suggested with a line of questioning and a string of silences that Sexton needed to take responsibility for what was clearly a mutually created scenario. Sexton never really questioned Orne's interpretations either. As the session approached its end, she reached a conclusion about the violence with Kayo that focused entirely on the transference. Suddenly, she confronted the reality of her feelings about Orne's departure from Boston:

Sexton: I don't know maybe I am more upset about you going away than I have been talking about.

Orne: Mmhmmm. I'm sure of that. [*silence*]

Sexton: But that doesn't make any sense. That's sick.

Orne: What is sick?

Sexton: Because I've got to leave you someday … and if you leave me then the problem is kind of solved.

Orne: Is it?

Sexton: But you know what the other night I couldn't sleep I kept thinking about it the last appointment. You know naturally we may have a long time but that's all I think about…. "How will it be at the last appointment? How can I really say good-bye to him?" Look at the trouble I have. I mean it centers on all my troubles. I never made up to irritate you the problem of leaving anyway.

Orne: Mmmmm.

Sexton: I mean it is just a problem....

Orne: Hmmm. [*very long silence*]

Sexton: Maybe I am too entangled to work I don't know. Kayo was talking about this excessive transference. I said, "Kayo I am excessive in my emotions."

Linking the fights with Kayo to the sexual violence and to the threat of Orne's departure, Sexton suggested that the trauma in the transference might be most important to her, that it might be related to the other issues she was describing. But at the same time, her statement about his departure also produced a long silence from Orne. Perhaps Orne was ambivalent about his departure, because for some reason he remained silent far longer than was his usual style. Sexton seemed to deflate in response, speculating about whether her transference was simply too intense, and enlisting Kayo as an ally in this interpretation. She used the word *entangled* to suggest the intensity of her relationship to Orne. Just as she moved readily away from discussing the reality of sexual abuse, she quickly protected Orne's silence at a moment when he should have said something. But her use of *entangled* suggests that she somehow knew she was involved in yet another cocreated situation in which Orne was not owning his role as participant. Left alone with her fears of losing him, she did what appeared to come very easily to her; she blamed herself for an "excessive transference."

Given the fact that Orne and Sexton had worked together for almost eight years, years in which her life had changed from a woman who could not care for herself or her children to a nationally recognized, prize-winning poet who would soon publish her third book, Sexton had a lot to lose if Orne left Boston. She saw Orne three times a week, wrote him in between sessions, and often called him in the midst of an argument with Kayo. She listened to and transcribed tapes for hours each week, and studied old transcripts to try to learn something about herself. She dedicated many of her poems to him, and he was her first and most important interlocutor. Although he must have realized her attachment to him and dependence on their work together, Orne did not seem equipped in this session to address it. He ended the session by telling Sexton that he would really prefer not to leave Boston, but that if he left it would be an opportunity for them to do some work together, just as they had worked on his departure when she was to be in Europe on the Ford Fellowship (from which she returned prematurely in October, with a "leaky ego").

As they discussed how Sexton might hold onto Orne even in his absence, something began to shift in the session. First, the topic turned to Sexton's expertise, the subject of writing:

Orne: You're going to have to learn ways to keep me, you know, that's real. Now in some ways you use some ego prostheses.

Sexton: I don't know what you mean.

Orne: Ego aids, artificial aids to help.

Sexton: What? Like writing.

Orne: I think taking a picture is a much better example. Writing [is] communication still. Taking a picture is a way you can manage it so that it is real.

Orne's suggestion that Sexton use a photograph as an ego prosthesis, which contradicts Sexton's idea that poetry might offer her a way to keep him, provides an enormously interesting contrast. Sexton offers writing as a way to hold onto their relationship; she might re-create in her writing what she has with him, a dialogue. But Orne, focused as he was on "reality," suggested she keep a picture of him. This visual representation of her beloved therapist would remind her of their work together. We can see that Sexton's idea has transformative possibilities; she can reinvent Orne on the page and continue their conversation. Although the Orne in her writing cannot speak back, he can through his patient-writer. Orne, however, does not seem to understand this. His idea that a photograph, a static image from the past, would provide a better transitional object for Sexton than her poem, turns the focus back onto himself and somehow undermines the fact that their work cannot be captured in a photo; only his image can.

As they continued to imagine preparing for his departure, Orne reminded her of a time when he wanted them to end the treatment prematurely, and he blamed himself for misunderstanding his role. He asked her to consider a six-month period in 1962 when he had requested major changes in the treatment. First, he wanted Sexton to review her old tapes to find out what she could learn about herself from them. Second, he wanted to see her twice a week instead of three times a week. Third, he would no longer hold her hand when she became very upset, something he had done for years. Finally, he wanted her to set a termination date. What he did not tell Sexton at the time was that he had recently married, and he was concerned that his marriage would have a destabilizing effect on Sexton unless she were healthier. After six months, Sexton had one of her most serious mental breakdowns, and Orne withdrew his demands, stating that he had been overconfident in his own ability to make her well.

Orne and Sexton were to discuss this difficult period in the treatment much more in the months to follow. In the November 30 session, he reminded her of it and acknowledged that he had made a mistake:

> *Orne:* Think back years ago I wanted to set termination dates. This wasn't stupid; it wasn't appropriate. The reason for it at that time was essentially sound but I wasn't sophisticated enough to understand that it wouldn't work.... I thought at times in the treatment that if I didn't light a fire under you to make you face an issue which you weren't about to discuss. I think this was right but the only catch to this was that I couldn't light the fire. If I did this, then we were no longer on the same team. This is very different. It isn't my doing; it isn't my choosing.
>
> *Sexton:* I don't think that way you must realize that. You must realize that I am not that reasonable inside.
>
> *Orne:* If I were doing it [trying to force her to terminate], I would have problems.... Very frankly, I would rather not leave Boston and if I do leave it will be for good reasons kind of, which are realities in my life.

Once they entered a direct conversation about Orne's departure, the feelings it evoked from a time when Sexton felt abandoned by Orne (see Chapter 5), and their work together, Sexton seemed much more capable of engaging her feelings. Until this point, both Orne and Sexton seemed locked in a rational discussion that was interrupted by outbursts from Sexton's other, "feeling" self. It is hard not to consider her shift into a language of feeling at the end of the session as directly related to Orne's own shift. One can almost hear the energy change in the room once Orne admitted that he might have made a mistake at one time. Sexton seemed heartened when he said that it was essential that he and Sexton stayed "on the same team," and that he would really prefer not to leave Boston. Once he became an ally rather than an expert trying to make her take control of her unconscious rage, Sexton was able to express the feelings she'd had, we must assume, when she entered the session.

Orne's reference to his past mistake and the necessity that he and Sexton share the agenda for her treatment provided an extremely useful model of therapeutic change in a situation where it had been severely deficient. Jill Gentile (2001) describes how patients and therapists can become locked in dyadic exchanges that appear to be intimate but only emphasize the isolation of the two parties:

> Psychoanalytic models of therapeutic action themselves have perpetuated such closed dyadic states, contributing to a perversion of agency for both the individual patient and psychoanalysis, with the attendant costs of keeping both the patient and psychoanalysis in a state of relative disenfranchisement from (and limited impact upon) the larger world. (p. 651)

For change to occur, she argues, an element of thirdness needs to become present, in which patient and doctor enter a shared intersubjective space. Sexton and Orne entered this space once he admitted that he had made an error in judgment in the past.

As a testament to their successful work together at the end of the session, and largely as a result of Orne's acknowledgment of his role in her healing process, Sexton finally expressed the affect that seemed to elude her throughout the hour. She revealed how she felt when Kayo told her about killing the young Korean soldier:

> *Sexton:* What I really wanted to do was cry.... I said to him I think I want to cry, and I told him I am really crying for the loss of innocence, some loss.... It's not just violence, it's something indelible on his brain ... this is crying for some part of us.

The "loss" that is "indelible on his brain" referred to the effects of trauma on the brain of Kayo, remnants of the past that influenced him to try to strangle his wife. But it might also, given the string of associations in the session, refer to the brain of the dead young president John F. Kennedy, which Sexton had watched shattering into fragments over and over again on national television. And of course it gestured to the possibility of another indelible loss, of Orne himself in his role as healer of Sexton's psychic world. Sexton was grieving losses that could not be fully articulated, and she was searching for a witness to her pain. But she was also grieving for "some part of us." Syntactically, "us" refers to her and Kayo, but we cannot help but hear Orne and Sexton as another "us," and finally, the "us" that is the United States, in full mourning for the loss of its president.

Living in the aftermath of the Kennedy assassination but affectively trapped in her powerless past, Sexton shows an uncanny knowledge of the neurological effects of trauma in her description of Kayo's "something indelible" here. It is as if she knew firsthand that the Greek word for *trauma* is "wound," and she suggests a kind of wound on Kayo's brain. Sexton seems to have known firsthand that "the mental imprints" of trauma are "replayed in the form of intense emotional reactions, nightmares, images, aggressive behavior, physical pain, and bodily states"; she had seen firsthand that traumatic experiences can "have profound effects on memory, affect regulation, biological stress modulation, and interpersonal relatedness" (van der Kolk, 2002, p. 383). An even better picture of what she knew about trauma can be found in her poetic representations of posttraumatic stress, which appear in more than a dozen of her poems.

The question in the title of this chapter—Did Anne Sexton kill John F. Kennedy?—presents a joke and a problem. Of course Sexton did not kill Kennedy, but in her husband's mind it was a possibility. This fantasy might have had all kinds of consequences, but knowing that it could not have happened leads us to dismiss the question almost out of hand. Throughout this session, Orne was eager to help Sexton "look at" her "problems," as if the looking at would produce the cure, but he did not really believe her version of at least one of these problems—her suspicion that she was sexually abused. Although very willing to blame herself for causing all kinds of violence, Sexton remained focused on the affects her problems produced, the actions that came out of them, and her suspicions about the power of understanding through the talking cure. She seemed to feel that she was powerless before her past, a feeling common to trauma survivors. This disparity—between Sexton's traumatic entrapment in the past and Orne's notion that understanding it (whatever it was) could cure her—would become more pronounced in the months that followed.

3

HOLDING HANDS AND LETTING GO—THE ROAD TO "FLEE ON YOUR DONKEY"

December 10–12, 1963

> But you, my doctor, my enthusiast,
> were better than Christ;
> you promised me another world
> to tell me who
> I was.
>
> **—"Flee on Your Donkey"**

In early December 1963, Sexton felt plagued by violence and loss. She told Orne that she could not stop thinking about the Kennedy assassination and Kayo's revelation that he had killed a prisoner of war in Korea. She also experienced tremendous anxiety as she considered the possibility of Orne's departure. At the same time, she continued to work on "Flee on Your Donkey," a long poem that she described as "the definitive poem about my illness." She told him she found the poem very difficult to finish (she did not, in fact, publish it until May 7, 1966, in *The New Yorker*). The poem addresses an earlier period in their treatment to which Orne himself had drawn her attention the week before. Over 200 lines in its final version, it conveys the months-long turmoil that ensued during the winter and spring of 1962 when Orne, fearing Sexton would discover that he had just married, attempted to help her "get better" so that she could end treatment. In a sudden shift of his behavior, he refused to hold her hand any longer, reduced her sessions to two per week, and attempted to set dates for termination of therapy. Sexton experienced these changes as a painful rejection, culminating in a breakdown outside Orne's office and her subsequent admission to Westwood Lodge psychiatric hospital for an overnight stay in "the scene of the disordered senses."

As we shall see, "Flee on Your Donkey" offered Sexton one way to narrate this multilayered therapeutic struggle. But her therapy notebooks and sessions provided another. In early December 1963, she tried to find ways to connect with Orne even though she knew his career might take him away from her the following fall. Carefully studying the period in 1962 when he had withdrawn from her and encouraged her to end the treatment, and fearful that Orne was about to push her away again, she raised important issues about their relationship. Her attention to the old notebooks provided an opportunity to make sense of the past, not only for repair, but as a way to prepare for the future. Sexton read and reread several of her therapy transcriptions and revealed feelings about the events they described that she had never before spoken aloud to her psychiatrist. Both in her current sessions and in the poem, however, the question of "what really happened" remained far less important than the effects of feeling abandoned by Orne to the solitary anguish of mental illness. Their work together on these sessions constituted one of the most productive collaborations in their history. It also led them into an exploration of other experiences of loss in Sexton's past, and even to a recent loss she had felt very keenly, that of John F. Kennedy.

This chapter considers two key December 1963 sessions in which the issues represented in the poem are addressed: December 10 and 12. Despite some initial reluctance on Orne's part, he and Sexton worked together to reconstruct the therapeutic impasse of the prior year. Orne took responsibility for pushing her too hard or pushing her away (depending on whose version we believe), which led Sexton to important insights about the nature of their ongoing efforts to make her well. The negotiation process itself led to a greater understanding of what had transpired between them during the earlier period in therapy and how that impasse might have related to her painful childhood experiences, offering possibilities for how she and Orne could work in the months to follow. It also illustrated two of the most prominent patterns in their interactions: Orne's persistence in pushing Sexton to identify what he saw as the intrapsychic nature of her emotional distress, and Sexton's insistence that her treatment, her poetry, and even her identity were created through the work they did together. This important step in Sexton's therapy offered her a new way to work through difficult personal problems, and it also pushed Orne toward a shift in technique. Through exploring her reactions to him, Sexton opened the way to learning more about how she related to others. But she also urged Orne to consider how his decisions and actions affected her. In important ways, their interactions became more relational than classical in these hours, as Orne embraced the notion of working as a team to make sense of the past. Stephen Mitchell succinctly explains the shift from classical to relational approaches in American psychoanalysis that would become much more pronounced in the 70s and 80s:

> For Freud, the relationship with the analyst was a re-creation of past relationships, a new version struck from the original "stereotype plate" (Freud, 1912). The here-and-now relationship was crucial, but as a replication, as a vehicle for the recovery of memories, the filling in of amnesias, which cured the patient. Contemporary views of the analytic relationship tend to put more emphasis on what is new in the analytic relationship. The past is still important, but as a vehicle for understanding the meaning of the present relationship with the analyst, and it is in the working through of that relationship that cure resides. (Mitchell, 1984, p. 483)

The "working through" that Sexton and Orne managed in these two sessions offered a relatively new version of their relationship, one that would become more developed in the months to come.

In the sessions I am about to discuss, Sexton drew Orne into an extended discussion of their relationship as she attempted to cope with her feelings about his departure. His willingness to take responsibility for his side of their dialogue is clear. He spoke more, responded directly to Sexton's comments, and even admitted that she might be correct in her views about what had happened between them in 1962. Orne acknowledged that his actions had caused her great pain, culminating a hospitalization, and that perhaps he had made an error. Forced to consider his own shaping role in what they usually identified as Sexton's illness, Orne articulated his participation in the therapeutic process in terms that are familiar to us today, but which were largely unrecognized in his time. Irwin Hoffman (1996) explains that we have come to understand that

> there is no objective interpretation and there is no affective attunement that is merely responsive to and reflective of what the patient brings to the situation ... there is always something personal and theoretical (the theoretical being an aspect of the personal) that is coming from the side of the analyst. (p. 110)

Sexton's examinations of old therapy notebooks forced Orne to confront "the something personal and theoretical" that he brought to his interactions with her, often in the guise of scientific objectivity.

And yet Orne also resisted a relational model in significant ways, as he attempted to show Sexton that the mistake he made had been the result of a misconception that she had "sold" him on, like a bad bill of goods. When he shared with Sexton a sense of responsibility for his part in their struggle, he spoke like a contemporary relational psychotherapist, owning his role in the therapeutic dialogue. But when he tried to encourage her to see that his actions resulted from her illness, rather than his own countertransference feelings, he lacked a contemporary appreciation of his role in the therapeutic process. Excusing an admitted mistake by claiming he was a victim of his patient's illness, he illustrated how psychiatrists—well-paid, prestigious professionals in American culture—can become ensnared in protecting institutional prejudices and inequities of power that their profession attempts to deconstruct in pursuit of the truth.

December 10, 1963

Sexton first mentioned "Flee on Your Donkey" to Orne on December 10, 1963, a day in which loss, violence, and the art of poetry were very much on her mind. She was struggling with her writing, attempting to capture her intense experiences of the past weeks. She had written about images of choking and a description of an affair. Although her husband, Kayo, did not seem bothered personally by Anne's depiction of an extramarital affair, he did not like it because he thought she would be criticized brutally when it was published. Maxine Kumin similarly told her she was making a mistake; she was "raping her life."

Sexton felt uncomfortable writing what was so true to her private experience, worrying that she might be revealing too much about her personal life. But she was having trouble finding a creative outlet for her pain:

> *Sexton:* I have been for a year and a half blocked on the poem that I wanted to write. What I might call the definitive poem about my illness. Couldn't do it. It was to you. It was—I don't know. It just didn't work. It's as though I were gonna write the whole thing up and then throw it out. It's a way of mastering experience but I'm putting it all in.
>
> *Orne:* That's what intrigues me. If you were writing it for yourself.... But you know your concern is how can you publish it. What can you do with it?
>
> *Sexton:* Well unfortunately if I write it, if I really write the whole thing I'll want to publish it. I mean any writer would tell you that.
>
> *Orne:* You haven't written for yourself.
>
> *Sexton:* I don't think about poems I just write them.... I know they'll be published eventually.
>
> *Orne:* You haven't written for yourself.
>
> *Sexton:* I think I do write for myself. I don't write to please a magazine. But this is a little bit different. I don't know what I am doing.... I don't know who I am.

It is clear from the tone of Orne's responses that he believed Sexton was concerned with writing for an audience rather than processing her own feelings. Orne seemed to want her to "master experience" for her own benefit, but Sexton correctly asserted that she was a publishing writer; of course she wrote to be published. She commented that she wrote poems all the time, knowing they would eventually come out in print, even if not immediately. His unwillingness to affirm her vocation as a poet, an accomplishment that afforded her a place in the public world, represented a "stuck" place in their treatment. Sexton had forged a professional identity for herself that Orne, in his insistence on poetry as therapy (at least in this example), refused to acknowledge.

On December 10, Sexton raised a number of issues that would also appear in her poem: the loss of a physical intimacy with Orne through his withdrawing his hand during their sessions, her childhood isolation and fear, her feelings that she would always be abandoned by someone close to her. She was not depressed now, she insisted, but trying to face his eventual departure by reading through her notebooks from the time period the prior year when she had felt abandoned by his change in behavior. Until that time, Orne had regularly held Sexton's hand when she became very upset. Sexton read about his sudden refusal to do so in her notebooks:

> *Sexton:* You wouldn't hold my hand, trying to stop the three times a week appointment. I started feeling pretty sorry for myself.... I started feeling so badly for myself because I am so manipulated by you. Your need to get me well created such a distance and hurt me so much and it reminded me of the hurt that I am about to feel. I suppose I am kind of angry about it. You wouldn't hold my hand. I begged you and you wouldn't. And your hand nowhere existed. And I thought to myself I'd rather have you go away than ever do that again ... the thing I couldn't bear was you suddenly decided to stop holding my hand.
>
> *Orne:* [*long silence*]
>
> *Sexton:* I read from January to May ... [*trails off and seems to go into a trance*]

In the first part of this exchange on the tape, Sexton spoke clearly and definitively as she articulated what she had discovered as she read through her notebooks. When she arrived at the point of saying she was angry with Orne, her voice became a bit uncertain: "I suppose I am angry about it." Sexton spoke of the thing she "could not bear" and how sudden it felt to her. She told Orne that it "hurt me so much" that, even though she "begged," his "hand nowhere existed." The word *hand* repeats again and again in these sentences, as if it were being taken away each time the word was uttered, her voice trailing off as she waited for a response. Her anger and frustration seemed to disappear as she fell silent, but Orne still did not speak. The silence was protracted, lasting around 10 seconds. Finally, she resumed talking, but she seemed deflated. She emphasized that she had done a lot of research, as she had read sessions "from January to May." With still no response from Orne, she went into a trance.

Orne: Anne, Anne, do you have to go through that again?

Sexton: Yes, only really worse.

Orne: No, at that point we weren't able to be close but this is something that we have to face and we can face it together.

Sexton: How? I don't know.

Orne: Anne, Anne [*seems to move to hold her hand, which she resists*] … You are not going to hold my hand? That doesn't solve it.

Sexton: You went away from me. You did.

Orne: Yes, it's true. I tried to force you to be well then. I recognized much later that that was wrong.

Sexton: You wouldn't be close to me. Well I don't want you at all.

Orne: It's not true, Anne. I know that you're angry with me. That doesn't mean we can't be honest.

Sexton: I don't want to be here when you tell me.

Orne: I think it's essential that we work together … Anne, Anne, Anne, Anne, now try to reason. You don't have to pull away.

Although she clearly felt rejected by his silence, Sexton was easily coaxed back into contact with Orne. He held her hand, acknowledged her anger, and admitted that he had tried to "force [her] to be well."

From Orne's point of view, Sexton's movement into a trance state might have been interpreted as resistance. In 1963, silence was very much respected as an appropriate response to even the most persistent patients. Ernest Bibring, a well-known Boston analyst at the time, wrote that an analyst's passivity or silence does not interfere with the treatment, but actually contributes to the patient's spontaneity. Of course, he admits, silence can sometimes be met with resistance:

> The relative passivity of the analyst intends not to interfere too much with the spontaneity of the patient. The usual "rituals" mean not to inhibit the spontaneity of the patient and the analyst. That they can be misused by the patient for purposes of resistance is well known and requires interpretive or manipulative measures. (1954, p. 765)

Note how the analyst's passivity here is "relative," as if it is not serious, and rather harmless. The patient's response to the silence, in contrast, is characterized as "misused … for the purpose of resistance." Seen from this perspective, Orne's initial long silence after Sexton's admission that she was angry might have provoked her movement into trance, which would require "interpretive or manipulative" measures on his part. But the interpretation of Sexton's movement into trance as a form of resistance did not take into account the amount of frustration Sexton might have felt when, after finally giving voice to her anger from the past, she was met not by acknowledgment or apology, but silence. In fact, when she told him she was angry, she qualified it, saying, "I suppose I am angry about it." Sexton rarely expressed anger at Orne, although she often did with Kayo. With Orne, she was tentative at best. When he failed to respond, she became despondent.

Orne seemed to recognize that he had made an error by not responding to Sexton's anger, as he told her when she was in trance: "I know that you're angry with me. That doesn't mean we can't be honest." He acknowledged that he had pushed her away in the past: "Yet, it's true." Once he had acknowledged her anger and the validity of her perception of what had happened, Sexton began to respond to him again. The previous July, she had told Orne, "When I'm that child in trance I can't grow up because then all these other things will happen. I want to turn around and start everything going backward." In this case, Sexton may have attempted to go back to a time when Orne had not abandoned her. Recognizing her flight as a direct response to his silence, Orne was able to coax her out of the trance. In fact, he moved to hold her hand, and she immediately began to speak again. In this exchange of words, silence, and gestures, Orne needed to take responsibility for his role in causing her feelings of abandonment. It might have been true that Sexton struggled throughout her treatment with a sense of abandonment, but in this particular case she had indeed been pushed away by her therapist.

In his review of the concept of enactment, James McLaughlin (McLaughlin & Johan, 1992) argues that "even silence, when it reflects a withdrawal to avoid anger, can be an enactment" (p. 829). In this instance, what might be interpreted as Orne's initial error of holding Sexton's hand was followed by a second error, of failing to acknowledge his patient's anger as justified. Sexton's rapid descent into trance and her emergence from it as soon as Orne began to take responsibility for his actions in the past suggest that silence was not a good choice of technique for him in response to her statement that she was angry about his abandonment of her in 1962. Theodore Jacobs (2001) points out that silence is not necessarily helpful for a patient facing her analyst's error:

> The patient may, and often does, experience the analyst as being unwilling or unable to face up to his own errors, seeking instead to conceal that fact behind the protective cover of proper and quite correct analytic technique. Such a situation, I believe, cannot foster growth. It can only lead to deception, collusions, and increased distrust, both of the analyst and of the patient's own perceptions. (p. 666)

When he directly addressed her anger and moved to hold her hand, Orne seemed to intend resumption of a posture that would "foster growth" and decrease her distrust in him. In his efforts to reconnect with Sexton, Orne would seem to have left behind his Freudian training to embrace a more Winnicottian vision of the patient as in need of affirmation. Stephen Mitchell's (1986) explanation of the difference between these two approaches aptly summarizes the difference between Orne's initial silence and his subsequent reaching out to Sexton:

> Whereas Freud saw the analytic situation in terms of abstinence (instinctual wishes emerge and find no gratification), Winnicott sees the analytic situation in terms of satisfaction, not of instinctual impulses per se, but of crucial developmental experiences, missed parental functions. The couch, the constancy of the sessions, the demeanor of the analyst, these become the holding environment which was not provided in infancy. Freud saw the analytic process in terms of renunciation; by bringing to light and renouncing infantile wishes, healthier and more mature forms of libidinal organization become possible. Winnicott sees the analytic process in terms of a kind of revitalization; the frozen, aborted self is able to reawaken and begin to develop as crucial ego needs are met. (p. 114)

Winnicott's theory that "crucial ego needs" remained unmet in a patient, while a "frozen aborted self" lies dormant, could aptly explain what Sexton seemed to want to communicate to Orne at the time. In fact, she often described herself as "frozen" to Orne, capturing her childhood experience in an image of hiding in the closet while the family ignored her from downstairs. Seen in Winnicottian terms, Orne reached out to that frozen child with his hand and his voice, and her literal reawakening from a trance was the result.

"Flee on Your Donkey," the poem Sexton was struggling to finish, presents a number of images that seem to be directly related to the above exchange. The poem addresses a therapist, whom the speaker refers to as a "new God" who works on Marlborough Street (where Orne's office was located). Its epigraph is from Rimbaud, "*Ma faim, Anne, Anne,/Fais sur ton ane*" ("My hunger, Anne, Anne,/Flee on your donkey"). The first lines present the speaker on a trip to a mental institution "because there was no other place to flee to":

> without luggage or defenses,
> giving up my car keys and my cash,
> keeping only a pack of Salem cigarettes
> the way a child holds on to a toy.

Surrendering her symbols of adult independence, keys and cash, while grasping her cigarettes as a child grips a teddy bear, the speaker is without "luggage or defenses." She is in flight, but the place she flees to "is a mental hospital/not a child's game." She uses the term *defenses*, from a psychiatric vocabulary, to characterize her mental state. She is a mentally ill woman, a poet, who has been left all alone with only her muse and her cigarettes to provide comfort or solace:

> Everyone has left me
> except my muse,
> that good nurse.
> She stays in my hand,
> a mild white mouse.

Unlike the dropped hand of Sexton's own psychiatrist, the muse "stays in [her] hand" in these lines, providing soft comfort. The muse remains with the speaker, providing benign promise of poems to come. And yet, the muse is likely to provide temporary comfort, for we cannot imagine a mouse staying in anyone's hand for a very long time.

After describing the other patients in the hospital, the speaker tells about the recent loss of both her parents:

Meanwhile,
they carried out my mother,
wrapped like somebody's doll, in sheets,
bandaged her jaw and stuffed up her holes.
My father, too. He went out on the rotten blood
he used up on other women in the Middle West.
He went out, a cured old alcoholic
on crooked feet and useless hands.

The speaker's mother, "wrapped like somebody's doll," and father, "a cured old alcoholic/on crooked feet and useless hands," are both dead. The mother appears as a childlike mummy, while the father, a former drunk and philanderer, seems physically handicapped, unable to use his hands or feet. The mother is wrapped like a plastic doll, a child's plaything rather than a maternal object. The image suggests that she might well have been emotionally dead for a very long time. The father, whose crooked feet might even denote the demonic, may have been "cured" of his disease, but he also is of no use to the poem's narrator. Not only are both parents recently deceased, but the images used to describe them suggest that they might not have been very nurturing even when alive. In the speaker's emotional world, they have been dead a long time.

The poem juxtaposes these helpless and utterly unparental images with those portraying a god/doctor/cheerleader. Addressing the doctor directly, the speaker pronounces him a savior. He is her doctor and enthusiast, "better than Christ," who promised her another world to tell her who she was.

I spent most of my time,
a stranger,
damned and in trance—that little hut,
that naked blue-veined place,
my eyes shut on the confusing office,
eyes circling into my childhood,
eyes newly cut.
Years of hints
strung out—a serialized case history—
thirty-three years of the same dull incest
that sustained us both.

The speaker, "damned and in trance," with "eyes circling into [her] childhood," remembers "thirty-three years of the same dull incest/ that sustained us both." Trapped in an endlessly repeating past, she characterizes her central issue as incest. It is "dull," a boring subject, one not fit for sharpened wits like hers and her doctor's. It sends her into a dissociative state, into the land of the dead. And yet, the incest also "sustained" them, as if it were food. Just as trauma can repeat endlessly even as each new wound feels like the first, incest both feeds and deadens in these lines. It is uninteresting or blunt, but paradoxically nourishing to one who cannot escape it. It causes its victim to go in "circles," consuming and consumed by childhood memories of victimization. The childhood she cannot escape from emerges in years of "hints/strung out," as if she were offering a soap opera to her doctor. Incest, at the crux of the history, sends her back into a childlike posture in a womblike office, with its blue veins.

> The "damned" speaker exists in contrast to her doctor/
>   savior:
> You, my bachelor analyst,
> who sat on Marlborough Street,
> sharing your office with your mother
> and giving up cigarettes each New Year,
> were the new God,
> the manager of the Gideon Bible.

An administrative god, who doles out bibles, the doctor is better than God but also more human. He is a comical exception to what the speaker has experienced, and a promise of something beyond her. But the ironically painted identity of the doctor becomes more complex in these lines, as his saving powers are tempered by human limitations. The speaker admittedly struggles more, circling as she does around her childhood pain, but her "bachelor" doctor is still entwined with his own mother and continually trying to give up cigarettes. Even as the patient waits for him to save her, he seems to have other preoccupations. He is an addict whose office, if womblike, is "confusing."

December 12, 1963

If the previous session confronted Sexton with the somewhat limited doctor that we find in the above lines, the next session, December 12, showed Sexton feeling much better. She told Orne that she had begun to "feel better [since] the last appointment." She attributed her relief to their conversation about hand holding and Orne's confirmation of his part in their impasse:

Sexton: You did say yes you did push me away.... Often you say after all these years why don't you trust me. But there were times when really I couldn't. Something happened that wasn't. Of course if you're going away it isn't necessary to push me away. For you, I mean.

Orne: This is undoubtedly so. You see pushing you away isn't really pushing you away. It's pushing you.

Sexton: Well! MMMMMMM I don't know. Well, on the ground that we work it—the arena, the stage, whatever you want—it was maybe pushing but it was pushing away.

Orne: Well, um, not …

Sexton: Or maybe. I am pretty sure I think that that's so.

Orne: Well because, you see, to you in your very concrete way, it felt like rejection.

Sexton: Mmmm very definitely.

Orne: I don't think it was. But it was pushing.

Sexton: It really was pushing; it really was pushing away. What else can you say? … I mean it was so obvious. You were also working on that I should come less often. You were trying to create a distance that I couldn't understand.

Orne: Well, I don't know whether it was a distance.

Sexton: It seemed so. I mean to me. Naturally it would.

Orne: It may well be.

Sexton: It was. Of course it was. It's so concrete. You were worried about this acting out and thinking "she ought to be better than this." You really were endeavoring to get me to intellectualize but instead….

Orne: Not intellectualize.

Sexton: Well *what*? Talk instead of act?

Orne: That's not intellectualizing. Intellectualizing is something different.

Sexton: Yeah but just all of a sudden. Holding my hand had had such meaning. All of a sudden you wouldn't, you know, and there wasn't anything I could do about it.

Orne: No, I see.

Sexton: If I read back over it I am very caught. I don't have it here now. But there are a couple of appointments where you really were … I was getting to feel kind of rejected but not talking about it because there wasn't anything I could do about it. There wasn't anything I could do.

Orne: You could have told me how you felt.

Sexton: No. Because we weren't doing it together at all. Besides, I *had* told you how I felt and it had no result. But now I have the feeling, *in contrast*, that if I tell you how I feel it means something to you. Though I do keep saying you wouldn't understand. Like all the time.

Sexton began this conversation relieved to know that Orne admitted that he had pushed her away in the past. It seemed very important to her to be able to distinguish between his past efforts to separate himself from her and his present situation, in which he might be forced to leave Boston. Orne did not echo Sexton's version of the past events or the past session, however. Instead, he argued that he had been pushing her to get well, while she maintained that he had pushed her away. Whatever they had shared the previous hour seemed to disappear. In short, they were at it again.

Sexton's expressions emphasized the powerful feelings his withdrawal from her had produced. Despite his unwillingness to confirm her view of the past, she said she was "pretty sure" that Orne was "very definitely" trying to create a distance. Even as Orne insisted that he was pushing her to get well, Sexton attempted to show him that he had "concretely" pushed her away. We can readily understand Sexton's point of view, for his method did in fact create distance: physical distance, in that he would not hold her hand, and temporal, in that he wanted to see her less and to set a date for the end of the treatment. Sexton was insistent but not stubborn in these exchanges. She held to her point of view that she and Orne "weren't doing it together." She drew their attention to the analytic space, "the ground … the arena, the stage on which we work," emphasizing the therapeutic space as a world in itself. Nor did Orne's attempt to blame her for not telling him how she felt seem correct to Sexton, who was pushing him to see that she did tell him her feelings, even if he refused to take them into account because they did not concur with his point of view on what would be helpful to her.

In this exchange, Orne once again revealed his idea of what would help Sexton: She needed to acknowledge and integrate her feelings, to see what she was doing and take responsibility for it. For Sexton, the only road to wellness was through a mutual dialogue based on trust. Established in the past, it must be maintained in the present. Unable to obtain Orne's corroboration of her version of the story, she was willing to agree to disagree on the semantics, while emphasizing how she felt that "now, in contrast" something quite different was happening. Yet Orne persisted in defending his version of the story:

> *Orne:* No, there is this thing I wanted to pick up on…. I don't believe that it was rejection.
>
> *Sexton:* Oh you wanna go back to that? Why do you want to go back to that?
>
> *Orne:* It's important. I think. I'm not saying that it was right. It wasn't helpful to you. I am very willing to recognize that. But I think it's important that, well, maybe it's important to me that you understand it.
>
> *Sexton:* I don't think I can. I don't really believe you. I mean I think you're being truthful but I don't think you know. Haha. I'm sorry….
>
> *Orne:* Maybe.
>
> *Sexton:* The minute you told me you were married, the thing you'd been worried about, you held my hand and you were willing to be close to me.
>
> *Orne:* Yes. Ah….
>
> *Sexton:* Of course at that moment you were sorry you know because …
>
> *Orne:* No.
>
> *Sexton:* Well I don't know. *What?* Why?

Orne: What happened was I wanted to spare you some discomfort and yet, you know, I knew that probabilities were sooner or later you'd run into someone who knew me, and so I was under a tremendous amount of pressure to force you to be well.

Sexton: So that you could tell me.

Orne: That's right

Sexton: And I just wasn't getting well that way. And it was getting more frustrating. But that's alright, I understand it. I mean everyone …

Orne: But that's not rejection.

Sexton: So the minute you told me …

Orne: Because at that point I no longer felt that there was a pressure.

Sexton: At what cost I don't know. I don't know how I would have reacted.

Orne: It happens that this had been a big thing with you for a long time.

Sexton: That you were gonna be married.

Orne: And my error was that I didn't trust you enough.

Orne revealed his thought process; he wanted to "spare her some discomfort," so he tried to "force [her] to get well." It is difficult to ascertain what theory Orne used when he determined how to proceed with Sexton's treatment, but he might have been thinking that he needed to teach Sexton to be more independent. While Sexton did not deny that she might have reacted badly to his marriage, she insisted that his recipe for her cure was misguided and ultimately harmful: "I just wasn't getting well that way." She was playful with Orne as she joked about how she "made so many problems," and also as she laughed about how unable she was to get well when he was pushing her to do so. Her laughter seemed to indicate a bit of discomfort, however, as she attempted to ally herself with her therapist, perhaps in order to protect his authority as a way to hold onto him?

Orne, whose tone was far more serious, seemed determined to teach her a lesson about what really happened.

Sexton: I was much more capable of dealing with that than of you not holding my hand. You see, I think you took my transference too literally. You thought it was primarily sexual.

Orne: Mmm? [*sounds questioning*]

Sexton: Well, how am I going to think about it? I mean now that I think about it, actually, I like it that you're married. I mean as long as it didn't change you. But of course what happened was it did change you. [*laughing*]

Orne: Well.

Sexton: I really wasn't entertaining any prolonged fantasies of marrying you myself. I was too disturbed about what you were doing if you weren't married. There was no security. I couldn't figure out what you were doing. I don't mean sexually. I mean I worried about it. Every time you said, "I have a life of my own," I wondered what it was.

Orne: You are correct. Well, actually what happened at the time is that I got caught in underestimating the effect my getting married had on some patients where I had not expected it to be a problem.

Sexton: And me who makes so many problems.

Sexton's willingness to work with Orne in this lively back and forth exchange illustrates her ability to play with ideas, and her willingness to believe that her doctor could help her to change her identity. She chuckled as she told him she wasn't entertaining any *prolonged* fantasies of marrying him herself, acknowledging that he was nonetheless an intimate partner. For Sexton, who seemed to become more enlivened every time Orne responded, it seemed clear that therapy was an intersubjective exchange. She asked Orne, "Well, how am I to think about it?" This comment signaled her ability to take Orne's way of thinking into account, and to allow it to influence her own. This was especially indicated in her shifting tone in these exchanges. She often seemed to mull over what he said, with an "mmmm" or "well…." It is as if Sexton understood that individuals do not exist apart from their interpersonal relationships. This more contemporary approach to the therapeutic relationship resonates in her comments to Orne, which emphasize their separate but also overlapping thought processes as they revisited the past together.

Sexton's own analysis of the situation, in fact, constituted an amazing reversal of roles, in which she used the terminology of Orne's profession to illustrate her understanding of his error: "I think you took my transference too literally." It is as if she saw it as her job to remind Orne of an essential component of treatment, that transference love is necessary to facilitate the patient's growth, but that it is not to be confused with love outside the consulting room. Sexton might well have read Freud's articulation of the subject, for she was an avid reader of psychoanalysis at the time. Freud (1915) explains:

> [The analyst] must keep firm hold of the transference love, but treat it as something unreal, as a situation which has to be gone through in the treatment and traced back to its unconscious origins and which must assist in bringing all that is most deeply hidden in the patient's erotic life into her consciousness and therefore under her control. The more plainly the analyst lets it be seen that he is proof against every temptation, the more readily will he be able to extract from the situation its analytic content. (p. 166)

The patient's erotic transference here is a fantasy that can be resisted by the analyst. Sexton's own fantasies, whether erotic or not, would, according to Freud, need to be resisted by Orne, rather than considered harmful. When she told Orne that he took her transference too literally, Sexton used words that were not that different from Freud's warning that analysts should treat the transference "as something unreal." Ironically, Orne, who was so fond of explaining "reality" to Sexton, fell into the role of having it explained to him by his patient.

Perhaps because she was beginning to sound like his supervisor rather than his patient, Orne abruptly turned the subject back to Sexton's role in the previous impasse:

> *Sexton:* You actually built more of a wall than your marriage, the knowledge of your marriage would have.
>
> *Orne:* My being married didn't build a wall from my side at all. But you see the important thing. And this is something that you need to understand. In a way this business of omnipotence and how important I am to you is what really hurt you. You somehow sold me on something which wasn't reality. Namely that you wouldn't have been able to tolerate it ... as a result, well, I bit.
>
> *Sexton:* Well ... [*tone is dubious*] Well, alright. I see what you're saying.

Orne: The difference this time around and why we can be close is
because I know on the one hand how on the other hand that
you know it's not that I'm irreplaceable.

Sexton: I'd still sell you on that.

Orne: You would, I know.

Sexton: Yeah.

Orne: It is just that I think I've learned a little since then.

Sexton: Dr. Orne, can't you see? Well, first of all, I compartmentalize
everything. What we are here together is very important to
me. And if something's going to happen to us here together
that's worse than if something happens in reality. Our relationship is real too but you do something with that and we're
in much more trouble than if you get married. If you had
said "I am married" and you wouldn't hold my hand, well,
then, that would have been real *trouble* ... because I would
interpret it in terms of *us.*...

Again Sexton distinguished between the consulting room and real
life, as she returned Orne's attention to the world they created together
through the treatment. Everything that happened in there, Sexton
warned, would be interpreted "in terms of *us.*" Orne's insistence that
Sexton had "sold" him on something did not strike Sexton as the correct interpretation, for she responded with a dubious "well...." Her
comment that she would still "sell him" on that has an ambiguous
ring, perhaps acknowledging his part but subtly mocking the hack-
neyed expression used by Orne. Nonetheless, she did not contradict
Orne's theory entirely. Her willingness to acknowledge his side of the
disagreement while continuing to present her own suggests that her
model of therapy, involving a "you," "me," and "us," was more similar
to a more current late 20th-century model of therapeutic interaction
than Orne's, which was firmly grounded on the disparity between the
clinician's sense of reality and the patient's manifest illness, which
the doctor must avoid being "sold" on. When he told her that his
marriage did not build a wall "on my side at all," he emphasized the
fact that he was the doctor, who, in reality, was able to distinguish
between personal events and transference effects. But Sexton knew
better, as she reminded him that "what happens in here" did in fact

involve Orne's "side" of the story about his marriage, which for his own reasons he needed to keep silent.

Orne's responses to Sexton resound with clichés that overlap and contradict each other. Of course this is common in human conversation, but here it becomes more obvious because Sexton's discourse is decidedly more sophisticated. While Sexton perhaps invoked the recently deceased (January 1963) Robert Frost to describe Orne's attempt to build a wall, Orne told Sexton that she had "sold" him on her attachment to him and that "well, [he] bit." Mixing images of a dishonest peddler with a fisherman offering bait, Orne then suggested that he had bought into the fantasy that he was indeed "irreplaceable." In his comments, he did not take up Sexton's thoughtful observations about their particular relationship, but instead suggested that he considered all of his patients together, as "patients." Orne needed to be reminded by Sexton that hers was a very particular subjectivity, as she pleaded with him to lower his professional blinders: "Can't you see?"

Although we can see that Sexton and Orne tried, however, unequally, to work together to reconstruct their past interaction in the session cited above, when she represented the painful impasse of a rejection in "Flee on Your Donkey," she portrayed the position of a patient who has been left alone without an interlocutor to help her make sense of her world. The poem's speaker explains to her listening doctor how she experienced a breakdown after a session:

> Once, outside your office,
> I collapsed in the old-fashioned swoon
> between the illegally parked cars.
> I threw myself down,
> pretending dead for eight hours.
> I thought I had died
> into a snowstorm.
> Above my head
> chains cracked along like teeth
> digging their way through the snowy street.
> I lay there
> like an overcoat
> that someone had thrown away.

You carried me back in,
awkwardly, tenderly,
with help of the red-haired secretary
who was built like a lifeguard.
My shoes,
I remember,
were lost in the snowbank
as if I planned never to walk again.

The speaker illustrates her helplessness and inability to function without the doctor's help, and there is no sense that they are working together. He is physically stronger, mentally more capable, and even accompanied by an assistant, who, like a linebacker, can defend him and assist him on the field. He has another teammate, in a sense, while the speaker must be rescued as if she has never played the game at all. Once she leaves the doctor's office she becomes "like an old overcoat," an object, waiting for death in the snow. She loses her shoes, "as if I planned never to walk again." Like her mother, wrapped in a sheet, and her father, on "useless feet," in the earlier lines, the speaker functions as if she is one of the dead. Her doctor and his secretary, in contrast, are able-bodied, if awkward, and the doctor "tenderly" performs the rescue.

The difference between this scene and that in Orne's office is important to consider. The speaker is describing a time when she and her doctor did not work together, and her metaphorical death was the result.

In contrast to this macabre scene, the speaker later turns to consider what she learned in her doctor's office:

You taught me
to believe in dreams;
thus I was the dredger.
I held them like an old woman with arthritic fingers,
carefully straining the water out—
sweet dark playthings,
and above all, mysterious
until they grew mournful and weak.
O my hunger! My hunger!
I was the one

who opened the warm eyelid
like a surgeon
and brought forth young girls
to grunt like fish.

Here the doctor values the patient's unconscious, which transforms her from an arthritic woman to a surgeon who awakens young girls and brings them to life. The value of the doctor's belief cannot be underestimated here, for with it the speaker can herself bring life, and even, we might imagine, reawaken her younger, frozen child self. In the presence of the doctor-teacher, the patient can become playful and flexible, a professional herself—a surgeon—who "brought forth young girls/to grunt like fish." Far from offering bait to a doctor who swallows it whole, this speaker-patient can actually summon life in the office. This ability is truncated in the poem, for the speaker returns to the mental hospital nonetheless, but ultimately, the power conferred by the doctor to a writing patient allows her to write the poem to record (and perhaps transform) experience.

Thus far we have visited three versions of Sexton's and Orne's 1962 impasse: hers, his, and the one she constructed in "Flee on Your Donkey." But one more important version of the story exists, that crafted by Diane Middlebrook in her biography of Sexton. Middlebrook too listened to the tapes, and she also benefited from 80 hours of interviews with Orne. She read Sexton's notebooks and drafts, and therefore would seem to be the most knowledgeable person about Sexton's experiences of the breakdown and the preceding events. To one of very few other listeners to these restricted tapes, Middlebrook seems remarkably protective of Orne as she explains what led to Sexton's breakdown in the summer of 1962, and how it was represented by Sexton in "Flee on Your Donkey." Middlebrook's reconstruction of what she heard on the tapes, read in the poem, and learned from interviewing Orne suggests what may have been an unconscious effort to ignore or simply to remain silent about his part in provoking Sexton's distress at that time.

Middlebrook describes the impasse with Orne as related to his efforts to encourage Sexton to "take a more analytical role in the treatment." She suggests that Sexton refused to play a more active role in "integrating and mixing important aspects of herself" (p. 174). When she describes the months preceding Sexton's June breakdown, she omits a number of essential components of the events that led to Sexton's deterioration. Most importantly, Orne's anxiety about Sexton finding out about his marriage was directly related to his effort to encourage her self-analysis. His motivation to push her into a premature recovery reveals what we might today consider an enactment. In addition, he cut her from three sessions per week to two, and suggested that they set a date for termination. From the outside, it is difficult not to interpret Orne's actions as intended to "break up" with Sexton. For Middlebrook, however, the transference was primarily Sexton's.

When Middlebrook turns to interpret the therapeutic situation as it appeared in Sexton's poem, she ignores several images that seem directly related to the events discussed above. She does not consider that the image of the "bachelor analyst" still sharing an office with his mother refers to Sexton's ignorance about the fact of Orne's marriage. Middlebrook links the "hand" in the poem to Sexton's childhood feeling that her Nana's hands were sexual, when it is obviously related to the one that Orne refused to hold. While Middlebrook does acknowledge that Sexton asked Orne to "be Nana" and hold her hand, she does not state that Orne did in fact hold Sexton's hand for many months and that the withdrawal of his hand (among other things) led to a deterioration culminating in her hospitalization. Moreover, Middlebrook takes Orne's position that he was simply "pushing" too hard for Anne to get well, as if that version of the events were the only one.

In Sexton's own reconstruction of these events, to which Middlebrook listened before she completed the biography, Sexton placed much more importance on Orne's withdrawal from her than his pushing. Indeed, when they revisited the period in their December 1963 conversations, Orne admitted that the real motive for his "pushing" Sexton was his fear of the effect of learning about his marriage on her. Middlebrook identifies the style of the poem as "more unconscious" than Sexton's usual style at the time, as it "channeled unconscious processes into artistic forms." But we must consider that the so-called "unconscious processes" related directly to Sexton's conscious life in Orne's office during the period. Moreover, Middlebrook argues that "the poem hitches a ride on a metaphor that combines Christ (riding to Jerusalem astride a donkey) with Rimbaud" (p. 177). The expression "hitches a ride" somehow resonates with Orne's statements that Sexton "sold him" a bill of goods to which he "bit." These two interpreters of her experiences leave the gifted writer Anne Sexton far behind. Her attempt to manage rejection led her into the metaphor of being rescued by a far superior being, but experts failed Sexton before and after her death, as they relegated her to an isolated world in which she was haunted and made mad by figures from the past. Her relapse or regression into the position of a helpless mental patient had something to do, of course, with her own internal processing of past and present events, but it also was influenced by the therapeutic perspective of her most important interlocutor in present reality, one who seemed caught up himself in a powerful transference-counter-transference enactment.

Read in the context of the sessions I cited above, the final lines of "Flee on Your Donkey" do not show a doctor riding into Jerusalem, but instead a speaker who cries directions to herself without success. The narrator attempts to mobilize her despair, to carve out a space for herself in a new world, when the old one, with its flat heart and rotted brains, is too familiar to be endured:

> Turn, my hungers!
> For once make a deliberate decision.
> There are brains that rot here
> like black bananas.
> Hearts have grown as flat as dinner plates.
> Anne, Anne,
> flee on your donkey,
> flee this sad hotel,
> ride out on some hairy beast,
> gallop backward pressing
> your buttocks to his withers,
> sit to his clumsy gait somehow.
> Ride out
> any old way you please!
> In this place everyone talks to his own mouth.

> That's what it means to be crazy.
> Those I loved best died of it—
> the fool's disease.

The speaker needs "somehow" to "ride out" of her pain, and yet, like the patient in her doctor's office in the early lines of the poem, she seems to go in circles. She is galloping backwards, the donkey's gait clumsy—much less satisfying than her awkward doctor's "tender" touch. The poem ends in death from "the fool's disease," and we can imagine that the speaker's best loves would include perhaps her parents. The place in which dialogue is impossible, because "everyone talks to his own mouth," is no place at all.

If Sexton's speaker "hitched a ride" on anything from Rimbaud (whose poem is notoriously difficult to interpret) in this poem, it was the idea that she had to flee, because she had nowhere to call home. Most importantly, the narrator ends the poem talking to herself, after remembering talking to a doctor in the past, a doctor who remains far from her listening ear, or who has no ears himself. Although she once knew how to carve life out of her dreams, she has no witness in these lines. She is bound to death herself, turning round and round on an ass.

After they had discussed the hand holding in the December 12 appointment, she asked Orne why she was always feeling abandoned, "even at the end of an appointment." She agreed that she felt left alone because she was very much alone as a child. But, she told Orne, the important thing was not what happened then but what happened between them in the here and now. As if to support her argument that the present moment could be the source of healing, Sexton told Orne about a dream she had the night before, a dream in which she was Jacquelyn Kennedy and Orne was the recently deceased president:

> *Sexton:* We were riding in a car and people started shooting. And we
> were lying in the gutter and people were shooting. And I
> think I said shouldn't we get somewhere safer and you said
> it's too late. And I tried to shield you so they wouldn't shoot
> you. [*laughing*] Sounds a lot like the Kennedy thing but it
> was on a street you see. I was trying to protect your face. I
> didn't know how to protect you. Whatever that means.
>
> *Orne:* Hmmm.

Sexton: Hmm?

Orne: Mmhmmm.

Sexton: People were shooting.

Orne: What did the street remind you of?

Sexton: I think I associate it to the Kennedy thing.

Orne: But what else? Anything strange about the street?

Sexton: Probably that I think it might have had cobblestones and that would make it a European street. But maybe because I associate Europe with war more. It might have been war.... I think I said, "Can't we get out of here to somewhere safer?" and you said, "No it's too late there's nothing we can do but just hope they don't notice."

Orne: Were you frightened?

Sexton: Mmm. [*15-second silence*] I know that they were shooting and I associated that to the fact that Kayo likes to shoot and it's just as though Kayo shot Kennedy. Kayo would kill us, you see. Or you. I don't know.... Well, it must have been some kind of war because I think I said to you and this doesn't make any sense, "Maybe they won't notice that we're German." ... Following the association, Nana lived in Germany.

Orne: Mmm.

Sexton: It's really about you though. Me and you.... I was putting my hand over your face thinking it would protect you. And I think I got shot in the hand, I don't remember. Maybe I got shot all over the place, I don't know.

Orne: That's the part of me you want to keep.

Orne made few comments in this exchange, although Sexton repeatedly urged him to take up her comparison of the two of them to the Kennedy couple. He did not express any curiosity about Sexton's sense of danger, her desire to protect him, or her wounded hand. Asking her about the street, Orne seemed to suggest that he had another reading of the dream. But until the end of the session, he did not articulate what it was. Like the long silence that led her into a trance early in the session, the absence of his point of view in response to the dream was palpable. Perhaps Orne was more anxious about being coupled with Sexton than he realized, for he missed a remarkable opportunity to tie together the themes they had discussed in the hour: separation as tragic death, protection as a part of intimacy, and perhaps most significantly, holding hands and saving face. Although it is impossible to know what Orne was thinking about Sexton's dream, he seemed remarkably reluctant to discuss the two of them as a married couple, even as a fantasy. For Orne, working together as doctor and patient and being married were very far apart, even in the realm of unconscious fantasy. When he said "that's the part of me you want to keep," however, he offered Sexton something to hold on to, something she would return to less than a week later.

If the December 1963 sessions provide an indication of why Sexton found it so hard to finish "Flee on Your Donkey," it may be that the poem could not substitute for a genuine dialogue, a human connection, which is perhaps even better than the reach of a real hand. The real hand is what Orne offered Sexton, and when he took it away he left her to stare into an abyss in which past, present, and future dissolved into one shapeless form. In her dream, Sexton tried to "save" his "face," even as she lost her own hand in the process. In their work together, it would be much harder to measure the consequences of Orne's ambivalence.

4

"This Terrible Ideal of the Happy Family"

December 14–19, 1963

Orne: Today is Tuesday the 17th of … um …

Sexton: [*softly*] December.

Orne: December 1963.

Sexton: [*chuckling*] That's what you need me for—the date!

Orne: Hmmph.

Sexton: I don't always know that either.

(December 17, 1963)

In mid-December 1963, after two productive sessions in which Sexton and Orne worked through a difficult period from the past, Sexton seemed to feel closer to Orne. At the same time, however, her relationship with her husband was becoming more violent. On December 14, they had an argument during which Kayo choked her once again and their older daughter Linda responded to Sexton's cry for help. Five days later, Sexton called Orne to report yet another battle. Orne attempted to help Sexton identify the ways in which she precipitated the violence by turning her rage about Orne's departure against her husband. Sexton attributed blame to herself, to Kayo, to Orne's possible departure, and to societal pressures to be a housewife in a happy American family—a role she loathed but also exploited as a key subject in her poetry.

Faithfully transcribing each therapy tape, even when she "didn't feel like working," Sexton tried to understand what she was doing as a way to stop the violence in her home. Unfortunately, understanding and subsequent action were separated in her mind. She told Orne she "just couldn't work that way," suggesting that she needed some other method to help her control her behavior. Knowing what she was doing, and why, did not dissipate her anger at her husband. Most importantly, it did not make her feel powerful in her own self.

But what would help? Sexton offered suggestions when she talked to Orne about what made her feel "hopeful" or "great." She praised Orne for his way of responding to her when they conversed about "real things," like psychoanalysis, or when he represented her to herself as a creative person. She gushed when she remembered his very useful interpretation of her John F. Kennedy dream, offering him four more dreams to interpret. Finally, she expressed her appreciation that he revealed that his decision to leave Boston was more about his duty to others than a wish to abandon her. Praising their mutual relationship as a sharp contrast to her marriage, she wished she could "really talk" to her husband the way she did with Orne.

But much as Sexton valued her relationship with Orne, her psychiatrist did not ground his technique in the more equal and reciprocal experiences of shared respect that most pleased his patient. He insisted in a rather didactic way that Sexton try to understand what she was doing so that she would stop acting out. Likewise, he issued warnings, as though he were reminding her of the rules. She was not to talk to Kayo about things that she should be addressing in therapy. She should talk about her feelings in therapy and not act them out at home. Although his points may have been useful to Sexton, Orne's tone was authoritative and sometimes paternalistic. For example, he repeatedly apprised her of things that she was forgetting, often beginning with "there's just one thing, Anne." He did not seem convinced when Sexton argued that she simply could not be what Kayo wanted: a perfect wife, who would market, maintain the house, take care of the children, and keep their guests entertained at dinner parties. It enraged her, for example, that Kayo once told Orne that Sexton's best attribute was that she was "a wonderful hostess." While Orne's tone was often both firm and loving, his message was always the same: "Please try to understand what you are doing here"—as if he knew exactly what that was.

Orne remained quite definitive in his approach, unwavering in his belief that Sexton was trying to avoid expressing her feelings with him and instead acting them out with her husband. His tone was insistent as he told Sexton that she was making her husband into her psychiatrist, using him as a sounding board for all of her troubles and relying on him to be the voice of reality for her. In a much less certain voice, Sexton questioned Orne's interpretation of her actions again and again. After saying, "I am not turning Kayo into my psychiatrist," for example, she then tentatively asked, "Am I?" When Orne failed to respond to a comment that clearly solicited his acknowledgment, such as when she reminded him of the date at the beginning of a session, ("That's what you need me for, the date!"), she undermined herself ("I don't always know that either"). And even when she became exasperated, as she did when Orne insisted that she was not expressing her feelings with him ("What? You want me to produce feelings on the spot?"), Sexton always assumed that she was in the wrong. After all, she was, at home and in the office, "the sick one." More often than not, Sexton would question and resist Orne's interpretations, only to conclude her effort with a sigh and an acquiescent, "I guess you're right."

If we attend to the dialogue in Orne's office in late December 1963, we can hear what Sándor Ferenczi, writing years earlier, called a "confusion of tongues." Ferenczi used the metaphor of a confusion of tongues to explain how an adult might speak and enact a sexual language in response to a child's need for tenderness. For the child, who holds far less power than the adult and needs love, such confusion can have very serious consequences. The child can, for example, become prematurely adept at adult functions but remain almost paralyzed emotionally. The adult, blinded to the child's actual needs by the power of his own desire, can inflict further damage. He may even convince himself that what he is doing is helpful to the child's growth. Ferenczi extended his analysis of the effects of unequal power relationships to consider the ways in which mental health professionals could become deaf to their patients in the service of their own power:

> Gradually, then, I came to the conclusion that the patients have an exceedingly refined sensitivity for the wishes, tendencies, whims, sympathies and antipathies of their analyst, even if the analyst is completely unaware of this sensitivity. Instead of contradicting the analyst or accusing him of errors and blindness, the patients identify themselves with him. (1949, p. 226)

Although she was at times very vocal about her own needs and problems, Sexton learned very early in the treatment to "identify herself" with Martin Orne's understanding of her illness. Like many patients, she was so attentive to his "wishes, tendencies, whims, sympathies, and antipathies" that she was only too ready to accept his version of the truth as her own. In the sessions and in her poetry, she did, however, offer Orne what Ferenczi might have called "a good deal of instructive material," although he did not generally hear what she might have been communicating in her own tongue. She offered him a good deal of instruction in the middle of December 1963, for example, when she discussed how her poem "Old Dwarf Heart" might help to explain what she was struggling with in her relationship with Kayo. Unfortunately, Orne did not seem to hear her.

Orne sounded like a one-track record in these sessions. He rarely professed an interest in the details of Sexton's latest battle in her home, despite her protests that she was physically bruised and that her life was in danger. He repeatedly asked Sexton if she "wanted to know what she was doing" and begged her to "try to understand" that she was acting out feelings of rage with Kayo that did not really belong to her relationship with him, but had origins deep in Sexton's past and in her present relationship with Orne. Although not necessarily useful to Sexton, who either resisted or could not learn from his method, Orne's approach can be traced to the very origins of psychoanalysis. Almost from the beginning of his career in the 1890s, Freud suggested that difficult emotional experiences could be remembered, reconnected to their original feelings, understood, and thereby worked through:

> Someone has experienced a psychical trauma without reacting to it sufficiently, we get him to experience it a second time, but under hypnosis; and we now compel him to complete his reaction to it. He can then get rid of the idea's affect, which was so to say "strangulated," and when this is done the operation of the idea is brought to an end. Thus we cure—not hysteria but some of its individual symptoms—by causing an unaccomplished reaction to be completed. (1893, p. 39)

This is one of Freud's first iterations of the working through of painful experiences, but it shows two key elements that would influence psychoanalytically informed treatments, including Sexton's, for decades. First, painful events, if unprocessed, cause a repetition. Second, in order to stop that repetition, the patient must learn to reconnect the feeling with the original experience. The result, like a scientific experiment in a lab, would be a kind of completion of a reaction. Much later, psychoanalysts would begin to argue that this form of insight was insufficient as a prescription for change and growth.

If we listen carefully to Sexton, it is clear that although she considered and repeated Orne's interpretations back to him, she quietly articulated her own theory of therapeutic action. Her theory becomes most evident when we listen for and study her affects in these sessions, and the content that accompanies them. When Orne lectured her about what she "needed to understand," she said, "Yes, I see," or "But how," or "Come on," sounding compliant, confused, or frustrated. But when her affects showed joy, curiosity, and appreciation, she used the words "great," "interesting," and "hopeful," offering her listener potential clues to what might actually help her change her life.

Sexton felt "hopeful" when she and Orne talked about her dreams, because they gave her access to "what might be going on under there." Sexton needed a "real" relationship with her analyst, one not constrained by a code of silence or an evaluative stance. She valued productive and creative dialogue, which gave her space or a sense of security to get to know her own mind and to develop new ways of thinking. She liked to discuss her poetry as a way of understanding what she was experiencing, and to hear Orne refer to it as if he knew it well. One might surmise that a therapeutic relationship based on shared experiences promised to make her feel powerful enough to address those relationships that caused her more pain. But her hope for this kind of interaction contrasted markedly with what was available to her in these sessions.

As I discussed in the previous chapters, Sexton seemed to anticipate a changing conception of what the analyst knows about the patient and how knowledge is constructed in the psychoanalytic setting. Labeled "the postmodern turn," the "intersubjective turn," or "the relational turn," the fundamental shift was from a model of an all-knowing analyst who objectively interprets what is in the patient's mind to the notion that the analyst participates in the construction of his patient's story. The analyst's participation in the patient's story is, as Modell argued in 1984, "significant, subjective, and undeniable." Irwin Hirsch (2002) summarized the ways in which interpersonal theorists confronted the reality that knowledge is perspectival and analysts can no longer be considered objective experts (p. 574). Steven Seligman (2003), writing from the perspective of developmental and dynamic systems theory, noted that "the image of the detached and objective analyst has been dislocated. Engagement, rather than positivist observation, [has been] placed at the center of the therapeutic action" (pp. 482–483).

As they reached the end of 1963, Orne seemed tied to what today's analysts would surely see as a one-person model of therapy, in which a disengaged doctor observes his patient objectively and informs her, through interpretations, of the reality that she avoids or distorts. Orne wanted Sexton to bring her angry and sad feelings to his office, where she could voice and then understand them. But Sexton, more in line with the theorists cited above, wanted to establish a sense of her own self through her conversations with Orne. She sought to replace a persistent negative identity with a new, cocreated one.

Longing to escape a repetition of patterns that could be traced back to her parents' violent struggles and her own unmetabolized rage, Sexton could not see how the cure could be found simply in knowing what the problem was. Instead, she sought more of what worked best for her—a real live model of new ways of being with another—and affirmation of how those new ways were not created by her psychiatrist alone, but instead *with him*. As the cocreator of her most important body of work, Orne was perceived as ideal for this job. But as a result of his training, his own history, and the cultural climate at the time, he had some difficulties filling the role she imagined for him.

December 14, 1963: "He's Going to Kill Me!"

On December 14, 1963, Sexton entered Orne's office to discuss an argument in which something new happened: She involved her daughter Linda directly in the violence between them. Kayo had returned from his therapy session with Dr. Tartakoff with the idea that they

hire a Swedish nanny to help with the childcare and household main-
tenance. They would have to buy a bigger house, he said, but that
would not be a terrible idea. Sexton countered that they would never
get any money out of their current house because although they had
added an extra room as her office, they lived in a "low-income neighborhood." She also resented that the nanny would be performing the
childcare duties, which she did enjoy, and which made her feel like
an effective mother. Frustration mounted; they "went four rounds"
before it was over. In the middle of the argument, the stereo system
suddenly turned itself on and began to play music. The Sextons agreed
that it was the ghost of their parents telling them to cut it out. They
talked about this for a half hour in the kitchen, but eventually, as
Kayo attempted to talk to her about his feelings of isolation, Anne
went into a trance. Kayo, furious, took her upstairs.

Once they were upstairs, Kayo began to hit Anne in frustration,
trying to bring her back to consciousness. When Kayo tried to choke
her again, she screamed for her daughters to come to her rescue. Ten-
year-old Linda ran into the bedroom to break it up. Later, she told
her mother: "Mummy. He had his arms around your neck!" Sexton
managed to calm her down, and Linda said, "It's okay as long as you
don't get a divorce." Linda had nightmares that night and ended up
in her mother's bed, and then was very upset the next day, seeming anxious and concerned that her parents would divorce. Sexton
tried to reassure her daughter that her father still loved her and her
parents were not divorcing. She also spent three hours on the phone
with Maxine Kumin the next morning, who "social-worked [her],"
urging her to leave Kayo. But Sexton thought it would "be so terrible
for the kids."

When she told Orne about this argument, Sexton sounded dramatic as she discussed being afraid for her life. Orne did not seem to
be impressed by Sexton's insistence. He countered that a divorce was
not only something Linda opposed, but it was also something that
Sexton did not want. Orne rejected Sexton's belief that Kayo might
very well kill her, and instead wanted her to look at what she was
doing to precipitate it:

Sexton: He might kill me! I told Rita, "Promise you'll testify if he kills me." It is temporary insanity. He doesn't know what he's doing. He doesn't really remember it. I can't tell you what he's like. He acts sorry and cries.... We can't talk and yet I can't leave it alone. It's just so terrible. I wish we could talk in front of a psychiatrist but I guess that's never done.

Orne: You want to talk in front of a psychiatrist or do you want a psychiatrist as a judge?

Sexton: I would like someone who is reasonable to be able to see what we're doing wrong. I know I am at fault. I know I am.

Orne: It's not a question of fault.

Sexton sought validation of the threat to her life here. She wanted it to be known that Kayo had the capacity to do terribly violent things, even to kill her. She had indeed elicited such a reaction from her best friend, Maxine. But she seemed to need an expert's affirmation that she was in danger. She suggested something that is very common today—couples therapy. We can only imagine that it might have been very useful for the Sextons to discuss their arguments in front of another mental health professional, but Orne did not seem to agree. If we follow Ferenczi's metaphor of the confusion of tongues, we can see that Orne already knew what the problem was, that it resided in Sexton, and that he and his patient could therefore resolve it. Orne's failure to consider Sexton's idea was a function of therapeutic practice at the time, but it also signaled his inability to hear his patient's idea as useful.

The fact of the argument was not as important to Orne as what he interpreted as its undisputable message. He attempted to redirect Sexton's attention to its meanings rather than its threat to her existence, but she was insistent on the danger she felt:

Sexton: Well, what are you going to do, Dr. Orne? Pretty soon I'll be dead and it will be a great big waste and no one will have understood. Now I know that I am kind of hysterical and maybe I exaggerate but there isn't any way to exaggerate this.

Orne: I am quite aware of what your fights mean…. I also am aware on the other side if Kayo were really choking you, you couldn't have screamed successfully.

Sexton: Well, it was when I was getting away from him….

Sexton: You don't believe me.

Orne: If you were that frightened …

Sexton: You don't believe me. I won't talk about it anymore.

Orne: Do you want to look at what's happening?

Sexton: No, because you don't believe me.

Orne: You know we are on the same side.

Sexton: Not if you don't … How can I, what am I going to do?! You frustrate me!

Orne: Then why don't you listen?

Sexton: Because you don't know and you are starting to say something all wrong.

Orne: Why don't you listen before you tell me it's wrong? If after you listen to me …

Sexton: All right I'll listen. [*sigh*]

Orne: Anne, you're not a child. What I don't understand is you tell me how frightened you are, that this is going to kill you. At the same time you tell me it used to stop with one round. And what you did was you in effect said I'm beaten. Now, it is very important for you for some reason not to do this. I am not saying it is healthy to do this. Frankly I don't think any of the fighting is healthy. It is acting out between you, which we both know, just as much acting out as the ghost of your parents turning on the hi-fi set.

Orne attempted to affirm Sexton's growing sense of self-esteem in this exchange. He thought that it was a positive development that she was not content to apologize to Kayo and say it was all her fault and end the argument. But he did not agree that Sexton might have been killed. His unwillingness to believe her was a problem for Sexton, and it made her retreat from his perhaps helpful assessment of her growing ego strength. Orne's statement "I am quite aware of what your fights mean" revealed his already existent interpretation of the situation, which he was patiently waiting to provide to Sexton, and attempted to redirect her from the issue of danger to her own agency. But his failure to empathize with her fear almost prevented him from being heard by her. In fact, in the next session, she was to remind him that his inability to believe her was a "faux pas" on his part.

As Orne attempted to articulate his understanding of what was going on, Sexton explained how she felt devalued by her husband:

> *Sexton:* All he does is criticize me. I'd like to give him a little criticism. I'd like someone who likes what I am. What is he perfect? I could dream up a better man to be married to. Always I have to change. If that's why somebody kills their wife it doesn't make sense to me. And I've stopped it now because physically I feel beaten. I don't feel well. That's the way I am. I couldn't change it without trading myself in for someone new. But everything had to be where it was … so when I got the Radcliffe grant with *my money* this is what I want to shout at him, with the thing that I've done, we built a room, the room is built with the thing I've done. A room is built so everything is out of the way…. I redecorate the living room to suit his taste. I'd like to paint it red but no, it has to look like his mother's house. She does everything perfect. Everything has to be charming and lovely. We repaper the hallway … that wasn't me. I was pretending from the word go. I was playing a part it's true. That's what he wants back; that is what he is waiting for.
>
> *Orne:* What *do you want*? [*loud voice*]
>
> *Sexton:* I'd like very much to be married to a man who loves me for what I am, you know, saw something positive in who I am.
>
> *Orne:* What do *you* want?
>
> *Sexton:* It's what I said …

The most difficult aspect of this conversation to describe to readers who will not hear it for themselves is its nonverbal components. Orne sighed a lot as Sexton railed on about her husband and his perfect little family. He sounded like he did not believe that what she was saying was what really mattered, as if it were a smokescreen for the real issue, which he knew to be a very different one indeed. And when he asked Sexton what she really wanted, he simply refused to accept her answer that she wanted to be respected as a poet rather than criticized as a poor housewife. In fact, Sexton's assessent that Kayo wanted her to be a good homemaker, just like his mother, was undoubtedly correct. Most of the household chores in their home were performed by Kayo or his mother, who visited often. The weekly maid, Mary, also cleaned and organized, but Sexton was a self-proclaimed slob, so the job was a big one. And it was no secret that Kayo was never fond of Sexton's poet-friends, nor did he appreciate how much poetry and therapy kept her out of the house at night (Middlebrook, 1991, pp. 154–156).

Orne agreed with Kayo, to a point; he thought that Sexton should do some part of the household chores:

Orne: I think it is a very healthy thing that you did the marketing. Not because you did the marketing. You were saying, "Alright I am trying my damnedest to give you something which you want." That's okay. This isn't sick. It can't be unilateral.

Sexton: My mother. My father just praised her and said she was brilliant. But she didn't move. And all we heard was praise about how wonderful she was. And all I get from him is criticism.

Orne: That's not true. Your mother had no bed of roses when your papa was drinking and beating her up.

Sexton: At least he praised her and thought she was wonderful.

Orne: When sober.

Sexton: I don't care. Let's discount when he drank.

Orne: Let's discount when Kayo hits you.

Sexton: All right we will but the rest of the time he's criticizing me. He acts like a martyr every minute.

Orne: It isn't you that he's having trouble with. It's his inability to be what you are trying to force him to be.

Orne was leading up to his belief that Sexton used Kayo as a psychiatrist, a theme he returned to repeatedly in the sessions to follow. Sexton, however, offered him an opportunity to discuss how she was repeating her parents' story, with one significant exception, which was that she, unlike her mother, was not the recipient of her husband's praise. Orne even raised the issue himself, pointing to Sexton's father's drunken attacks on her mother. But Orne did not explore the feelings Sexton had about the battles, nor the feelings she must have had about being unappreciated by both her parents. His failure to empathize with his patient in any way did not facilitate his patient's growth.

Given that Winnicott's and Kohut's theories were far from the center of the clinical discourse in 1963, it makes sense that Orne would not approach Sexton with the empathic stance of a self psychologist. But had Orne even a more rigidly Freudian approach, which was available to him at the time, he might at the very least have interpreted Sexton's repetition of her parents' story. Freud (1914) understood the repetition compulsion in "Remembering, Repeating and Working-Through" as the tendency to repeatedly act out unresolved neurotic problems, instead of remembering them. Later, in *Beyond the Pleasure Principle* (1920), Freud further elaborated upon the postulation that the repetition is in the service of control—of making oneself master of an overwhelming (traumatic) situation. Freud came to understand that the repetition permitted patients to reverse the roles of victim and perpetrator, and so gain some control over the helplessness they experienced in the past. Moreover, he argued for the importance of the conflict being repeated in an intense transference. From this vantage point, Sexton may have been attempting to choose her own suffering, perhaps by inviting Kayo to make her his victim, rather than having it thrust upon her? If so, she had also found a psychiatrist who was reluctant to see her as a victim, which would correspond to Freud's notion of the value of an intense transference as a means of mastering helplessness and victimization.

A more contemporary view of Sexton's repetition of her parents' violent drunken arguments might involve an understanding of how patients with posttraumatic stress disorder (for which Sexton exhibited all of the symptoms) "repeatedly enact roles of either victim or victimizer, and revictimization is a consistent finding" (van der Kolk, 2002, p. 391). Another perspective, from self psychology, might contend that Sexton was trying to gain recognition and appreciation of her traumatic experience with her parents. Finally, a developmental model would offer an understanding of how Sexton, deprived as a young child of self-regulatory functions, illustrated in her arguments that "so much of what is known is never put into words, but instead preserved in affect-intereaction schemas" (Beebe & Lachmann, 1998, p. 15). Whichever of these contemporary interpretations we might prefer, each of them offers a way to understand Sexton's dilemma that is based on dialogue, discovery, and the creation of something new, rather than on recognition, understanding, and working through something from the past. The fact that Sexton anticipated this way of thinking long before it was in mainstream practice is part of what we might identify as a confusion of tongues in her therapy.

December 17, 1963: "Old Dwarf Heart"

The next session began with the epigraph of this chapter, in which Sexton quietly suggested that Orne "needed her" for the date, while Orne seemed to disagree in a "hmmph." Sexton did not seem offended, although to an outside listener he seems withholding not to be able to acknowledge that she plays some important role in the therapeutic relationship. Sexton ignored Orne's dismissal and moved on to attempt to draw him into interpreting her dreams rather than her battles. She had written down four dreams, the titles of which were like "the titles of poems" to her. In the first, she imagined stabbing herself. In the second, her daughter and another boy were running around on a beach without clothing, and Sexton was thinking that they were too old for that. In the third, Sexton was being reintroduced to a surgeon, Johnny, for whom she had considered leaving Kayo after they were first married. In the dream, Johnny was wealthy and wanted her back. In the fourth dream, she was shopping for a new skin:

> *Sexton:* And then I am somewhere and I'm trying to buy a new skin. It's made of chain armor and they hold the left arm up. I am feeling this skin and I complain to someone this is kind of rusty and it really isn't any good.
>
> *Orne:* [*silence*]
>
> *Sexton:* Well, that's all that. And then I'm going through my mother's things like makeup. Things that would be on her dressing table. And there's no good stuff. And I wish at that moment, and I'm thinking, "Why did I sell her all this stuff? I cheated her. If only I'd known later I'd inherit it and it wasn't worth it to be cheating her."

Orne: [*silence*]

Sexton: What funny dreams. They never get complete and they don't mean anything. You can dream all of that in one night and none of it is resolved in any way.

Orne: Mm. You don't remember much of the detail of it.

Sexton: Nooo.

Orne: The first dream, you know, several themes keep coming up.

Sexton: Which one? The leprosy?

Orne: No. No. The one you told me about in the beginning. About stabbing yourself. It's something we've been talking about a good deal here.

Sexton: And we're trying to understand. You're going to dismiss all these as things we can't understand. I'm trying so hard.

Orne: It's not what I'm saying. I am saying that you feel I can't understand you. How much of theses dreams is kind of a testing thing I don't know.

Sexton: Remember the dream I had last week, and I was afraid to bring it in, thinking it might have a sexual meaning? The one from last week where they were shooting? You gave a very good interpretation: "That is what you are trying to keep of me."

Orne: My face.

Sexton: I know that that was positive. I thought gee, you can read your unconscious like a palm. It might tell me what do I feel down there. And here I thought it would be something that I wouldn't like it. But I am always hopeful. I'd like that my unconscious is ready to keep something I thought I should work a little more with my unconscious and see what it reads. Which is why this effort. You see, I know I can't make up a dream at all.... I'd just like to know what is happening. I need a few more signs. When I want away and was running everything consciously I was ruined. For a change I'd like to know how things are going a little bit. Bad or good. Which is why the effort.

Orne: [*silence*]

Sexton: So I suppose that means you don't understand. But why did
I make an effort? Well, because my unconscious wanted to
make an effort and have you not understand.

Orne: It's only sometimes that I don't understand

Sexton: But what about all the rest of these? You see I've wasted my
time writing these down?

Orne: Is that what you wanted?

Sexton: I wouldn't have written them down if I didn't have some hope.

If reading this long exchange provides some sense of the disconnection between psychiatrist and patient here, listening to it can only be described as painful. Orne's responses to Sexton sounded halfhearted at best. Mostly, he remained silent. Sexton attempted in a number of different ways to draw him into the process of playing with the meanings of her dreams, but Orne dismissed them with a "you don't remember much detail" and suggested that their sole purpose was to show Orne that Sexton believed he could not understand her, to "trick" him. Sexton told Orne that his interpretation of her Kennedy dream was "positive" and it made her feel "hopeful" that she could learn something about herself by listening to her unconscious. She did not learn from being told she was to blame for her problems, but she was willing to consider that her unconscious was leading her in directions she was not always able to control or understand. It gave her "hope" to offer them to Orne for interpretation, and she wanted acknowledgment of her "effort."

Although Orne's inability to understand ("because you're a man, because you're not sick, because you married late") was indeed a theme in Sexton's treatment, it did not sound like Sexton wanted to convey a sense of disconnection from her tone. She sounded optimistic as she used the word "hopeful" about finding some new ways of understanding herself in the dreams, and she offered Orne far more to understand in these dreams than he decided to address. She emphasized the amount of "effort" she was putting into the process, even as Orne expressed his suspicions that she was "testing" him. After Sexton made several attempts to draw him into a discussion of the dreams, Orne finally offered an idea, that the new skin dream reminded him of a poem she had composed almost four years before.

Sexton said, "That's 'Old Dwarf Heart,' the hideous one." Although Orne initially made an analogy to Dorian Gray, Oscar Wilde's terrifying story of the man who did not age, Sexton insisted that "Old Dwarf Heart" captured her sentiments much more accurately, in her own language. She seemed to be trying to find her own way to understand the dreams as she sought answers in her poem; Orne's approach had offered her nothing.

Sexton then attempted to remember the lines of the poem, mixing them up. Her voice changed into a deep, slow, sonorific one, and she began to recite the first three lines:

> When I lie down to love,
> old dwarf heart shakes her head.
> Like an imbecile she was born old.

Sexton could not remember the rest and said she'd have to bring in her books to refer to. The lines that followed are:

> her eyes wobble as thirty-one thick folds
> of skin open to glare at me on my flickering bed.
> She knows the decay we're made of.

As she attempted to remember the lines, Sexton associated to how Maxine Kumin and her analyst had a coded language they used to understand her, a language grounded in Kumin's writing. In a soft voice, Sexton almost asked Orne why they could not develop such a language, but then dismissed her own wish by stating, "Well, she writes prose and I write poetry." Nonetheless, she continued to work on remembering her poem, reciting the very last lines of the final stanza: "even if I put on seventy coats I could not cover you/mother, father, I'm made of." The image of 70 coats seemed to interest her, as she repeated it several times. Like the rusty chain armor coat in her dream, the image of 70 coats offered no real protection for Sexton's speaker. Her effort to work with the image in this context and in the memory of her poem suggested that the problem lay within Sexton as it does within the speaker of her poem, rather than on the surface, where it might be covered or protected.

The part of the final stanza that Sexton was forgetting reads this way:

Oh now I lay me down to love,
how awkwardly her arms undo,
how patiently I untangle her wrists
like knots. Old ornament, old naked fist,
even if I put on seventy coats I could not cover you.
Mother, father, I'm made of.

Considered in the terms of the lines that were embossed in Sexton's memory on December 17, 1963, the poem's first and last stanzas tell a story of desire, thwarted connection, deceit, and decay. It also tells a tale of a confusion of tongues in which an outsider's disease infects the speaker's own inner world. The poem's speaker attempts to "lie down to love" (perhaps to *make* love), but experiences the disapproving gaze of "old dwarf heart." Even worse than the actual doctor, who watches and interprets his patient, making her afraid, Old Dwarf Heart "shakes her head" at the speaker. Old Dwarf Heart is like an "imbecile," a dolt, who was "born old." Her "thirty-one/thick folds of skin" glare at the speaker, reminding her of "the decay we're made of." The use of the first person plural pronoun in "we're made of" makes it evident that both the speaker and her listener are infected. The speaker's own decay seems to have been present even before the poem began, but Old Dwarf Heart's clingy disapproval makes it oppressive. She utterly envelops the speaker in a gaze, a knotted grasp, a rotting that seems to start from the outside but also oozes from within.

Although in the first line of the poem "Old Dwarf Heart" stands outside the speaker, by the end of the poem, the withered up observer and the speaker herself are completely enmeshed. The speaker "patiently" works to disengage, "her wrists/like knots," but it is difficult to determine whose wrists she means. The speaker's best intentions, "to love," become directed instead toward freeing herself from a locking grip that might almost be her own. In the last lines, Old Dwarf Heart is in her body and on her body, unable to be concealed "by seventy coats." In a final statement that takes us back to her conception, the speaker concludes "mother, father, I'm made of." Born old, she bears the mark of parents who could not protect her. The result is a feeling of never having been young and innocent, a sense of deprivation and disease at her core.

Sexton herself was never far from feeling the exposure, disapproval, and decay represented in this poem. We can locate its history in the harsh criticism and intrusive caretaking of her parents (who died a year before the poem was written), and the strangely sexual loving touch of her aunt Nana. We can sense Sexton's almost omnipresent feeling that there was something terribly lacking or diseased where her real self should be. When she mentioned her poem to Orne, she was trying to capture the feeling of a dream she'd had in which she was shopping for a new skin; there was a sense in the dream that she might have leprosy. She felt diseased, unsafe, and alone, and she was searching for something or someone to protect her.

Sitting in Orne's office three years after she first wrote "Old Dwarf Heart," Sexton sounded magnetically drawn to its images of confinement and decay. Its language still captured Sexton's feelings about who she was and what she could do. The images came to the fore as she worked "to love" her husband at a time when her psychiatrist, who wanted her to try to love herself, was probably going to go away. She seemed to feel vulnerable, diseased, and alone, but Orne did not work with Sexton to understand any feelings that the dream and the poem could be communicating.

Instead, Orne asked why she wanted to talk about dreams when of late they had been talking so much about Kayo. He spoke as if there were no possible relationships between her poem about untangling herself from someone's wrists in a desire to "love" without intrusion and her ongoing battles in which she ended up with her husband's wrists around her neck. Nor did he interpret a dream about shopping for a new "armor," with her feeling of being attacked for not being a good housewife while being unacknowledged for her identity as a poet. Finally, the image of rummaging through her mother's drawers, linked to the "mother, father, I'm made of" in the poem, did not seem, for Orne, to relate to Sexton's rage at him, her husband, and her repetition of her parents' arguments.

Orne changed the subject, suggesting that Sexton was avoiding the real issue:

Orne: I was wondering you came in and start out with your dreams and last time you came in very upset about what was happening with Kayo.

Sexton: I was trying to work on me and forget that.

Orne: Why?

Sexton: I don't want to talk about it. I listened. I can't stand me and Kayo. You had some points to make. I think you're against me too fast. Still I can't forgive me for not believing he tried to choke me. This was a big faux pas you shouldn't have said that you don't understand me you don't believe me. It's my whole tendency not to discuss him. He frustrates me too much.

Orne persisted in his attempt to get Sexton to pay more attention to what she was doing with Kayo, while Sexton focused on feeling negated by him and her husband. In the comment above, she cited Orne for being "against [her] too fast," and for not believing the story she told him. As the conversation continued, Sexton expressed sadness about the loss of innocence in her marriage:

Sexton: I could cry for what we started. The thing we still have is this terrible ideal of the American dream … such innocence that even the country had … but these ideals, they don't exist anymore. I love him for his innocence but when I hear it doesn't exist … you wouldn't understand, because you were married so late and we were so stupid and so idealistic.

Sexton sounded wistful as she told Orne that her arguments with Kayo, like the death of John F. Kennedy, represented a loss of innocence, a loss of the idea of the American dream. She said that the dream was F. Scott Fitzgerald's too, "for all he drank himself to death," and that it was "sweet." The feelings Sexton had when she married Kayo, filled as they were with fantasies of a rich life before them, could not "anymore be found" in her marriage. But they could be voiced with Orne, and his responses to them did not seem to take that into account. Once again, it was almost as if the language of tenderness that Sexton's memories of marriage evoked could not be echoed by Orne. Sexton excused him even before she gave him a chance to speak, saying he would not understand because he "married so late," but we can hear the hope in her voice that he might contradict her with a sentimental gesture of his own. Apparently faithful to his own agenda, Orne remained silent.

For the remainder of the session, Sexton associated to the failure of ideals in her marriage, threatening to leave Kayo once and for all if he ever hit the children "like he hits me." Orne pointed out that both Kayo and Sexton were affected by the Kennedy assassination and they were "shaken up." Urging Sexton to stop setting up a dichotomy in which Kayo was bad and Orne good, Orne turned her attention back to the good parts of her marriage, which seemed to influence the more positive tone in the sessions to come. Nonetheless, he missed an opportunity to link this discussion of the "decay" in their marriage to the very creative material of her dreams, which spoke to the content and the affect of the session, as well as to the solidity of her own intellect. We might wonder how the conversation might have shifted had Orne been working to help her to establish a better appreciation of her own self, through an analysis of the latent shame in her dreams. Perhaps a better feeling about her own creative powers might have given her the personal freedom to recognize and acknowledge Kayo's position a bit more?

Of course we cannot but speculate as we confront this rich material and the absence of discussion by Orne, but one thing is clear: Working with the content of Sexton's dreams might have led Sexton and Orne in any number of different directions. In the first dream, Sexton was stabbing herself. This dream interested Orne, who said they had been talking about that theme a lot in their sessions. Considered in conjunction with Orne's interest in getting Sexton to do more in her marriage, the dream could be seen as a fantasy relating to Sexton's masochistic need to elicit punishment from her husband, her lack of self-worth, and her need to find a way to protect herself from a dangerous world. Fond as he was of identifying phallic imagery, we might at least have expected Orne to tell Sexton that the image of stabbing herself showed her turning the phallic power against herself. The speaker of "Old Dwarf Heart" fears the intrusion of outsiders, whose disapproval becomes identified with her too vulnerable self. In real life, Sexton the dreamer searched for a new skin only to find a suit of armor would not do. The search led her to her mother's makeup drawer, the contents of which, we might infer, were her mother's own armor, and a terribly insufficient inheritance. In the end she is "made of" her parents, and cannot undo the knot of their legacy. Any interpretaton of Sexton's feelings of vulnerability and emptiness might have addressed her struggles in a way that facilitated the self-mastery Orne clearly sought from her. His silence did not seem to do that, unfortunately.

December 19, 1963

In the next session, December 19, Sexton insisted that she had married Kayo to get love, which she desperately needed. She regretted her decision because she could not love him, because he had "no soul." If he had a soul, she argued, then he would not love her most when she helped around the house: "I think it's beneath me … a woman's place is not in the home a servant's place is in the home." Orne clearly did not agree, as he told Sexton that doing housework was a way of being a partner in a marriage. Sexton did not take him up on this point, and instead offered a way that she did feel recognized by her husband. When she asked him why he loved her, Kayo told her that he loved her because she was like "a many sided diamond, though rough":

> *Sexton:* I asked him I said, "What do you love about me?" and he said, "Because you're such a many sided diamond, though rough." And I liked that. He didn't have to put it so poetically but it said a lot.
>
> *Orne:* For somebody whose got no soul it's a remarkable statement.

Here Sexton offered Orne a loud clue about her need for affirmation, while he proffered an "I told you so" defense of Sexton's husband. Sexton did not comment on his irony, but continued to appreciate her husband's representation of her as a complex person. Note that her poet-self was met "poetically" by her husband this time, although she generously offered that he did not have to express himself so.

If we need further evidence that Sexton was happy to hear Kayo praise her many sides, we need only to see what happened to Kayo's comment in her own poetic imagination. Less than a week later, she had completed "Christmas Eve," in which she used Kayo's image to explore her ties to her mother, who had died of breast cancer in 1961. The poem's speaker sits by the Christmas tree staring at her mother's portrait as her family sleeps upstairs. She begins by addressing the portrait:

> Oh sharp diamond, my mother!
> I could not count the cost
> of all your faces, your moods—
> that present that I lost.
> Sweet girl, my deathbed,
> my jewel-fingered lady,
> your portrait flickered all night
> by the bulbs of the tree.

Here Sexton has transformed Kayo's representation of a sparkling and complex figure into a string of negatives. The Anne Sexton who lived in her husband's mind was a "many sided diamond"; this speaker's mother is a "sharp diamond," whose many sides signify her many moods. The speaker moves the diamond imagery from that of a natural gem to a mercenary one when she says that she "could not count the cost/of all your faces, your moods." The sense of worth here becomes one of expense; the mother exacts a cost from the daughter, who cannot "count" how much. The gift of a mother's presence, that "present I lost," exists only in the flickering image lit by the tree. Twice removed from the speaker, by the fact of the portrait and its dimly lit image, the speaker's mother is almost her daughter, in a reversal of roles: "sweet girl, my deathbed."

The end of the second stanza confirms that the mother's deficient love exacts a cost on the daughter. The speaker feels like an imitation of her mother, striving to be her while knowing that she never can:

> your aging daughters, each one a wife,
> each one talking to the family cook,
> each one avoiding your portrait,
> each one aping your life.

All of the daughters here are inadequate and less evolved, "aping" their mother's life. Each one imitates not her mother but her "mother's life," suggesting that they want to be like her, as all children do when they are young, but they do not seem to know what they are mimicking. Like rhesus monkeys left to raise themselves, they cannot find the real mother's gaze, and so "avoid" their mother's portrait. Perhaps they cannot be the wife and hostess that their mother was, but there is not much evidence of her domestic prowess in the poem. The mother becomes a kind of an angel in the third stanza, "a halo over [her] forehead," while the daughter stares at her image "forcing" herself, "waiting, inexhaustible, thirty-five." The feeling is of stasis. The daughter seems to be waiting for a sign, and it can only come from the two-dimensional figure on the wall. Despite her awareness of the futility of her effort, the speaker cannot be exhausted in her quest to become the mother whose love she did not have.

In the fourth stanza the speaker voices desire for her mother. She wants her mother to return to the land of the living, where things change and women age. Although the painting offers her the promise of connection with her mother, the flat image is a kind of a reproach:

> I wanted your eyes, like the shadows
> of two small birds, to change
> But they did not age.
> The smile that gathered me in, all wit,
> all charm, was invincible.
> Hour after hour I looked at your face
> but I could not pull the roots out of it.

The mother will not "age" or "change" in these lines, which renders her somehow "invincible" and impenetrable. Because the mother is merely an image, the daughter cannot get to the root of her own history. Nor can she find herself in memories of a relationship with her mother, for the implication is that it is a relationship that never was. Collectively, the images suggest that the speaker's mother was more interested in appearing in the portrait than in mothering a child.

Gradually, the speaker's envy of the ageless mother in the painting turns to unmistakeable rage, as she remembers being "led by the nose," as if her mother dragged her through life:

Then I watched how the sun hit your red sweater, your
withered neck,
your badly-painted flesh-pink skin.
You who led me by the nose, I saw you as you were.
Then I thought of your body
as one thinks of murder—

When she examines the painting on its own terms, the way the
"sun hit your red sweater, your/withered neck," the daughter suddenly
sees through the painting back to her real mother, as she was. As soon
as she remembers her actual mother, she becomes enraged. The image
is "badly-painted," as if created by an amateur. It itself, rather than
the daughter and her sisters, is an imitation. But almost as soon as she
voices her rage, the idea that she would like to murder her mother, the
speaker rushes to beg her mother's forgiveness:

Then I said Mary—
Mary, Mary, forgive me
and then I touched a present for the child,
the last I bred before your death;
and then I touched my breast
and then I touched the floor
and then my breast again as if,
somehow, it were one of yours.

Like the observing crone who becomes the diseased speaker in
"Old Dwarf Heart," this mother-daughter dyad becomes fused in a
portrait that captures death in life. Mother, father, and daughter are
one in the final lines of in "Old Dwarf Heart"; here too do mother and
daughter in the final stanza become as one body. The mother's diseased breast becomes the daughter's. Knowing that Mary Gray died
of breast cancer, we cannot but think that the image, which might
suggest nurturing contentment, reeks of disease: an identification that
is much like the image in "Old Dwarf Heart." But the rage that leads
the speaker toward an identification with her mother is new in this
poem. It does not exist in "Old Dwarf Heart." It is as if the daughter's rage can only be metabolized through an absolute union with her

mother, a merging that can only leave her half-dead and "waiting" for something that will never come.

At the end of the session, Sexton and Orne began to talk about her arguments with Kayo as a way of processing Orne's departure. Orne argued that by putting her feelings about his departure onto her husband, if she could establish a transference to Kayo, perhaps she would not need her doctor anymore anyway. Sexton denied that she was trying to make Kayo into her therapist, while Orne persisted, noting that Kayo could not be her psychiatrist "even if he went to the finest medical school, did his residency, etc.," because he was in the family.

Sexton clearly disagreed with Orne about the therapist's job versus the husband's. Orne told her that the therapist's job is "to point out the reality" to the patient, while the husband is "someone you share your life with." Sexton commented that Linda had asked Sexton what psychiatrists do, and Sexton had told her that psychiatrists talk over feelings. Linda asked if Sexton could be her psychiatrist, and Sexton said no, because Linda might need to talk about her feelings about her mother. Orne said, "See it is a family fantasy" that one person in the Sexton household could heal another. Sexton countered that she had actually told Linda to talk to the school psychologist, which she had. Orne said not to rush it. Sexton said that it was already happening.

As they discussed what Orne called the "family fantasy" of Sexton or Kayo acting as therapists, Orne seemed less than convincing to Sexton, although she attempted to understand what he meant. Orne raised the issue of Sexton's relationship to James Wright, with whom, Orne argued, Sexton had acted like a patient, "passing out all over the place." Sexton contended that they were fighting all the time, making her enraged, which caused her to pass out. For Sexton, her own feelings, and talking about them, constituted the heart of the therapy. Thus, she suggested, people can "social work" each other even if they are not trained to do so. The final confusion of tongues in the session became pronounced as Sexton outlined a doctor-patient relationship based on genuine dialogue and Orne offered a very different point of view:

> *Orne:* You have not been crying here at all. That's something we can behaviorally observe.

Sexton: I'm not getting upset here because I am acting out so much at home.

Orne: As long as it's in the context of trying to get him to fix it. But he can't do that.

Sexton: But you're gonna leave.

Orne: If I leave it's a long way off and we have …

Sexton: I don't want to trust you. I don't want to bring my emotions in here if you want to leave, do I?

Orne: Well. [*stutters*] Look my leaving or not leaving you've had trouble with that.

Sexton: I'll die at home, anyway. He'll kill me. I've got to stop it. That's even a better motivation.

Orne: That's not. Well.

Sexton: Well I should come in here and cry.

Orne: Anne …

Sexton: You know, it's just a symbol.

Orne: You should bring in your emotions in here.

Sexton: I brought in dreams and you didn't want them last time.

Orne: I wanted feelings.

Sexton: There will be feelings after dreams. I don't know. No feelings, just a dream?

Orne: Anne …

Sexton: I don't know how to produce feelings. I don't know where they come from.

Orne: Anne, Anne, I am asking you *not* to produce them at home. I am asking you not to act out at home.

Sexton: I'll start acting out here and then *you'll* get angry.

Orne: Act them out, that's true. But I won't let you. But [not with Kayo]. Your neuroses interdigitate too much. When you were saying you wanted him in analysis that's the fantasy then you will have your own analyst.

Sexton: It wouldn't hurt him.

Orne: That's not what I am arguing.

Sexton: Yeah, I know.

Orne: If you want to do what you call social work, that's okay. That's what you're doing, that's what all of us do. It's very helpful and successful. But don't get it mixed up with going into depth.

Sexton: I want him to understand me in depth.

Orne: Yep.

Sexton: I decided that this was a phony marriage. He didn't know me. The only way …

Orne: The only person who will ever know you that way … [is me].

Sexton: That's one of my troubles in writing. I am either completely open or it's got to be some fantasy that's no good.… I almost have the same trouble with people.

Orne: I know.

Sexton: I am either all the way there or I am not. I don't know how to walk this middle line … either it's all revealing, oh boy I am so open and it's not a secret … or it's a lie.

Orne: This is what we've been, you know, working on for a long time.

If Ferenczi's "Confusion of Tongues" helps us to understand something important about the way that Sexton and Orne spoke different languages in these mid-December sessions, it is that Sexton was telling Orne that she was angry at him in at least three different ways. She identified her anger at Kayo as a displaced transference of her rage at Orne onto her husband. She shared the insight that if Linda were angry with her it would be impossible for her to share those feelings with her mother. She also corrected Orne's interpretation of her affair with James Wright, identifying their arguments as the reason for her acting out. Sexton could not have been clearer. She even said it: "I'm mad because you're gonna go." Nonetheless, Orne remained fixated on an abstract idea that she needed to bring her feelings to him rather than acting them out at home. It was not that he was wrong, but that he could not hear it in Sexton's terms. His rigidity placed his patient in a position to say she was "such a mess," but it sounds to at least one listener, half a century later, that her psychiatrist was the one who was confused.

5

DANCING FOR YOUR DOCTOR—NOTES ON NARCISSISM

December 21–24, 1963

Sexton: Listen, I've been thinking while you were talking to me. When I'm talking I'm really kind of hiding. But I figure if when you're really talking then you're really thinking about what you're saying. So you couldn't really be looking at me. You know. Maybe that doesn't make any sense.

Orne: You don't have to be afraid at that moment.

Sexton: Yeah. Because you're not really figuring me out. So I spend the time figuring me out instead…. Isn't that kind of interesting?

(December 24, 1963)

In the final days of 1963, Sexton and Orne became, in Orne's words, "quite close." Sexton was not yet sure that Orne was leaving Boston, but she knew that it terrified her to think of losing him. She also realized that despite their arguments, she missed Kayo terribly when he left on business for 24 hours; she was "nothing, nothing!" without him. As snow began to threaten her trips into Boston to see Orne and the holidays arrived, Sexton even experienced a therapeutic breakthrough. She described with joy how she had come to discovered something "so interesting" about herself while she and Orne were discussing his practice of taping patients' therapy sessions. She learned most about herself and felt most understood when she felt that Orne was not looking at her and trying to figure her out, but, instead, engaging in genuine dialogue. She often felt "afraid" of his clinical gaze, as if she were facing imminent exposure. But when Orne was

111

busy thinking and responding to her, she could both listen to Orne and analyze herself. In short, Sexton seemed to be saying she worked best if she and Orne were mutual, if differently able subjects in the room, rather than when she felt as if she were the object and he the empowered subject supposed to know (see Lacan, 1977, p. 234).

Sexton had asserted in her poem "Said the Poet to the Analyst" that the analyst's business was "watching my words." Three years later, she presented quite an opposite view of therapeutic action in her own therapy, one based on watching her doctor's words to find her own. Her discovery of her own capacity for self-analysis came at a time when the business of therapy was very much on her mind. As the possibility of Orne's departure loomed, she and Orne spoke a lot about other doctors Sexton had seen. They discussed how they had helped her or failed to help her, and why they would not be her choice if she had to choose another doctor. Dr. Brunner-Orne, Orne's mother, was Sexton's somewhat rigid first psychiatrist; she occupied the office downstairs and still saw Sexton if Orne was away for a few days. Dr. Leiderman, who treated both Sextons when Orne left on a sabbatical, did not "get" Sexton, and worse, he had not helped Kayo to "transfer" to him (establish a transference). Dr. Riggs, who also saw Sexton when Orne was on vacation, encouraged a patient Sexton had recommended to him to write for him; the patient said he had a copy of Sexton's book on his desk. Dr. Harrison, who had also seen Sexton for a consultation, sat behind a desk rather than across the room, and thus she felt closer to him than most therapists; he had charged Sexton a poem rather than money for her visit, which displeased Orne.

Sexton talked most about Dr. Helen Tartakoff, who saw both her and Kayo in November and December 1963 to assess the value of Sexton's therapy and look for a therapist for Kayo. She thought it was "just great" that Tartakoff held open phone hours for her patients in the evening "like a pediatrician." She also loved her office, with its library waiting room full of all kinds of books and art. Fascinated by psychoanalysis and psychology, Sexton had amassed a huge library of her own in the effort "to find someone like me." She had developed a vocabulary that included words like *defense* and *transference* and *affect* and *ego*, and she regularly used these terms to describe her own mental processes or to discern what Orne might be thinking about when he looked at her with one of his particularly enigmatic facial expressions. In mid-December, she used the term *negative transference* to describe her reactions to Orne's refusal to hold her hand. When Orne said the terminology was not important, she disagreed, claiming that the words meant something. Likewise, she often described a time before she was "transferred" to Orne, a time when she was so naïve about how therapy was conducted that she wrote Orne a letter stating, "I must end therapy; I find I've fallen in love with you!" Sexton reminded him of this at the end of the session on December 21, a session in which she also told him, "I think you are smiling because you think I have developed a new defense."

Although it has been sometimes considered a performance, Sexton's pleasure at using psychoanalytic terms and discussing the field with her psychiatrist offered her another expert vocabulary to add to her growing knowledge of the languages of poetry and literature.* If we closely examine the December 21 and 24 sessions, in which Sexton spent a long time discussing Dr. Tartakoff and Orne himself, we can see that talking about her interactions with doctors was a way of exploring her relationship to herself. Generally speaking, Sexton wanted to feel that she was somebody. Too often, as when Kayo went away, she felt that she was "nobody," walking around the house without direction. Whether she was competing with her daughters for her husband's attention, working with fellow poets in a seminar, flirting with other women's husbands, or reading her poetry in a sexy red dress, Sexton usually demanded most of the attention in the room (Ostriker, 1989, pp. 154–169). While Orne knew about and tried to analyze Sexton's seemingly insatiable desire to be admired and recognized, his responses to her "entitled" need to feel "special" did not appear to include an awareness of how very "special" he felt about his own abilities and research.

As they discussed Sexton's need to impress Dr. Tartakoff for much of the December 21 session, Orne seemed fixated on Sexton's sense of entitlement, as if intending to analyze it away, rather than recognizing it as a need that she wanted to have met in order to grow.

---

* Middlebrook (1991) interprets Sexton's early interest in reading psychoanalysis as a performance for her doctor (pp. 53–54).

But in the very next session, on Christmas Eve, he offered Sexton a long description of his own position at the leading edge of his field. Describing himself as a maverick and a lone wolf in a very conservative city for psychiatry (a city he would soon leave to accept a prestigious research position), Orne speculated that he was one of very few nonanalysts in Boston who held the respect of the psychoanalysts. It is tempting to view Orne's own narcissism through the same lens that he used to interpret Sexton's; he did, after all, sound rather self-centered as he described his special position in the Boston psychiatric scene. Considered in terms of the theories that were to gain a following in the decades to follow, however, this picture of both Orne and his patient begins to appear rather different. In back-to-back sessions, these two very successful professionals, a research psychiatrist and his poet-patient, provide an opportunity to view narcissism from contrasting perspectives: as a pathology to be understood and overcome, or as the root of the mature, creative self.

December 21, 1963

Sexton began with a comment that she "thought we'd gotten somewhere last time," announcing that she had been trying harder to be "less hostile." She and Kayo bickered about Sexton's tendency to lean back in her chair, but it had not escalated into a battle. She insisted on her right to do so: "because I spend a lot of time *thinking* or reading. And I like to put my feet up. I like to lean back." She did concede, however, that perhaps Kayo was brittle because he had decided to give up smoking. Orne suggested that he agreed with Kayo; Sexton's desire to put her feet up, which scratched her bookcase and broke all of their chairs, conveyed that she was entitled to do whatever pleased her, without regard for others. She countered with "I don't have enough things that give me pleasure" and began to discuss a new friend, Anne Wilder, a psychiatrist with whom she had been corresponding and conversing (and with whom she would eventually have a love affair). Orne warned her that she needed to see Wilder as a friend, not her doctor, although Sexton insisted that the terms of the friendship included discussing psychological issues.

Orne changed the subject, noting that Sexton had become very upset, telephoning him the night before she was to see Dr. Tartakoff. Sexton said she was not sure what she wanted when she had called, but she did know that he might be interested in the fact that she had given Tartakoff a copy of her book. She commented, "I wanted her to remember me," noting that she completely understood why she had given Tartakoff the book. She then described her visit to Tartakoff's office in detail, focusing on the wonderful library/waiting room and her desire to have her books in there too:

Sexton: I understand it totally [*laughing*]. I want to impress her in case
   you go away and I have to find another therapist and Maxine
   said, "And she can be your therapist," and I said, "Well I
   don't know she's kind of cool," and Maxine said, "Well what
   do you mean by that," and she said, "You mean the regular
   hours?" In and out like a machine. Nothing can happen in
   50 minutes.

Orne: So it has to be special?

Sexton: I don't know what. It's a short amount of time for me.

Orne: How come?

Sexton: But I guess that was the idea behind it. Maxine said, "Yeah
   you want to con her," and "oh then she'll be fascinated to
   have you for a patient." Maxine thinks analysts run around
   thinking it would be fascinating to have writers, that analysts
   actually look for interesting patients. Maybe they do. I mean
   someone interesting to work with. I don't mean just interesting in some field.

Orne: What's more relevant is what you're looking for.

Sexton: Why I gave her the books? Well first of all, her waiting room is
   her living room, and it's very tastefully done. And there are
   all sorts of books. In other words this woman is intelligent.
   She's thinking. There are quarterlies for instance that I print
   in. She has books of poetry, although not just poetry, all sorts
   of things. Nice paintings. See I am sizing her up. And a horrible fish tank with big great huge kissing gourami fish and
   they look like they are drowning! It's fantastic! I keep thinking that can't be hers they must be her husband's. Horrible.

> These were monsters—this big! So I viewed the whole place and thought it as very tasteful and thought, "Now this woman is very intelligent," and I thought, "I'd kind of like to have my books there too." It's an ego thing.

Sexton's affect when she describes Tartakoff's office is energizing. She exclaims with delight when she says, "This woman is intelligent. This woman is thinking," reminding us of how she defended her chair-tipping habit a few minutes earlier: "I spend a lot of time *thinking* or reading!" When she noted that the quarterlies in the library include those that "I print in," she sounded shy, almost as if she denied her own authorship by calling attention to the print of the poem rather than its publication. Then, when she described the giant gourami fish, she sounded at once horrified and excited, like a little girl with her hands over her eyes at a scary movie, peeking through her fingers to see if it is safe to watch. And her attribution of the fish to Tartakoff's husband is curious; perhaps she wants to attribute the aggression in the marriage to the husband?

Orne did not respond to Sexton's queries about whether doctors prefer to have interesting patients, like writers. Nor did he pursue any aspect of the richness of Sexton's description of Tartakoff's office. As if she had not articulated her desire to have her books in an intelligent woman's library, or as if such a desire could not be considered valid in itself, he persisted in trying to find her "real motives." He did not recognize the need to be appreciated as a need in itself, but instead looked for her unconscious motives:

> *Orne:* What are you looking for?
>
> *Sexton:* What am I looking for? I don't know.... I'd like to impress her with my books. I was very careful the first time I saw her to somehow get in that I'd been at the institute because I don't want her to think I'm just a nobody—just some girl who's fighting with her husband. I want her to think I'm worth something. Is that so strange?
>
> *Orne:* Oh no. That's not so strange. You aren't answering what I asked you.
>
> *Sexton:* What do I want? Well, that she'll read them and she'll like them and she'll be impressed.

Orne: And what should she then do?

Sexton: Nothing.

Orne: Really?

Sexton: Well it depends on whether I need her or not.

Orne: And if you need her?

Sexton: Well then what should she do? Well it depends on whether I need her or not. Well, either take me as a patient or … get me somebody good. It's got to be somebody special like you're special.

Orne: Special, like I'm special.

In a persistent line of questions and emphatic tone, Orne responded as if he had discovered what Sexton really wanted, something that he believed she did not understand herself. He emphasized the word *special* every time Sexton uttered it, as if she did not know she was using it. His insistence on offering an interpretation that she had already provided herself elicited anger and frustration from his patient, but Orne persisted. He seemed committed to offering her Freudian ideas about the neurotic origins of entitlement, simply by naming the words *special* and *entitled* over and over again. It was as if what she felt was not as significant as her unconscious motives. To the listener, his refusal to hear what Sexton was saying is enraging; it is difficult to understand how Sexton remained relatively calm, if frustrated, unless we consider the trust and love she felt for her psychiatrist. In that context, of course, Orne's responses are even more enraging to an outside audience.

Orne's focus on the term *entitlement* reflects a perspective on narcissism that had its origins in Freudian theory but had been popularized by one of his colleagues at Massachusetts Mental in the months preceding this December appointment. According to Freud (1914), not only are we all born narcissists, but every human being seeks to repair early narcissistic injuries of the most basic kind:

> We all think we have reason to reproach Nature and our destiny for congenital and infantile disadvantages; we all demand reparation for early wounds to our narcissism, our self-love. Why did not Nature give us the golden curls of Balder or the strength of Siegfried or the lofty brow of genius or the noble profile of aristocracy? Why were we born in a middle-class home instead of in a royal palace? (p. 316)

Freud speaks of narcissistic needs arising in childhood to be someone we are not. In time, these needs are replaced by the healthier aims of adulthood, in which beloved objects take the place of narcissistic desires. But in some "special cases," individuals who have been deprived of being heard and understood by early caregivers come to think that there is something wrong with them (often with their bodies), and as a result, that they deserve special treatment. Freud uses King Richard's soliloquy to illustrate:

> Nature has done me a grievous wrong in denying me the beauty of form
> which wins human love. Life owes me reparation for this, and I will see
> that I get it. I have a right to be an exception, to disregard the scruples
> by which others let themselves be held back. (p. 314)

A man of his era, Freud also includes women in this category of special cases:

> Women regard themselves as having been damaged in infancy, as hav-
> ing been undeservedly cut short of something and unfairly treated; and
> the embitterment of so many daughters against their mother derives,
> ultimately, from the reproach against her of having brought them into
> the world as women instead of as men. (p. 314)

Freud's conception of pathological narcissism was termed entitlement in an important lecture by John M. Murray, a faculty member where Orne trained, that was delivered in March 1963 at the Boston Psychoanalytic Institute; it was published soon after in the *Journal of the American Psychoanalytic Association* in 1964. Murray notes:

> If the narcissistic world of omnipotence, with its unlimited power of
> magical thinking and unlimited entitlement to the lusts and destruc-
> tions of pregenital excitements, is not given up in favor of the more ideal-
> oriented relationships with mature libidinal fulfillments, individual and
> social aims and relations, the resultant therapeutic achievements will
> be critically limited, circumscribed, and perhaps only passing. (p. 495)

Murray's argument is the first mentioned in the Psychoanalytic Electronic Publishing (PEP) archive to emphasize the concept of entitlement as the main product of narcissism, and it certainly summarizes Orne's position in his sessions with Sexton. For 20

minutes, in many different ways, Orne urged Sexton to acknowledge her entitled wishes to be unlike all other patients in Tartakoff's
eyes. Entitlement seems clearly to have been on Orne's mind as
a way to understand Sexton's psychology, and he jumped at the
chance to convince her of what he knew. If so, his interpretation
was inaccurate, for if we look at Freud, he is speaking of narcissistic resentment because of who one is not, rather than pride in
who one is. Sexton was already a published poet; her poems were
already in Tartakoff's library! So her sense of entitlement to special treatment stemmed from the fact that she was indeed considered special in one field—poetry—special enough to have won two
prestigious prizes and published two books in less than four years.
Her desire to use her accomplishments to find a special therapist
does not seem completely unrealistic; she wanted to exploit her
cachet in order to find someone "special," just as one might try to
find an outstanding doctor by taking advantage of contacts in the
referral process.

To a contemporary listener, Sexton's desire to be thought of as
"worth something" makes very good sense. Why wouldn't she want
to be seen as an intelligent woman rather than a girl? Why not have
her book displayed in a "tasteful" library? Why wouldn't she want
to be respected as an equal by someone who stocks her library with
quarterlies that include her own poems? Orne's questions about her
real motives cannot be heard as anything but negating and deflating.
Although he could not refrain from pursuing his point about Sexton's
need to feel special, she had already told him that she might have a
selfish reason for giving Tartakoff the book when she began the conversation. In fact, she commented, "I understand it perfectly," emphasizing her manipulative wishes by drawing on Maxine's remark that
she wanted to "con" Tartakoff. Sexton obviously knew that she had
ulterior motives, but she likely knew that her desire to be recognized
as special, as a gifted writer, would elicit Orne's criticism. It was a
point between them. And so she herself may have been overly suspicious of her motives (to the degree that harsh self-criticism is today
seen as an important component of narcissism).

If we hear Orne differently today, it is in part because educated
readers have gained a different appreciation of a woman's worth than

was common in Orne's time. It is also because important challenges to the mainstream Freudian theory of narcissism were already gaining ground at the time of this session and have become almost common-place in contemporary psychoanalysis. For Winnicott and Kohut, for example, a healthy narcissism lies at the very core of personal growth. When it is impinged upon by early nurturing failures, the self can become stalled in an early stage of development. Winnicott sees the analytic process as a kind of rebirth; the frozen, aborted self reawakens and begins to develop as crucial ego needs are met. The job of the analyst is to join the patient in "going to meet and match the moment of hope" (1965, p. 309). Kohut (1966), at a later date, argues for the therapeutic restoration of "healthy" narcissism in cases of early object failure in which caregivers ignored or silenced the child's needs for special attention and affirmation. To counter this early developmental deficit, the therapist must welcome and nurture the nascent narcissism, supporting the patient's ideals and creativity.

> In any normal human life narcissistic issues of triumph and defeat play a tremendous role. What kind of life would it be if this were not so? I find nothing wrong with it. We all want to be victorious. We all want to enhance our self-esteem. We all want to shine. As I said, there is a lot of hypocrisy about that. (Kohut, Tolpin, & Tolpin, 1996, p. 73)

In keeping with Kohut's and Winnicott's theories of self-development, Sexton's creative work famously drew from her own experiences as the subject of her poetry. While her early high school writing was rife with romantic images of love and loss, the adult poems she wrote with Orne's encouragement focused on her breakdown, the painful separations from her children, and her ongoing mental anguish. If her "confessional" style was immediately popular with fellow sufferers like Robert Lowell, it also earned her a considerable amount of criticism. As Alicia Ostriker (1983) has noted, "Sexton is the easiest poet in the world to condescend to. Critics get in line for the pleasure of filing her under N for Narcissist" (p. 263). James Dickey (1963) was one of the first to get in line. The previous April, his review of *All My Pretty Ones* denounced Sexton's autobiographical style as unliterary: "Anne Sexton's poems so obviously come out of deep, painful sections of the author's life that one's literary opinions scarcely seem to matter;

one feels tempted to drop them furtively in the ashcan, rather than be caught with them in the presence of so much naked suffering" (p. 28). Sexton told Orne that she carried this review "all over Europe" the previous fall, and it was found in her wallet the day of her death (McClatchy, 1978).

Like Sexton's severe critics, Orne was suspicious of the value of her use of herself as a poet, but for different reasons. He proclaimed himself inexpert as a judge of the poetry itself, but he did draw from his expertise as a psychiatrist to encourage her to recognize and overcome the notion that she could use her accomplishments to obtain special treatment:

Orne: Somebody special like I'm special. Can you elaborate on that?

Sexton: I suppose someone who's going to care about me a little bit.

Orne: A little bit?

Sexton: Yeah. A little more than their other patients. [*giggling*]

Orne: That, if they work on a regular 50-minute hour, would at least spend 55 minutes …

Sexton: Yeah or 65. You know someone who's not too awfully orthodox. Not just the time. Someone who will hold my hand.

Orne: Time is a symbol.

Sexton: Yeah so is holding hands, so is a million other things … and not someone like Dr. Riggs who's gonna charge all that money.

Orne: But you see what is important to you in it is that you get something special.

Sexton: We've talked about this before. This is such an old conversation. You've always told me that and it makes me mad. [*laughing uneasily*]

Orne: That's why you brought her the books.

Sexton: Why? Why? I mean I don't understand the connection.

Orne: Because, you see, you had the same need before. You've had this need always for as long as I've known you. You've now accomplished something.

Sexton: So I can use it.

Orne: And you now feel that this is the basis on which you are entitled.

Sexton: I don't think I'm entitled to it.

Orne: Well, I think you demand it.

Sexton: You make me sound awful. I am not coming here anymore. You
    are awfully critical of me.

Orne: It's not critical.

Sexton: Well I don't like that. I don't demand it.

Orne's view of Sexton's entitlement, consistent with Murray's
reading of Freud's theory, was not news to Sexton. Exasperated,
she told him she had heard it before, and it had never taught her
anything about herself. His reply that he was not being "critical"
seems disingenuous. He was indeed critical, using the phrase,
"you've had this need as long as I've known you," and insisting on
the idea that she "demands" special treatment. Orne was clearly
motivated by the notion that Sexton needed to face her narcissistic
entitlement. But she would not agree, perhaps because he made
it sound as if she were unlike other people in having such needs.
Sexton did not recognize her needs as demands, but as deeply connected to her poetry and self-worth. Perhaps Lacan would have
said they represented her desire. Kohut, writing just a few years
after this session, was to argue that narcissism offers generative
fuel for the creative artist. In "Forms and Transformations of
Narcissism" (1966), he contends that the "unrestricted narcissism
of early childhood" underlies the "creative artist's relationship to
his work" (p. 112). Later (1977), he was to admire the grandiosity
of the creative self, as well as its ability to assimilate the world to
its own purposes.* In fact, for both Winnicott and Kohut, what
might be labeled narcissism can be considered necessary for the
development of creativity. Stephen Mitchell (1986) notes that "the
prototypical 'narcissist' is not the child, madman, or savage, but
the creative artist, drawing on overvaluing illusions for inspiration" (p. 114). Sexton seemed to share their vision, as she made
self-exposure into a poetic genre.

Kohut and Winnicott, in different ways, would have addressed
Sexton's desire to be seen as special as an opportunity to help her
complete a developmental process of self-affirmation. Although he
could not affirm Sexton's need to feel special, Orne did credit her

---

* See "Forms and Transformations of Narcissism" for an excellent overview of Kohut
  on creativity.

for using her fame to "set up a security operation" that might be of use if he left Boston and she needed a new therapist. Grateful for a reprieve from the entitlement issue, Sexton intuitively included Orne's own narcissist pleasure when she turned the conversation back to propose that perhaps her sudden fame offered narcissistic pleasure for him as well:

Orne: I think it's kind of nice that you have some ego tools now that you didn't have a few years ago.

Sexton: And you're kind of proud.

Orne: In a way.

Sexton: Practically you gave them to me.... Actually, it was good for your ego. Think about that for a moment, you know.

Orne: I guess the important thing to keep in mind is that neither ego really needed it.

Sexton: Not mine, not yours?

Orne: Yeah.

Sexton: I don't feel like I'm a poet anymore so I have to use them more.

Orne: What I wonder how long you will need proof that you are special before you can own that you are a real person.

Sexton: [*long silence*] I don't know. I feel about the books really the way I felt when I was writing them. I wanted to have a book as something that I can hold as visible proof. It is something I did. A child, you know, is not like that.

Orne: A child is not like that.

Sexton: A child is not something you did. A child is just.

Orne: Just...?

Sexton: I don't know how else to get back to anything real. I don't know exactly how to control myself you know. I don't know how to get what I want.

Orne: I guess we've got to know what you want.

Sexton: I think I want to be close but I don't act it at all.

As in the many instances I have cited from other sessions, Orne remained committed to the idea that Sexton should learn to feel special just for being herself. Neither her poetry nor her fame could be owned as aspects of her real self. But her children might be, as Orne's question about them suggested. When Sexton moved from this subject to issues of how to "control" herself and her difficulties in "getting close," her comments suggested a link between Orne's theory of her and her biggest conflicts. We might imagine an interpretation based on the richness of her developing self, with its many sides. Perhaps the rigidity of his model of self inhibited her growth in some way; we cannot know. But we do know that Orne did not address this fear, nor did he own that his departure might be seen as a "pushing away." At the very least, he refused to recognize Sexton's claim that he liked to feel special himself, and thus her difficulties in getting close would seem to relate directly to him in this instance!

The session ended with Sexton attempting another kind of recognition, as Orne's improved patient. She told him that she had been wondering what she had been like at the beginning of her treatment: "What did I act like?" She laughed as she told Orne that she had found a note she had written to him in their early days:

> *Sexton:* The funniest thing the other day I ran across a copy of a letter or one of the versions that I wrote you when we were first in therapy I guess two months or something saying, "I must stop treatment, I find that I've fallen in love with you."
>
> *Orne:* Mmm.
>
> *Sexton:* It's the most innocent! It's funny. Huh. You know I mean I wasn't really transferred to you then.
>
> *Orne:* Mmm.
>
> *Sexton:* You know really.
>
> *Orne:* Mmm.
>
> *Sexton:* In a way it was a way of not transferring to fall in love with you.
>
> *Orne:* Hmmm.
>
> *Sexton:* But I wasn't used to men, I didn't know what other emotions you could have.
>
> *Orne:* I'm afraid we'll have to stop in a little while.

Sexton speculated that sexualizing her relationship with Orne might have at first prevented her from establishing a proper transference. Her observation that she "wasn't used to men" begged for some kind of comment. And given Orne's interest in aggrandizing transferences, he certainly was in a very good position to comment on Sexton's use of sex as a way to remain distant from himself and her husband. Sexton insisted that her erotic transference was a way to avoid transference. Orne might have chosen one from any number of possible responses about their relationship at this moment. Instead, he reminded her that it was time to stop, avoiding any implications of her comment about "other emotions you could have."

Although Orne responded by saying their time was almost up, they then talked for another five minutes about the timing of the next session, and whether Sexton really needed to come to therapy on Christmas Eve. Orne made a decision:

> *Orne:* I think I'd better see you.
>
> *Sexton:* Hahaha. I really was aware I was testing you and you gave the right answer. You realize my indecision. I think, "He doesn't care if he sees me or not." Tssk. [*tape runs out*]

Orne finally stated that he thought she should come in, and Sexton commented that his response meant that he had "passed the test," that he was not trying to get rid of her after all. It is tempting to speculate that Orne was intimidated by Sexton's impulse to sexualize her relationships with powerful men, including him, and steered clear of it at all costs. But given what happened with her next therapist, it does seem like an opportunity lost. Is it possible that Orne believed a sexual transference was unanalyzable in Sexton's case? Orne seemed attached to an abstract theory of narcissistic entitlement in this hour, which blinded him to the loving feelings his patient expressed for him and to her desire to experience herself as a powerful and famous publishing poet. Difficult as it was for her to articulate her need for him and attachment to him, Sexton had done so, when he did not respond to her obvious desire to be told that she was important to him, that he did care "whether he [saw her] or not." Orne's theory might be interpreted as Orne's defense in this case, as it protected him from analyzing his own narcissism, his countertransference to his patient, and the fact that he was indeed abandoning his patients to pursue a more prestigious position.

December 24, 1963

If Orne claimed with certainty that his ego did not need the gratification that his patient's fame provided, it may be because his own ego had gotten quite a few boosts in the years he was treating Sexton. He had earned two advanced degrees, his reputation as a research scholar in the field of hypnosis and memory studies was clearly on the ascent, and he had already published six major articles in important journals in his field (one when he was still a Harvard undergraduate). Like his patient, he had won several prizes, including a Fulbright that took him to Australia for a term, and he was about to head an experimental psychiatry unit at the University of Pennsylvania.

He had also procured the first of dozens of grants from the National Institute of Mental Health and the U.S. military for memory studies. His *curriculum vita* cites that in the years he treated Sexton, he had grants from the U.S. Army, Navy, and Air Force for research in the detection of deception. This work would eventually earn him a reputation as an expert in False Memory Syndrome, and he would testify as an expert witness on the subject for many trials, including that of Patti Hearst. Sexton did not know about Orne's research and his involvement in military contracts, but she certainly expressed her curiosity about her psychiatrist's innovative method of taping therapy sessions. Toward the end of the session, Sexton began to question Orne about his place in his field (he was happy to answer). Their conversation exhilarated Sexton, resulting in her unconscious critique of Orne's own theory about what might help her to get well.

But before they turned to Orne's innovative therapeutic technique, they discussed domestic affairs and other doctors and patients. In the initial minutes of the session, Sexton described a Christmas card they had received that morning from a quintessential happy family: "Just the kind of thing Kayo thinks is the ideal wonderful life." She did not focus on this, however, and moved on to detail her very restless day, the result of Kayo's overnight business trip. She played Monopoly with the girls, invited herself to a neighbor's for a drink because she was "so lonely," and wandered restlessly back and forth from her writing room, even though she had a poem to work on. She marveled that despite all of their arguing, she still seemed to find his absence unbearable.

Sexton: The thing is I'm bored with him when I'm with him. When he's
away I am nothing. I am no longer bored because I am nothing. I feel like I've lost my whole identity. It maybe that it's
just that I am sick … if he died there would be no me. That's
pretty frightening.…

Orne: It's only because you've been threatening the relationship that
you can't let it go.

Sexton agreed, but turned the conversation to discuss what she
most disliked about other doctors; "they don't talk to me *as if* I'm
sick." Orne suggested that what she meant was that she needed her
doctor to speak to the child in her while also helping her to find
another voice within herself that could exist alongside that of the
child. If Orne had more consistently followed his advice in the sessions I am citing here, Sexton might have felt differently about her
desire to be recognized and admired.

In this explanation, which included his assertion that she did not
need the analytic couch because it was designed to bring out the
child, a process that came quite naturally to her, Orne sounded a bit
like Winnicott, attending to the lost inner child of his patient much
as Winnicott was willing to do with a patient like Margaret Little
(1990). His attention to the wounded part of her was much appreciated by his patient, and seemed almost soothing, as the conversation
that followed had an energized but relaxed tone.

The conversation turned to a patient of Dr. Riggs who had been
calling Sexton, but Sexton had not taken her calls until that day.
Sexton expressed her frustration that the people to whom she gave
wonderful referrals often wanted to call her to discuss their doctors.
But she conceded that she should understand the desire to talk to
someone who knows the doctor:

Sexton: She said, "Oh, I just love him he's so wonderful." I said, "He's
really very good looking, I knew you'd like him." She gives
him writing and he wants her to write. And I said, "Well
gee, Amy, I think you should concentrate on your dancing."
He can't wait for it. He grabs it from her and reads it right
there. I know she wants me to read it and help her make
it better. It really is no more than a hobby. I said, "That's

the trouble with dancing. You can't dance for your doctor."
And she said, "Well, I've been thinking of it. And I said that
would really be acting out."

Orne: No more than writing for him.

Sexton: No more than writing for him, but a little bit more…. I said the
thing you've got to learn how to do is live. She thinks you
can just write and it's easy. It takes awhile. You have to be as
smart as I am to do it as fast as I could. Or as innocent.

Orne: You have to work. [*seeming to be suggesting something about his
patient*]

Sexton: [*seeming to disagree with Orne's emphasis on work*] She doesn't
know the process of working on it.

Orne: One thing intrigues me is that you recognize that it is destructive
for her to dance for her doctor….

Sexton: Yeah, but I don't count this as talking about me at all. It's
very different she had very ambitious parents…. The way I
achieved was by doing nothing…. My parents weren't ambitious for me at all.

Orne: That's true.

If Sexton's parents had no ambitions for her, it is difficult to see how
Orne's refusal to accept her poetry as an accomplishment would not
repeat that pattern. In fact, however, Orne seemed to think that Sexton
was referring to another time in the therapy, when he had urged her
to write prose, a task that she attempted and failed at, miserably. Her
frustration with Orne's suggestion did perhaps fuel the example she
provided, but it also sounded like Sexton was trying on Orne's way of
seeing the world. In fact, she told Orne, "See, I sound just like you"
when she told the patient that maybe her doctor would like her just for
being herself, that she did not have to dance for him. As she relayed the
conversation, however, she did not sound terribly convinced that writing for one's doctor was such a bad thing. She did know that Orne was
convinced, however, and his conviction led her to question hers.

As they considered yet again the possibility of other doctors,
Sexton wondered about whether she would continue to tape her sessions if she were working with someone else, to which Orne answered
a definitive yes. Orne responded to Sexton's question about how his

practice of taped psychotherapy was received in his field, especially by the "analysts," becoming animated and emphatic. As if he were letting Sexton in on a secret, he admitted that he was one of very few people using the technique. This delighted her:

> *Sexton:* My experimenting doctor! I thought that, so I thought I'd say it. That's one of the qualities I like about you. You're really not rigid. Of course you can be very stubborn. But that's different. You're not rigid.
>
> *Orne:* True. This I don't think is unrealistic.
>
> *Sexton:* What do the analysts think about this? Terrible, they say.
>
> *Orne:* No. On the contrary, I am probably the only nonanalyst in Boston who is accepted as a therapist.
>
> *Sexton:* But I mean do they experiment?
>
> *Orne:* Some.
>
> *Sexton:* It seems to me their whole code is so rigid, their jargon is rigid. After they go through this long brainwashing.
>
> *Orne:* Again, we are training a new breed. This is psychiatry 10, 15 years hence. Actually the difference between myself and the two or three analysts I know is very small. You are right if you're talking about somebody in their 60s, since medicine is a status profession and age is necessary for certain things. The people who are currently acknowledged leaders don't represent the best part of the field … the frontiers of the field are with the relatively younger people…. I really couldn't care less…. It's changing. You happen to live in the most conservative psychiatric city in the country. You know, if you compare Boston psychiatry with psychiatry anywhere else you'll find it's an anachronism. Not that it isn't good, it's just …
>
> *Sexton:* I know. You told me this. I mean I know this anyway. I am lucky I don't live in some little town in the Midwest where there aren't any psychiatrists, or just one.
>
> *Orne:* Or a shock artist.

Orne used big terms, proclaiming himself one of "one or two" psychiatrists in Boston to have the respect of the analysts, suggesting that he might indeed be one of the "best in the field," and sketching out the invention of "psychiatry 10 or 15 years hence." Unlike the technique of the aged 60-year-old analysts about whom he purportedly "couldn't care less," Orne was "at the frontiers of his field." He did admit that he was generous enough to send referrals to them if his patients were in need of "that kind of approach." Orne emphasized that he was like the analysts and liked by them, but he also suggested that he was far beyond them in his *avant-garde* approach to psychiatry.

Sexton seemed somewhat bored by Orne's statements about his colleagues, but also impressed by Orne's place among them. Most decidedly, she liked it that Orne offered her an opportunity to study her own self without feeling herself as the object of his gaze. As my epigraph attests, alongside her admiration for Orne's "experiments" came Sexton's pleasure at watching the working of her own mind. Sexton was, after all, experimenting with a new brand of poetry in her home office. Just as she could not have made herself into a poet without Orne's help, it gave her pleasure to be a part of her psychiatrist's groundbreaking therapeutic technique. Unlike her doctor, however, Sexton did not equate professional pride with a narcissistic entitlement that lay at the core of a neurosis.

Sexton's position on hers and Orne's expertise becomes more complex when seen in terms of what Sexton said about Orne's pride in having helped her become the poet she was in the previous session— "It's good for your ego too! Think about that for a minute." In urging Orne to think about his own subjectivity rather than hers, we can see that Sexton, like Kohut and many others to follow, interpreted creativity as a means of reinventing the self, a process that ideally occurred between two working minds:

> For Kohut (1966/1977) creativity is a path of meaningful transformation. The creative unknown terrifies and exhilarates, challenges and strengthens self-experience. Transferences of creativity at their best enhance forward edge strivings and encourage the creative process. They may be based on needs for idealization, mirroring, or twinship. He identifies Freud's idealizing transference of creativity with Fliess as fulfilling such a significant but passing need while Freud wrote *The Interpretation of Dreams* … that the American playwright Eugene O'Neill experienced a mirroring transference of creativity with his wife that was continually supportive … and that Picasso experienced

a twinship transference with the painter Georges Braque, helping to sustain Picasso's sense of self. (Press, 2005, pp. 121–122)

Press's summary of Kohut's arguments about a creative transference that can be mirroring or idealizing or a form of twinship most certainly applies in Sexton's case. She is quick to remind Orne that she was "nothing" before she met him, and that her poetry is her most important accomplishment. Her representation of him as "God of our block" in "You Doctor Martin" did not shift in her other doctor poems, although she always qualified it so as to include herself as a possible creator as well. Despite his striving to help her find an "I" outside of the products of their cocreative bond, Sexton remained insistent on her theory of both her origins as a poet and its worth. She also remained committed to a view of creativity as a dialogue, and therapy itself as a kind of teamwork.

Perhaps the best reply to Orne's and her critics' charges of narcissism appeared a few years before these sessions, in the form of a poem in which a "cracked bowl" substitutes for the pool into which the mythical Narcissus gazed and fell in love. One of her earliest and most beautiful poems, written in 1958, "For John, Who Begs Me Not to Enquire Further," answers a letter from a mentor, John Holmes, who suggested that she write less personal poetry. The poem celebrates self-revelation and exploration as central to the "order" and "hope" for which anyone might strive. It ends in a celebration of creativity that emerges from the kind of mutual recognition that Sexton sought and sometimes found with Orne. In fact, the poem suggests that empathy lies at the core of the creative imagination.

In order to discuss the poem's celebration of self-study as something quite different from narcissism, I shall parse it into sections. But because it is one of Sexton's best poems, from which I take the title of this book, I quote the entire poem first:

> Not that it was beautiful,
> but that, in the end, there was
> a certain sense of order there;
> something worth learning
> in that narrow diary of my mind,
> in the commonplaces of the asylum
> where the cracked mirror

or my own selfish death
outstared me.
And if I tried
to give you something else,
something outside of myself,
you would not know
that the worst of anyone
can be, finally,
an accident of hope.
I tapped my own head;
it was a glass, an inverted bowl.
It is a small thing
to rage in your own bowl.
At first it was private.
Then it was more than myself;
it was you, or your house
or your kitchen.
And if you turn away
because there is no lesson here
I will hold my awkward bowl,
with all its cracked stars shining
like a complicated lie,
and fasten a new skin around it
as if I were dressing an orange
or a strange sun.
Not that it was beautiful,
but that I found some order there.
There ought to be something special
for someone
in this kind of hope.
This is something I would never find
in a lovelier place, my dear,
although your fear is anyone's fear,
like an invisible veil between us all ...
and sometimes in private,
my kitchen, your kitchen,
my face, your face.

The first line plunges us into a conversation that has already begun. As if to answer a charge, the speaker starts by saying, "No, but." The speaker claims not to be interested in beauty, urging her listener to consider that she knows about a "certain sense of order/ something worth learning." She wants to teach her reader about another way of being, based on what is possible rather than how things appear.

The listener's charge of narcissism immediately becomes the speaker's subject matter. The source of her lesson is a "narrow diary of [her] mind." She emphasizes the pejorative "narrow" by calling the language of the asylum a language of "commonplaces" or cliché. The image of the "diary" tells us that her source, her mind, is an instrument capable of recording things in words. The diary tells of her "own selfish death," produced by the "cracked mirror" of a fragmented self. Sexton's speaker stares at her distorted image, "a cracked mirror," producing a self-destructive impulse:

> where the cracked mirror
> or my own selfish death
> outstared me.

Note the broken, unmirrored self of the speaker who attempted to take her own life. This fragmented self is the "worst" of her, we are to learn, but it is also the source of all of the lessons she has for her listener. In fact, the broken self, the self without a whole mirror to affirm it, is both teacher and learner in the poem:

> And if I tried
> to give you something else,
> something outside of myself,
> you would not know
> that the worst of anyone
> can be, finally,
> an accident of hope.
> I tapped my own head;
> it was a glass, an inverted bowl.
> It is a small thing
> to rage in your own bowl.

The speaker asks an implicit rhetorical question: What if I tried to do something else, "something outside of myself"? If so, she argues, she would deprive her listener of a valuable lesson. Yes, she says, it is a "small thing" to "rage in your own bowl," and the cracked mirror becomes a glass, then a bowl, a container for rage that offers a domesticated image of private suffering. But as she narrates this small thing, she makes it look rather large. She makes it beneath her to rage only in this confined space, a kind of petty act. The rage can only be useful when it leads her outward, to a world that includes "more than myself." Although "it was private," soon it was "you." The "small thing," once tapped, provides a font of wisdom for others, in the form of a poem.

Once she has transformed the poem into a container for feelings, the speaker illustrates how useful this activity might be to her listener. Taking not only her worst qualities but also those of "anyone" to be of value, the speaker offers a new world order based on hope:

> There ought to be something special
> for someone
> in this kind of hope.

Notice that the word *special* does not have the pejorative meaning for this speaker that it did for Martin Orne. The "kind of hope" this speaker imagines provides a gift to the reader, an offering. Her insistence on the value in what seems to be of least value provides a reordering of the world of self and other as well as that of poetry itself. When the worst of herself becomes a subject deserving of attention, the speaker claims that her work is not for herself only, but for the "hope" of the whole human race—for who among us, she eventually will ask, has not felt the shame that I see in the "commonplace of the asylum"? What might seem a cliché—the asylum—becomes a productive language on its own terms. It, like the cracked head of the speaker, provides a place from which new meanings might emerge.

Entertaining the idea that the listener might again turn away from recognizing himself in her lines, the speaker tries another tack. She cannot concede that there is "no lesson here," no matter how "awkward" the "bowl" of her psyche. In fact, she transforms the bowl, "with all its cracked stars shining" into an orange with a new skin, or even a "strange sun." By this point in the poem the speaker has become a god in the act of creation, and her listener, who once subjected her to his objectifying critical gaze, is but one of her creatures. She has made a sky of stars and sun, an orchard from her own head.

Notice that talking to her listener about her torn psyche and her rage makes the speaker feel more powerful. She knows that it was not beautiful, but she "found some order there." And in a world of her making, "there ought to be something special/for someone/in this kind of hope." "Hope" cannot be found in "a lovelier place" than that this speaker has made, this place of her own recreated subjectivity, and the listener, who prompted her to narrate her own rebirth, is invited to dwell in it as well, not without his "fear," but as a "dear." She befriends her enemy and remakes him as almost lovely, just as her own cracked head becomes a place of instruction beyond compare. The "invisible veil between us all," like the squirrel's heartbeat in George Eliot's *Middlemarch*, marks her inevitable loneliness. But it is also thin as a veil and not even visible. It brings us together: "my kitchen, your kitchen,/my face, your face."

Although Sexton wrote "For John" to her mentor, it is not difficult to imagine that its lessons might have held messages for her psychiatrist as well. Sexton crafted a poem in which there is a world to be discovered in the "cracked bowl" of an individual's most painful feelings and thoughts. These can be transformed, through metaphor, into something beautiful. But for the untrained, naïve reader, the "cracks" themselves might act as a decoy and elicit criticism. It is only for the reader who can see himself in her lines that understanding is possible:

> This is something I would never find
> in a lovelier place, my dear,
> although your fear is anyone's fear,
> like an invisible veil between us all …
> and sometimes in private,
> my kitchen, your kitchen,
> my face, your face.

The final lesson of this poem is about the transformative power of empathic connection. For the reader who can see that "his kitchen" is "[her] kitchen," can also see that his pain is hers as well. Hardly cracked, the final image of this poem is of two human beings, mirroring each other, in a harmony that contrasts markedly with the sessions that I just cited. Clearly, Orne would have benefited from either reading a bit of Kohutian self psychology, soon to appear in print, or reading his patient's poems. But whatever his theory, he needed to listen a bit more carefully to his patient's versions of her experiences before interpreting them away, and he also needed to see his own face, or countertransference, as a crucial part of the entire picture that would become Anne Sexton's therapy.

6
THE BLACK PANTS
AND THE NEW BIKINI—
OEDIPAL SCRIPTS

February–March 1964

Sexton's therapy notebooks prove that she attended many sessions in January and February, but the actual archive of recorded tapes proceeds directly from December 24, 1963 to February 29, 1964. My purpose here is to pursue the story as we hear it in Sexton's own voice, so I turn to the next four sessions, from February 29 to March 12, 1964. Of all the tapes in the collection, these show Sexton and Orne at their most playful. In the first meeting, Sexton toyed with the idea of pursuing an old love in hopes of teaching his Wellesley-educated wife a lesson about the power of poetic prestige. In the next, with this man in mind, Sexton went shopping in the village of Wellesley and bought black fringed underwear as a prelude to very satisfying sex with her husband. Then, just before she departed on a vacation trip to Florida with a friend, Sexton engaged Orne in a role-play that involved meeting in a bar to begin an affair. Finally, in the session following Sexton's return, she tossed Orne a number of pictures of herself wearing a bikini and asked him to pick out the one Kayo liked most. Orne explained his choice with the comment, "That happens to be an excellent picture of you."

Although in the past her erotic transference to Orne was "underground," it became more evident in these sessions. Orne's handling of this material and her split-off sexuality in general was markedly different from his constraining silences of the previous year. Indeed, with their time together coming to an end, he seemed almost eager to take up the issues of Sexton's loving transference to him, her apparent acting out of it with other men, her on-again, off-again intimacy with Kayo, and her desire to "show" how smart she was. He said that he was trying to help her "fit the pieces together." Both Orne and Sexton appeared to believe that "the pieces" of her feelings about men could be understood in classically Oedipal terms, although neither elaborated in much detail what that might mean. Their use of Oedipal terminology did offer a language for Sexton to understand behavior that otherwise did not seem to make much sense. But unfortunately, the idea of the Oedipus complex that was available to Sexton did not really match the story she was acting out.

In Orne's time, it was common to offer Oedipal interpretations to patients as a form of insight into their actual life situations. If a patient could identify the repetition of this early conflict in his current relationships, it was thought, he or she would be able to develop new ways of relating to others. Interpretations of the Oedipus myth abound, but the basic facts of the plot are fixed. In the terrifying incestuous drama, Oedipus killed his father and married his mother. Whether this represented his fate, an enactment of his unconscious desires, or the outcome of his parents' abandonment of him, it seems already at a distance from Freud's application of it to young children.* But the label stuck and became a staple of traditional psychoanalytic practice. With Orne's coaxing, Sexton could see that she was acting out a female version of an Oedipal plot in her interactions with men, including her husband. For instance, in late February, she agreed that her desire to win the doctor-husband of a Wellesley College "snob" mirrored a wish to show her own Wellesley-educated mother that she had far surpassed her achievements. Similarly, she thought she might now be intellectually equipped to charm her critical father, were he still alive. She also understood that the doctor-husband was a stand-in for the unavailable Doctor Orne, whose loving attention she cherished and would soon lose. And it was also no surprise to her that she wanted her own husband to take the role of her father, which she and Kayo both interpreted as "part of her problem."

---

* For several excellent reviews of the Oedipus story and its interpretations, see Simon (1992).

In some of their most playful and seemingly productive sessions of the entire treatment, Orne attempted to convince Sexton to own her sexual acting out by understanding what she was "setting up," and Sexton worked hard to listen to him, understand herself, control her behavior, and become "more constructive." She could see that sexual fulfillment in her marriage satisfied her, but it felt dangerous, because it made her feel guilty and ashamed, and she feared rejection if she wanted sex more often than her husband. Sexton sought liberation and freedom by seducing other men, who made her feel good when they began to act sexually powerful toward her as they attempted to get her to sleep with them. But the actual sex often made her freeze up. She invariably sought permission from her lovers to feel sexy, as if it were bad to express her own desire. In these affairs, she often remained trapped in scenarios of acquiring power through winning the sexual partner of another woman.

If Orne pushed Sexton to understand her sexual acting out as manifestations of what he called omnipotent fantasies to control all who entered her world, he saw the origins of those fantasies in aggressive and sexual Oedipal wishes to overthrow her mother and win her father (in a female version of the mythic scenario). Sexton was only too willing to agree about her Oedipal plotting, and almost gleefully commented, "It's all there." The unfortunate fact, however, was that the Oedipal interpretations did not seem to stop her from repeating the pattern—perhaps because they were pursuing a story that did not fit her own. Although the evidence of emotional deprivation and abuse was right in front of them, the Oedipal plot that Sexton and Orne applied to her story was Freud's, in which the child competes with the same-sex parent for the love of the other. This recycled myth did not account for the part of Sexton's story that was missing, the part in which narcissistic parents thwart their daughter's developing sense of self, leaving her yearning for their love and incapable of taking charge of her own life. In Sexton's case, a mother competed with her daughter, as the daughter sought her approval. Sexton's high school creativity was met with accusations of plagiarism, and her mother began to write poems once Sexton started to publish hers. And her father, rather than being desired as the privileged love object of his daughter, seemed to impose his own sexual fantasy on Sexton by making inappropriate sexualized comments to her and possibly expressing direct sexual interest.

Rather than special objects of love for a beloved child, Sexton's parents seemed more like figures of hurt, rejection, and devaluation of an abused child. To his credit, Orne tried to help Sexton elaborate her understanding of her actions by asking questions about the parents in her mental landscape and encouraging her to confront how they had treated her when they were alive. Unable to tolerate the reality that Ralph Harvey and Mary Gray had been (to all appearances) self-centered, critical, emotionally and sometimes physically abusive parents, Sexton both raged against them and defended them to Orne. Orne himself seemed caught between blaming Sexton's parents for neglecting and abusing her, and blaming Sexton herself for failing to take responsibility for her behavior. Living at a time in which Fairbairn's and Winnicott's ideas emphasizing "object relations" (actual relationships with parents) over sexual drives were largely rejected by mainstream psychoanalysis in the United States and a "spare the rod" approach to child rearing was prevalent in the culture, Sexton and Orne did not have the resources to go much further in understanding her actions than a sketchy outline of the Freudian Oedipal myth.

Whatever validity the Oedipus story may retain as a developmental metaphor, it does not come close to describing the family story Anne Sexton told in her therapy or her poetry. Rather than seeking an illicit parental love in fantasy, Sexton seems engaged in an endless search for a missing parental love in her relationships. In an early letter to W. D. Snodgrass, she put it this way: "I want everyone to hold up large signs saying 'YOU'RE A GOOD GIRL!'" (Hall, 1989, p. 21).

To understand Sexton's voracious need for love and approval, we might turn to studies in self psychology, infant research, and child development that became popular in America only after Sexton's death. Writing in England, where he was already recognized for his innovative approach to the normative processes involved in development of the self, Winnicott was among the first to argue that "where parental care-giving is extremely insensitive and misattuned we assume a fault is created in the construction of the psychological self" (Fonagy & Target, 2002, p. 11). He moved the crucial issues back to the early years of development, which, if "good enough," paved the way for a relatively conflict-free Oedipal phase. In 1977, Kohut elaborated this notion by proposing that the origins of Oedipal conflict might lie in "frequently occurring failures from the side of narcissistically disturbed parents" (p. 247).

Recalling Mary Gray's invasive inspections of her daughter's body when she was a toddler and Ralph Harvey's sarcastic remarks about his daughter's acne and her sexuality, in the context of both parents' seeming disregard of or even disdain for their daughter's achievements, it seems safe to conclude that their parenting was "insensitive" and "misattuned," perhaps at times abusive. Their focus on their own lives and pleasures at the expense of their daughters' (not only Anne's but her sisters') developmental needs testifies to the "narcissistic failures" emphasized by Kohut. Sexton's repetitive reenactments of a story in which she sought basic self-affirmation and love through sexual affairs while jeopardizing her marriage, and even perhaps the presence of innumerable bees in her poetry, suggest her similarity to Kohut's portrayal of the faulty construction of her "psychological self."

With an understanding of self-development based on the child's need for mirroring and empathy, as Winnicott and Kohut proposed, Sexton and Orne might have considered how Sexton's story depicted a kind of Oedipus complex in reverse, the child who must protect her parents at all costs for fear of losing them. In 1952, Fairbairn described "the dilemma of a child who must protect the image of goodness in [her] needed objects by internalizing and identifying with (absorbing) [her] object's badness so as to survive" (Grotstein, 1991, p. 20). Sexton's pattern of entering into "bad" extramarital affairs with other women's husbands might have illustrated a need to identify with both her sexualizing father and her competitive mother in order to feel that she was okay. She would thus acquire a special relationship to demonstrate her worth to another woman while acting out of her father's fantasy that her value was principally as a sexual object. Her basic value, as she often confessed feeling to Orne, was as an object of men's desire, not any intrinsic worth in herself. She repeatedly told Orne that she could not stop herself from entering into sexual relationships outside her marriage, reflecting the unconsciously driven nature of her behavior. She felt "trapped" in a story that was truly not her own, a story in which she was not really the central character at all.

Orne's commonsense emphasis on Sexton's responsibility for her own compulsive actions neglected other feelings that were part of the entire scenario and that may have been more crucial than her sexuality per se—namely, her intense shame, sense of abandonment, and hunger for loving approval. Although they did discuss her most important formative experiences, Sexton and Orne rarely addressed these kinds of complex feelings about her earliest memories in the family. Orne suggested that Sexton was enraged at her parents, but he seemed to think that acknowledging that she was angry could cure her. It makes sense that she would have been enraged by Mary Gray's intense competition with her, but Sexton seemed to feel more than anger, as she repeatedly pointed out that she loved her mother, "adored her!" So too did she love her father, even as she felt ashamed when he accused her of being so hideous she turned his stomach, and confused when he said she was "going out to get fucked" as she left the house for a date. It made Sexton feel dirty to think about these comments. It also made her feel ashamed when she thought about what it meant to have her genitals examined on the cold bathroom floor, the same floor where enemas were administered. Protective of her mother to the end, she wondered if she somehow needed this treatment to be healthy, thereby seeming to illustrate the child's need to hang on desperately even to bad objects.

Instead of developing her own unique subjectivity, Sexton became caught in an endless struggle to return, in Winnicottian terms, to the point at which her development was frozen, seeking the missing responsive affirmation from her parents. Most often, she was compelled to do so by attempting to seduce people to love her. Freud wrote that the repetition compulsion was an attempt to master a traumatic situation. But her efforts at mastery through repetition were in the end self-defeating rather than affirming. What was missing in her schemes of illicit affairs and seduction was a secure basis in a loving developmental triangle (Herzog, 2004) in which she was held in esteem by an admiring mother and an equally admiring father. As if acting out a scene from a Greek tragedy with a dead-end plot, Sexton failed to gain any real satisfaction in her pursuit of forbidden love and was compelled to begin again. But in four sessions just before the end of her treatment with Orne, she worked very hard to capture the meaning of her behavior, explored the details of her fantasies and feelings, and sought to express her needs in her marriage rather than elsewhere.

February 29, 1964: "I'd Like to Title a Book Called *Fuck You!*"

Many weeks had passed since the December sessions in which Sexton focused mainly on her arguments with Kayo. She now knew that Orne was leaving Boston, and she seemed to have become almost hypomanic as a way to ward off the painful feelings elicited by this fact. From the first minutes of this session, we can hear a shift in the tone of the therapeutic interactions. Sexton sounds overly excited, as if she were using denial to defend against the feelings of loss that Orne's imminent departure aroused, including terrible fears that woke her from nightmares. Orne himself comes across as calmer and more playful, perhaps more sure of his role as he tries to help Sexton find a new therapist and manage the transition. He also sounds more connected to her for the most part, and less easily angered or frustrated. Orne asks more pointed questions and raises issues she would rather ignore, such as why she would not allow herself to recognize that she was hurting her husband by sleeping with other men.

Sexton began the session thanking Orne for speaking to her on the phone in the middle of a fight with Kayo two nights before. Kayo had discovered sometime during the previous month that she had had an affair, although it is not clear when he found out or with whom she had the affair. In their telephone conversation, Sexton told Orne about Kayo's criticism of her for the affair, as Kayo listened in. She called Kayo "old eavesdropper" when she discovered him listening, but did not engage in further arguing. Instead, she heeded Orne's advice to ignore Kayo (who subsequently began crying and banging on the bed next to hers) and go to sleep. The next day, she reported, still enraged at Kayo, she went around her house in a furious mood. But she refrained from acting on her rage, exactly as Orne was counseling her. As she had told him in December, she understood his message to be, "Think. Don't act. Understand." Proudly, she showed him what she had learned:

Sexton: Then I got over it all by myself.... Partly by listening to the tape. I get more constructive after I listen to it in my other life. I was feeling very rebellious. I wanted to write a poem. I'd like to title a book called *Fuck You!* Stick my tongue out at the whole world! Anyone who's conventional—for instance, Kayo. I hate him and then I get over it. It is healthy for me to get angry with him, and then get over it. It's a healthy progression.

As she spoke more with Orne about her new ability to feel angry in her "other life" without acting on the feelings, Sexton used the word *constructive* several times. She was trying to construct a new way of being with Orne's help, but the process was challenging. She knew that feeling angry but not acting on it would help her, yet she found this restraint difficult. She could work on this lesson best when she felt she had permission to have the feelings. As she articulated her effort to contain her rage, she confronted her split perspective on her husband. On the one hand, she wanted to get along with Kayo, and she said she loved him. On the other hand, Kayo's criticisms of her behavior evoked her desire to defy any form of convention imposed on her.

Although Sexton claimed that she was rebelling against Kayo's refusal to accept her for who she was, Orne attributed her attitude to a wish for omnipotence. He questioned the extent to which she could tolerate any limits whatsoever:

Sexton: I don't like him running around spying on me.

Orne: It's not so dumb on his part. It's about time he did.

Sexton: I don't like it.

Orne: You don't like anything which controls you. And this does place some limits on you.

Sexton: [*loudly*] The minute somebody gives me a limit I have to hurdle over it.

Orne: Do you want him to approve of your affair? Honestly, would you?

Sexton: No, but I don't like the vein in which he does it ... he's like his mother. If anyone, any stranger asked her why she didn't wear a wedding ring, she'd say, "George broke his vows to me." [*Sexton speaks mockingly in a low grim tone*] ... Any man would have an affair having to deal with that.

Sexton did not deny her resistance to accepting limits in this conversation; she screamed it aloud. But she did not seem to care about understanding why she detested limits, perhaps because she felt it was another piece of evidence that she was "no good." Given Orne's emphasis on her taking responsibility for her actions, it would seem that the only answer would be for her to acknowledge her defiance of limits as selfish and narcissistic. Perhaps to avoid this self-condemnation, she shifted the conversation to Kayo's mother, who often said that Sexton had much to learn in the wife and mother departments. Sexton seemed to be looking for a way to justify her own behavior by criticizing the tone of Kayo's disapproval; he sounded just like his mother. By focusing on Kayo's mother, she could justify her anger at both of them.

Sexton hypothesized that her newly formed poet self made a conventional marriage more difficult. She speculated that it was her manic "alter," Elizabeth, whom Orne had banished early in the treatment, with whom Kayo had fallen in love. Orne then suggested that Elizabeth actually had some appealing qualities that Sexton might not want to discard. He seemed to want her to own the sexual side of herself, the side that was, in Sexton's words, "a star girl":

Sexton: The queen of the prom. That's who I was, that was the only thing I had.

Orne: A star, a catch?

Sexton: Well, she isn't that way now. She's the underground woman. [*laughing*]

Orne: Doesn't sound like a part of you that you'd want to relinquish.

Sexton: Well, Dr. Orne, you know the poem I wrote to you that said, "Once I was beautiful and now I am myself"? I never really was beautiful, but if a woman thinks she is beautiful she can convince anyone. It's an aura. Of course underneath it I had all the self-doubt in the world. This was my game. It was the only thing I had. "Once I was beautiful and now I am myself." You taught me how to be something really of my own, that I was in some degree a real person. Because, you know, part of me knew this was shallow and stupid. Part of me knew all this was wrong. That's all. So I've changed

> a little bit. I now take pride in the real part of me that's a
> poet. And the real part of me that's a mother.... I don't have
> to take pride in the marriage because that is no accomplish-
> ment. That just is.
>
> *Orne:* It's no accomplishment?
>
> *Sexton:* Well, let's not talk about this marriage that's foundering on the
> rocks as an accomplishment.... My kids are like a miracle to
> me. My marriage is like breathing. You don't congratulate
> yourself for breathing.
>
> *Orne:* Not until you stop.

This conversation moved quickly from Sexton's youthful sexy appeal
to her sense of self-worth as a poet, to her pride in her mothering of
her children, to her feeling that one does not work on a marriage
because it "just is." Perhaps seeing his chance to help Sexton integrate
her current marriage with her status as a professional poet and mother
of two thriving daughters, Orne praised her prom girl self, even as he
pushed her to see that a marriage could end, that she was jeopardizing
the relationship if she treated it as a given, "like breathing." Her reference to her first poem in her first volume, "You, Doctor Martin," presents a poignant reminder of what she created through her relationship
to Orne, a "real self," who could be proud of far more than her ability
to attract attention for her physical attractiveness, but also who could
be proud of more than being a mother. She was a public figure who
received daily recognition, via fan mail, of her importance to others.

The contrast between Elizabeth, Sexton's sexy younger manic self,
and the self "who is a poet" is striking. She "takes pride" in her poet
self as a sign that she is now a "real person." Elizabeth, the beautiful
queen of the prom, had one job: to convince men to fall in love with
her. If her power used to come from seducing men, Sexton said, it was
because it was the only thing she had. She told Orne that now she had
something else. But it is difficult to believe her, for "Elizabeth," the
beautiful manic Anne who can "get men to fall in love with [her]" was
still very much on the scene. Orne struggled to get her to acknowledge this part of herself without success. He did not inquire about
how Sexton's power as a sexual object for men figured in her life as "a
poet." But Orne knew, as we do, that the seduction of her audience

and her fellow poets was often on the agenda at a reading. Sexton wore a red dress that unbuttoned from the bottom up to the knee as she recited her poems. She often flirted with the (usually male) professor who was her host at a university reading, drinking from his glass, leaning into him, or blatantly propositioning him.

Joan Riviere's explanation of "Womanliness as Masquerade" (1929) offers a way to understand Sexton's paradoxical representation of the beautiful versus creative woman here. Riviere explains a case in which a woman who fears being perceived as too "masculine," or too powerful in the world, attempts to seduce men every time she needs to deliver a public lecture. She defines her seductive behavior as "womanliness":

> Womanliness therefore could be assumed and worn as a mask, both to hide the possession of masculinity and to avert the reprisals expected if she was found to possess it—much as a thief will turn out his pockets and ask to be searched to prove that he has not the stolen goods … owing to her conflicts it did not represent her main development, and was used far more as a device for avoiding anxiety than as a primary mode of sexual enjoyment. (pp. 306–307)

If we take Riviere's point here, we might hypothesize that for Sexton, sexuality was most often a "device for avoiding anxiety" rather than a mode for physical pleasure. Sexton too became terrified before a public reading, requiring thermoses of martinis to calm herself down before she performed. She often spoke of her performances as if she had to don a mask to survive them. And as I noted, seducing her host and the entire audience was always a part of her performance. Riviere's explanation would further suggest that Sexton might have perceived her power in the public space as a usurpation of the "masculine" power that both of her parents sought for themselves. Thus she acted out their "badness" by becoming a "bad girl" before the crowd whenever the threat of surpassing her parents arose.

"You, Doctor Martin" makes a distinction between a poet, who is an agent, making sense of the world, and a "beautiful" woman who makes men feel good. If Sexton believed her poem, which she claimed in this session, she should not have needed to encourage men to "make" her and so feel better about themselves, nor should she have needed to seduce the Wellesley-educated Gloria's husband to show

Gloria something about her Phi Beta Kappa membership. Orne never directly pursued the issue of anxiety in their conversations; indeed I cannot remember him ever uttering the word *anxiety*. But it would seem that anxiety about losing the love of her parents, and the desire to have it, were very much on the scene in these sessions.

Orne saw the discrepancy between Sexton's poem and the Elizabeth persona, although he interpreted it somewhat differently. He pushed Sexton to see that banishing Elizabeth, the "beautiful" Anne, did not solve the problem of Sexton's infidelity and its effects on her marriage. He returned to the previous night's scene:

> *Orne:* But you didn't want to believe that he was crying? … How do you
>   feel about his crying?
> *Sexton:* I don't like it. I can't bear to hurt him…. He said he is aware
>   that one of our problems is that I see him as a father … and
>   I said why don't you let me mother you sometimes? He never
>   really will … he said this is all very abnormal; we're supposed
>   to be a husband and wife. But it's part of my capability.

When she quoted Kayo's comment that it was a problem that she saw him as a father, Sexton shifted the inquiry about infidelity and her marital problems to their genetic origins. In Oedipal repetitions, she sought the love of other men, including Orne, to counteract feelings of worthlessness and emptiness. Kayo commented that her wanting a father sounded "very abnormal" to his early 1960s ears, but in reality Kayo did act like a parent to Sexton, taking care of her and often speaking to her as if she were a child. He sometimes seemed to play the mother figure in these triangles for Sexton, as she claimed that she was seeking solace from his disapproval. Sexton appeared to want to mother him, and insists that it is part of her "capability" to do so. But Orne does not discuss this with her, nor does Kayo. Moreover, Kayo performed many of the traditional female tasks in their home, such as shopping for food, making dinner, and caring for their two daughters. Like Orne, he could function as either father or mother in Sexton's efforts to capture the lost love of her parents, but her role seemed to be relegated perpetually to that of the child.

Orne told Sexton that he thought she had fought with Kayo because Kayo went away. In doing so, he had elicited Sexton's rage because she was worrying about Orne's own forthcoming departure. Sexton agreed: "It's always something to do with you going away" [*laughing*]. Orne remained silent at this important moment when Sexton jokingly found a way to talk about the threat of his departure. Perhaps he believed that simply acknowledging the fact that she had feelings about his leaving would produce a change. For Sexton, as I have argued in previous chapters, simply knowing what and why she felt something did not change her feelings or the actions that often accompanied them. She seemed to find it terribly painful to speak about her need for Orne and her dependency on him, instead turning the conversation to a dream she'd had the night before, in which she was pursuing a man she thought was Orne but then realized was Johnny, the young surgeon with whom she had flirted. Sexton became almost hypomanic as she considered the meaning of the dream and whether she might actually pursue Johnny in Wellesley and show his wife something about intellect. Once again, she became interested in an erotic pursuit just as the anxiety about her dependence on Orne arose and was ignored by him:

> *Sexton:* Must be my father and his attitude towards my mother.... I can't wait till I can say to them, "Tell me what you've done with your Phi Beta Kappa key!"
>
> *Orne:* Go on.
>
> *Sexton:* I rise to the bait immediately to convince him that I am smart.... [Johnny] would say, "You really have a lot of potential you really are smart." Fascinating. Same thing you ended up saying! It would just kill her [Gloria]. Now I want to do it. I want to throw it at him.
>
> *Orne:* At him or at her?
>
> *Sexton:* At him. At her. At him.
>
> *Orne:* I don't know who's the more important one of the two.
>
> *Sexton:* Him. But her too. But him. I'd just as soon go marry him. He's very manic. Manages things. A doctor.
>
> *Orne:* Hmmm.
>
> *Sexton:* I'd just as soon marry him. A doctor. Part of him I hate. He is the snob I fingered in you.
>
> *Orne:* Your father was a snob too.

Orne's comment brings the three men into focus as Oedipal objects. Whether Johnny the surgeon, Orne the psychiatrist, or Ralph Harvey, the drunk but powerful father, Sexton's goal was to win the man's admiration. She wanted to impress the man with her intellectual abilities, and to prove that the women they loved were inferior to her: Gloria, Mary Gray, Kayo's mother, or any other woman who needed to learn a lesson about Sexton's power. "At him or at her?" Clearly it was both. But she did not immediately understand it as an Oedipal constellation, although as Orne pointed out, the terms were rather blatant.

In fact, once the conversation turned to her parents, Sexton became embroiled in an old struggle between feeling abandoned, yearning for approval, and fearing and hating their disapproval. Sexton did not agree with Orne that her father was a snob, nor was she able to hear what any listener would identify as Orne's obvious disdain for her mother:

> *Sexton:* I don't know what they were. No, my father wasn't a snob.
> *Orne:* With his custom-made shirts.
> *Sexton:* That was his way of trying to seem … My mother was not …
>   For my father, everything had to look big.
> *Orne:* Your mother was what? Wasn't your mother Phi Beta Kappa by
>   the way?
> *Sexton:* No.
> *Orne:* She just had the highest score at Wellesley?
> *Sexton:* Yes, but she didn't try. But my father spent every minute saying,
>   "Your mother was such a brilliant woman." My sisters agree
>   on this. My father's admiration was … If my father had been
>   married to me now, he'd be so proud.

Orne seemed to point out that this was a classic Oedipal situation in which Sexton sought to replace her mother as the star in her father's eyes. But Sexton's description of her parents' relationship and her place in it does not match what we might consider as a classical Oedipal configuration. In Oedipal theory, a girl must ambivalently reject her mother and seek her father's exclusive love as a step in her own individuation. But to make this move effectively, the parents must exist as a loving couple in the first place, loving each other and the child, and the child herself must feel loved separately by each as well as by the two together. In Sexton's mind, and in her home, as she and her sisters agreed, her mother received "top billing," while she and her sisters frantically competed for both of their parents' love. Indeed, neither her mother's love nor her father's was sure. At times, in fact, it seemed to Sexton that their disdain was more reliable than their praise.

If Sexton did not feel that she existed as an object of love for either parent, she also did not feel her presence in their lives and minds as a couple. As a result, she never really entered what we might identify as a healthy Oedipal phase of individuation. Instead, she tried to find her parents in proxy, through a search for loving attention, while expressing her rage for its absence. James Herzog (2005) draws from research in child psychoanalysis to explain how the Oedipal period must be preceded by one in which a child feels loved by both parents if the child is to develop into a healthy, mature adult:

> The self develops optimally if robust representations are present of self with mother, self with father, and self with mother and father together. Such representations … are only constructed if the actual familial constellation favors their emergence … entrance into the Oedipus [is] facilitated by such a construction, and in its absence narcissistic fixation was a more likely outcome. (pp. 1031–1032)

It was already clear in Sexton's poetry that the "familial constellation" in her childhood home did not facilitate the emergence of a healthy self. Sexton was often banished to play in her room because she was considered too messy to be in her parents' company. And as was discussed in the last chapter, her narcissistic needs and behavior certainly did seem to pose issues for her, but we might include in this context her parents' narcissistic problems as well. The history suggests an extreme lack of empathy on their parts.

Sexton's father, with his custom-made shirts, ironed underwear, and flashy cars, and her mother, sporting her fur and jewels and presiding over an active social life and enormous home, were regular characters in Sexton's poetry as well as her therapy. And her child self, a hollowed, lifeless, imprisoned doll, also figures prominently in these poems. In "Young," published in *All My Pretty Ones* in 1962, the speaker takes us into her childhood home:

A thousand doors ago
when I was a lonely kid
in a big house with four
garages and it was summer
as long as I could remember
[...]
my mother's window a funnel
of yellow heat running out,
my father's window, half shut,
an eye where sleepers pass

These lines represent both parents as unavailable to the little girl in a big house. The mother is a funnel from whom the love runs out, while father is unconscious. With two unavailable objects, the speaker is "lonely" despite her enormous house with its four garages. In the same volume, in "The House," the family of dolls includes a father, "his face bloated and pink" after a bender, and "his mouth" open "as wide as his kiss." The mother seems preoccupied with money: "sorting her diamonds like a bank teller/to see if they add up." In both of these poems, Sexton portrays a familial scene that became almost a trope in her writing and therapy.

The same family scenario was to be repeated in poems in her next volume, *Live or Die*, which she was working on in the final year of her therapy with Orne. In "Self in 1958," published in *Live or Die*, the speaker tells her audience, "I am a plaster doll." She proclaims herself "some shellacked and grinning person," an "I. Magnin transplant." Living "in a doll's house," the speaker depicts herself as a plaything of others, "walled in by their noise" and without a friend. Like the evil parents in a fairy tale, the parents in the poem force-feed the doll-child: "They pry my mouth for their cups of gin/and their stale bread." The final stanza begins with a question of how this doll-child can find a way to "reality," and it ends with a statement that she cannot. She depicts herself as a prisoner:

What is reality
To this synthetic doll
Who should smile, who should shift gears,
Should spring the doors open in a wholesome disorder,

And have no evidence of ruin or fears?
But I would cry,
Rooted into the wall that
was once my mother,
if I could remember how
and if I had the tears

The doll-child in these lines cannot "shift gears" or rebel by spring-ing open the doors "in a wholesome disorder." She cannot find a real-ity, for, like so many of Sexton's speakers, she is frozen, a traumatized victim. Her gin-swilling parents offer a kind of warmth that "is not a friend." A "synthetic doll," she cannot escape by climbing back into the womb, for she is rooted into a "wall that/was once my mother." The image of maternal love here is a solid barrier, and entirely without human features. For this speaker, "ruin" and "fears" are more promi-nent than parental nurturing. Left without feeling, a numbed doll, she does not even seem to yearn for them, for she cannot "remember how" to cry, nor does she have "the tears."

If the frozen doll-children in Sexton's poems remain fixed in emo-tional prisons, Sexton's actual self, in 1964, made continual efforts to escape. Orne tried to get Sexton to see that she was repeating classic Oedipal triangles in order to free herself, and she did recognize this pattern, albeit not always immediately. In their conversation about Johnny, when she did not immediately follow Orne's line of thought, he became more explicit:

Orne: Do you think he'd be a good father?
Sexton: Father? I'm not sure. Gloria never wanted to have children.
Orne: I don't mean father of your children I mean father of you.
Sexton: [*laughing*] Oh, father of me. I don't think he was like a father.
He was too challenging. He used to say to me, "If you were with me you wouldn't need to talk baby talk."

Orne asked if that were true, and Sexton said that Johnny was a lot like Orne. Rather than pursuing the link between him and Johnny, which was, in his words "undoubtedly true," Orne turned the conversa-tion back to Sexton's parents. Sexton reminded him that he had met her mother, and wondered what he thought. Did he think she was "rather straight and human"? She sounded perfectly convinced that the mother others saw was not the one represented in her poems. Orne, however, seemed to agree with Sexton's poetic image of her mother more than she recognized. He did not take advantage of the opportunity to compare Johnny to himself, an opportunity Sexton had offered him herself. Like her parents, Orne did not seem invested in nurturing the child in Sexton. His failure to recognize her dependency needs became more apparent as they discussed her childhood in more detail.

To the listener, it is obvious that Orne did not like Sexton's mother at all. While Sexton remembered how her mother was "always very much the lady," and "people did not get away with telling dirty jokes around my mother," Orne pushed her to link these observations to the fact that Sexton had wanted to write a poem called "Fuck You!" Orne quietly pointed out the contrast between her representation of her mother and her rage toward her. It was very difficult for Sexton to recognize the extent to which she sounded protective of her mother:

Orne: The thing that impressed me about her was that she was very controlling. Trying to control the situation.

Sexton: But did you like her, or didn't you have time to judge that?

Orne: I didn't think whether I liked her or didn't.

Sexton: You must have gotten an impression.

Orne: I thought she was a tough cookie.

Sexton: What do you mean? Strong.

Orne: No, tough. There's a difference…. I guess her behavior towards Blanche.

Sexton: Oh, that was terrible, wasn't it? Well, yeah, if anyone doesn't do what she wants, that's it. She took it as a personal insult when I was seeing Dr. Brunner and I went up there and started to cry and said, "Please love me!" It was an insult to her motherhood that I would say such a thing.

With Orne's encouragement, Sexton identified her mother's cruelty to her older sister Blanche, whom Mary Gray had written out of her will. Agreeing that that was "terrible," Sexton then remembered that her mother was disgusted when she begged her for her love after her first breakdown. She used the present tense, as if her mother was still very much alive in her mind. On other occasions, she and Orne had discussed how Sexton's mother had competed with her to the point of falsely charging her with plagiarism when she wrote her first poems to refusing to pay for her to go to college when she decided she would like to do that after her breakdown. When Orne called Sexton's mother "a tough cookie," he seemed to suggest that she was cruel and heartless. But he did not say so to Sexton. We might read his omission as an empathic failure, for he did not emphasize his patient's need for another kind of mother. Given Sexton's loyalty, however, we might wonder if he was protecting his patient's fragile defense.

Although Orne did not interpret it, Mary Gray's rivalry with her daughter may best be understood from the perspective of narcissistic parenting. Jane Knox (2007) explains:

> The narcissist parent disdains the child for being dependent, but unconsciously cannot bear the possibility of being surpassed by the child, and so must undermine the child's efforts toward independence.... The caregiver's needs are prioritized over those of the child's. Although Alice Miller highlighted the damaging effects of parental narcissistic demands, she describes the resulting inhibition of the child's capacity to express hate, but only hints at the child's experience that his or her love is a demand which parents cannot tolerate. (p. 546)

When Sexton described her desperate attempt to extract her mother's love after she left the mental hospital, her mother clearly experienced it as a "demand" she could not "tolerate." Likewise, Sexton's rage seems to be displaced from her mother. Sexton sounds very protective of her mother in this excerpt, seeming to anticipate that Orne too would think her a powerful and "human" woman. But Orne worked hard to get Sexton to link her feelings about her mother to the Oedipal triangle she was constructing. He seemed to understand that her "capacity to express hate" was a problem, as well as her mother's experience of Sexton's love "as a demand which [she could not] tolerate." At the same time, it would seem that Sexton's love was difficult for him to tolerate, as he averted her every effort to declare it to him.

Today we might argue that Sexton's search for Johnny had at its center a longing for her mother's love that was denied. Sexton addressed this subject by referring to one of her few published short stories, "Dancing the Jig," in which a young girl attempts to win her mother's love. Diane Middlebrook (1991) explains that Sexton invented the term to describe her reaction to her mother's need "to squelch Anne or compete with her." Middlebrook argues that Mary Gray doled out approval parsimoniously—just enough to keep Anne "dancing the jig" (p. 37). Sexton used the term with Orne in this session to explain the effort to impress her mother by holding up her own version of a Phi Beta Kappa key in the form of her published poetry:

Sexton: I adored her, Dr. Orne, I did.

Orne: Indeed, but you do want to write a poem "Fuck You!"

Sexton: I want to shock Billie and Kayo and all these suburban moralists. Why don't I live in Cambridge, married to someone.... Jeepers, we don't have anything in common, but you know, nothing.

Orne: We're going to have to come to terms with mother before you can ...

Sexton: ... worry about these things?

Orne: Yep. Because you know when you talk about finding Johnny and Gloria it's not just Johnny. I mean Johnny meant a great part to you but in large part because it meant you were beating Gloria.

Sexton: Mmm. I am better than her with her Phi Beta Kappa key.

Orne: That's right.

Orne: And her money and her ...

Sexton: And now I can't wait to race in to say, "Look what I've got!" It makes me immediately manic.

Orne: That's right.

Sexton: I would do that. It's called dancing the jig. I don't even know what I'm doing.

Orne: That's exactly it. You were talking a good while ago about how you wanted to impress your mother.

Sexton: But to win your father!

Orne: I pointed out to you her response. But before I did you were just as excited about the prospect.

Sexton: Well, it's even added when he's walking around this country. [And he is a] doctor yet!

Orne: Yep.

Sexton: Got any medical directories where I can look him up?

Orne: I suggest we understand it first.

One aspect of the dance that she does not define completely here is that it continually shifts from mother to father then back to mother in sequence, between the cast of couples, as if only the love of both could be satisfying. But her methods force her to annihilate one on the journey to the other. This movement back and forth, to win mother, then father, seems to be an unconscious attempt to experience the love of both together. But it also meant that when Sexton found fulfillment with one partner, as she did with Orne, she eagerly turned to another, such as Kayo, to complete the picture. Although for the most part this kind of triangle worked well for her, it was about to be destroyed by Orne's departure.

Perhaps the most prominent finding in recent studies of child development is that, contrary to what was once considered the normal path of development, children do not attach themselves first to their mother, then to their father, and then to the parental couple. We now understand that children form simultaneous representations of themselves with mother, father, and parental couple together, and that each of these self-representations must be robust for the child to thrive. In a series of papers on this subject, James Herzog (2004) has argued that children need to internalize a "viable and structuralizing paternal authority" and an "endorsing and reciprocating maternal authority" (p. 908) if they are to move into a healthy separation from their parents. The absence of both led to a lack of an organizing self-presence at Sexton's core.

Sexton's approach to both men and women seemed most often unattuned, a direct consequence of her experience as a child. She sought the attention of all around her in almost every situation, while seemingly ignoring some of the most obvious social cues. Her desire to seduce men (and sometimes women) seems to have been one of her primary form(s) of being with another, and it often led to destruction, as in her failed affair with the poet James Wright, who apparently was so moved by Sexton that he invited her to marry him and wrote arguably his most successful poem, "The Blessing," about their relationship. In his poem, the speaker proclaims in the final line, "If I could step out of my body I would burst into blossom." Beautiful as this line is, in real life, Sexton had already rejected him, proclaiming that she needed to return to her husband and family, and their relationship would not blossom in the future, despite Sexton's attempts to woo him again.

March 3, 1964

If on February 29, Orne had to push Sexton to recognize the Oedipal elements in her talk of Johnny and Gloria, in the next session, after she had listened to the tape, she could see them clearly. Sexton began the session with the pronouncement that "it's a very Oedipal thing, but nonetheless it can still work me. Listening to it I was thinking of how I could find Gloria now." Sexton told Orne that even though she understood how the Oedipal triangle was "working [her]," she could not help herself from jumping "right back into it" as she listened. She wondered at how she could see what was happening and then begin to do it all over again. Orne responded with an expected "mmhmm." But in a truly surprising move, Sexton then made an abrupt turn in a new direction and narrated a trip to Wellesley in which she had not looked for Gloria or Johnny at all. Instead, she went to a lingerie store and purchased a pair of black sexy underwear.

Sexton's description of her trip to Wellesley and its aftermath is lively and entertaining. I will quote only some of it here, but it would seem that she found a way to use her libidinal energy in her own marriage:

> *Sexton:* This is funny for old moralist Anne. It goes back to my mother saying that a woman never buys lingerie for or jewelry for herself … a lady never does…. They had some black ones with fringe, about two-inch fringe and that was really, you know, quite possessed me and I said, "Ooh I've got to buy these. My husband … my husband would have a fit!" I mean, he would like them…. Soooo, I get home and I put them on and they really look great [*laughing*] you know, I'm just fascinated so I think, well, we're not having a drink with Kayo I'll pull up my skirt and show him these pants. Why, he gets home I show him right off [*laughing*] so I also showed him half the time we were drinking and I kept saying, "I think a neighbor can see in here," but he kept saying no…. So I came upstairs and I'm showing him the pants so he gets, you know,

very interested again and that movie that he wanted to look at about Frogman and I'm showing him the pants and I said to him, and I meant it very seriously, "Honey, these pants you know won't die. Go to sleep. You know, I'll wear them another night." And he says back to the bed, says, "You don't want to have sex with me." Now that's stupid cause I didn't mean that I, of course I didn't want to get caught, but I, in other words but he was having fun, you know, cause he liked them … and it was fun but I didn't necessarily mean we had to have sex. I know what I meant was, you know, go to sleep. Well, he gets all, "You don't wanna have sex with me," and I said, "Oh I don't know about … 'bout that," so I went on and put on a black bra that, you know, so I had nothing on with the pants and the bra … and so, and then I pull the covers up and I'm looking at the Frogman too [*laughs*] but I have on the black bra on and he's still saying, "You don't wanna have sex with me." He's so, you know … and I said, "Well, I don't know," and he said, "Well, you had three martinis," and I said, "I know but I'm totally sober." So he said, "Well …," and I said, "I don't wanna put in the diaphragm," but at any rate I was putting up enough obstacles. Finally he … this … he went downstairs and got some wine and we had wine and we had, you know, a lot of fun.

The purchase of the black underwear, "funny for old moralist Anne," sounds like an act of rebellion against her mother who had taught that a woman does not buy her own lingerie. Laughing as she tells Orne, Sexton suggests that in order to enjoy her sex life with her husband, she must rebel against the mother in her head. Sexton went on to say that she thought that the sexual interlude was an important part of her case history and that she wanted to tell him so that Orne knew she and Kayo were not fighting all the time, that they shared a very fulfilling sex life. The long description of their sexual adventure is quite unusual for Sexton. To the listener, her enthusiasm sounds liberating. She seems to have experienced a brief release from the prison of her marital troubles, and she wants to show the evidence to Orne. It is especially telling that she initiated the sexual encounter after noticing how "sexy" she looked in the mirror. Able to appreciate her own body as sexual, she could then turn to share her desire with her husband. It is as if she was able to find in the mirror the beloved Anne who so escaped her parents' eyes.

Sexton sounded very proud of herself for initiating a sexual adventure with her husband. But then she admitted that despite her newfound love for her husband, she had not forgotten about Johnny:

> *Sexton:* I called Kayo at the office when he was busy for no reason except to say I love you. Because that was my feeling at the moment. And yet when I listen to the tape I am trying to remember how Johnny spelled his last name and I'm thinking about calling up Wellesley and finding out where they are, and I'm thinking, making little plots. It doesn't really make sense together.
>
> *Orne:* Why do you want to keep it apart?
>
> *Sexton:* Keep what apart?
>
> *Orne:* The feelings. In the past you've ... you haven't tried to put it together.
>
> *Sexton:* Put what together?
>
> *Orne:* Enjoying sex with Kayo and wanting to call Johnny.
>
> *Sexton:* They don't even have anything to do with each other, I don't understand them! Neither of them. I don't even understand sex, really. I know sex feels good but it's something way beyond that. I don't un ... well, I just think that we're very compatible and I don't know why and I don't ... don't understand it.
>
> *Orne:* Hmm.
>
> *Sexton:* I don't understand why. I guess I do from the tape but it doesn't.... I figure that if I knew *really* some of the, uh ... what's the word ... well, some of the drive to do this would disappear if I really understood it.
>
> *Orne:* Mmhmm.

Orne is oddly silent here. He professed that he wanted to help Sexton put the story together, but she cannot seem to do so on her own. She is plagued by a question: How can she be content with her husband's love and also need to pursue Johnny? She tries to understand it as a libidinal issue, even using Freud's term "drive to do so," but she makes no sense of it. It is hard to know what Orne might have had in mind about this conflict, because he does not say, but it certainly seems possible that he thought that Sexton was desperately trying to keep her sexual self separate from her intellectual side. Seducing Johnny would be a victory for the mind, while seducing Kayo was evidence of her sexiest side. Alternatively, it might have been that Orne felt that once Sexton had seduced Kayo, her "Elizabeth self" could move on to another project—seducing yet another man.

Despite its deeply personal and somewhat enigmatic meanings, we must acknowledge that Sexton's conflict was not all that unusual for a woman living in the suburbs in 1964. Messages about being a wife and mother, complete with newfangled vacuum cleaners and fancy *hors d'oeuvres*, did not also include sexy black underwear or role-playing with one's husband. In some way, both the poet and the sexy woman were "outlaw identities" in the wake of the 1950s, when women were deposited firmly in their suburban houses behind picture windows, waving goodbye as their husbands went off to work. Just a year earlier, in *The Feminine Mystique* (1963), which Sexton read and highlighted copiously, Betty Friedan had argued:

> We need a drastic reshaping of the cultural image of femininity that will permit women to reach maturity, identity, completeness of self, without conflict with sexual fulfillment. A massive attempt must be made by educators and parents—and ministers, magazine editors, manipulators, guidance counselors—to stop girls from growing up wanting to be "just a housewife," stop it by insisting, with the same attention from childhood on that parents and educators give to boys, that girls develop the resources of self, goals that will permit them to find their own identity. (p. 318)

In her poetry and therapy, Sexton herself had explored this conflict between "completeness of self" as poet and "sexual fulfillment," which to her usually meant making men feel fulfilled. She was developing "resources of self" with Orne, but they indeed conflicted with what she had learned about sex from her culture and in her home, from her puritanical mother and perverse drunken father. In the 1940s and 1950s America, sexual fulfillment for women meant appealing to men's desires and women's identities had more to do with being beautiful objects than desiring subjects.*

"Housewife" presents perhaps the most literal depiction of the image of woman that was prevalent in Sexton's time. But Sexton takes it to an extreme, as she shows how the housewife merges with her house in a macabre and grossly sexual image:

> Some women marry houses.
> It's another kind of skin; it has a heart,
> a mouth, a liver and bowel movements.
> The walls are permanent and pink.
> See how she sits on her knees all day,
> faithfully washing herself down.
> Men enter by force, drawn back like Jonah
> into their fleshy mothers.
> A woman is her mother.
> That's the main thing.

The paradigmatic women in this poem cannot stand on their own two feet, and their identities seem reduced to cleaning the "house" of their own wombs. Each is a kind of whale, a mother figure, into which "men enter by force." By the end of the poem, mother, house, womb and daughter are one. "That's the main thing," in a collapsing of identities, that precludes any subjective perspective for the woman. Nonetheless, the speaker of the poem, most probably a woman, lays it all out for us, teaching us a lesson. "See," she says, "this is how we learn to be a woman in this culture." It is important to note that her lesson is about women who do not express sexual desire, for they are, like their houses and the houses of their wombs, shapeless and inanimate, destined to be raped if the species is to continue.

To his credit, in his conversations with Sexton, Orne seemed to move beyond the entrapment Sexton outlined in this and her other early poems and to agree with Friedan that sexuality should be a part of a woman's desiring self. In this session, he repeatedly asked her

---

* See Alicia Ostriker's *Stealing The Language: The Emergence of Women's Poetry in America* (1986) for an elegant review of women's poetry as a product of and resistance to patriarchal structures.

what was wrong with sexual desire, why she needed to keep it at bay. Sexton answered that she wanted to feel desired, rather than rejected by Kayo, who had criticized her for wanting too much sex on their honeymoon. She said that she was afraid that she would be turned on all the time, without knowing how to "turn it off." Finally, she was afraid of feeling sexually attracted to Orne in his office, because she "didn't know how to control [herself]." Sexton told Orne, "There's nothing that makes a woman feel worse than to be not desired. I would rather never enjoy sex, truthfully, taking all my pleasure and throw it out the window, than to feel not wanted." We might imagine him asking if she felt unwanted by him, if that was how she thought about his decision to leave Boston, but he did not take up the invitation.

Orne deflected Sexton's comments about feeling sexy with him, and hypothesized that perhaps she wanted to be "forced" to make love with Kayo, which made Sexton laugh: "With the black pants and the bra? I don't think so. I want to be desired. Is that odd? I want him to want me. Is that odd?" Although he clearly agreed that wanting to be desired was normal for a woman, Orne pursued the question as relating to purely sexual desire, leaving aside Sexton's hurt feelings from her honeymoon when Kayo criticized her for her sexual appetite. Sexton insisted that she did enjoy sex but she forgot or repressed it afterwards because "it is a disturbing thing that I can't get out of my mind." Orne commented that she *needed* Kayo for sex, that perhaps the needing was the problem. He seemed to want her to admit that needing her husband was not comfortable for her, and I suspect it was because he felt that she wanted to be omnipotent. At the same time, Orne did not seem comfortable discussing Sexton's need for him, which was also at times a sexual need, as she had just told him. His silence left her once again when she was seeking some kind of affirmation, repeating a parental pattern of unmet emotional needs that fueled her extramarital affairs. Sexton's own discomfort also signaled her reluctance to play a role that would in the end lead her to usurp her husband as the desiring subject in their household. It also illustrated how terribly uncomfortable she was for needing the doctor who would soon leave her.

Sexton added that to have sex with Kayo in the way they had the night before, she "had to play a role," which she did not want to do all the time. The role was the polar opposite of the housewife. She had to become a seductress, almost a prostitute, with black lingerie and a coy smile, luring her husband toward carnal pleasure while *Frogman* played on the television. Orne, sounding eager to develop Sexton's understanding that sexual desire could be more primitive, asked, "What do you think those things are for?" In this line of inquiry, he playfully inquired about another identity that his patient might assume. Sexton veered away from this potential meaning, returning to the idea that it felt dangerous to be sexual in Orne's office:

> *Sexton:* Husband, doctor, father. Who can you feel sexy for?
>
> *Orne:* [*coughs*]
>
> *Sexton:* Husband …
>
> *Orne:* Mmm.
>
> *Sexton:* Lover. Not doctor, not father.
>
> *Orne:* Mmm … and yet, uh … you were thinking about calling Johnny.
>
> *Sexton:* I don't think that had much to do with sex.

Here they were back where they had started the session, in the Oedipal configurations she was pursuing in her fantasies about Johnny, which she clearly linked to her feelings about Orne as well. In her mind, husband, lover, doctor, and father were always in danger of becoming confused. Inviting Orne to pursue the emotional realities of these mixed signals, she said, "You know, the Oedipal conflict that everybody thinks, you know, they're so well acquainted with it they forget to recognize it … emotionally." Sexton seems to be asking Orne to consider the emotional world in which father, lover, doctor, and husband might become merged. Orne was soon to pursue Sexton's feelings about her father, but in response to Sexton's use of the word *emotionally* he did not ask any questions.

Listening today, we might interpret Sexton's comment about understanding Oedipal material "emotionally" as relating to the particularity of her experience of the Oedipus complex, her own complex matrix of unique feelings and meanings for which a cultural symbol worked as a frame. What analysts call the Oedipus complex in psychoanalytic shorthand is in truth an attempt to generalize the singular experience of each person's development in a particular family dynamic. In 1964, it was common to interpret Oedipal conflict in relation to libidinal drives: The child moves toward maturity by shifting sexual drives and impulses from the same-sex parent to the parent of the opposite sex. But in the decades to follow, analysts would shift their focus from libidinal interpretations of Oedipal material to more personal, relational stories. Arnold Cooper (1986), writing 20 years after these sessions, outlines the consequences of this shift:

> The various speculations in the literature about particular family constellations of the hysteric must now be viewed from a different perspective. Weak father, dominant mother; or, submissive mother, seductive father were thought to be important because they were assumed to affect both the stimulation and the resolution of the libidinally based Oedipal conflict. When we move away from the libidinal model, we can explore what was experienced, learned, and what was inattended to within the family relationships. Formulas pertaining to various Oedipal triangles give way to a careful study of the individual experience. (p. 600)

In her own terms, Sexton seems to be articulating much of what is described by Cooper here in 1983. If the cultural myth worked as a frame for her experience, it also helped her to distinguish her own of version of that myth, her personal story, which was and was not like "that story," the one she would tell in her poetry. She was curious about "what was experienced, learned and what was inattended to within [her] family relationships." In poem after poem and session after session, she attempted to come to new understandings of how these stories from the past shaped her choices in the present.

In this session, Sexton pushed to explore the Oedipal material directly in relation to Orne. She told him that she was afraid she would spend "years dreaming about [him]" if she were not careful:

Sexton: Because I don't want to feel that way here, then I'll get it stuck on you and I don't want that. I don't want to go through, you know, years of dreaming about you.

Orne: Mmhmm.

Sexton: That isn't the intention of the relationship.

Orne: Mmhmm.

Sexton: You know? That's not the idea.

Orne: Hmm.

Sexton: I don't call that very therapeutic.

Orne: Mmhmm. You feel that's what would happen?

Sexton: What would happen? That I'd be sexy and it wouldn't be therapeutic?

Orne: That you would just spend years of dreaming about me?

Sexton: I'm afraid I might, yes.

Orne: Mmm ... instead of years of dreaming about your father.

Sexton: I don't remember dreaming about my father.

Orne: I know.

Sexton: I should better get rid of him.

Orne: Get rid of him?

Sexton: Mmm.

Orne: What do you mean?

Sexton: [*sigh*] Ah, I wouldn't want to sleep with my father. That's probably the biggest joke of any therapy. [*laughing*] A nice hysterical girl sitting there saying, "I really wouldn't want to sleep with my father," and we all know that's funny but ...

Orne: Why?

Sexton: ... Well, it doesn't appeal to me.

Sexton here links her love for Orne with her feelings about her father. Orne does not continue the analogy, but pushes Sexton to understand that her feelings about her father should not be "gotten rid of," but analyzed. She knows that she did not ever think of sleeping with her father, but she also knows that this is what the Oedipal story suggests for her. Laughing at herself, she almost suggested that she must be resisting the truth. But then she reminds Orne of when she learned to associate sex with guilt:

Sexton: I don't know why I feel so guilty about sex. I do, talking about it in here.

Orne: Mmhmm.

Sexton: And you're poppa. I suppose.

Orne: And they are mommy.

Sexton: Poppa was as bad about sex as anyone.

Orne: That's right. And he's so ...

Sexton: When he was drunk he seemed to me horrible.
Orne: Mmhmm.
Sexton: Mean and … saying awful things.
Orne: He said sex things when he was drunk. You know, like you were
        going to screw some guys.
Sexton: Hmm, he used the word *fuck.*
Orne: Mmhmm. He would never when he was sober.
Sexton: Oh! He was vulgar and awful.
Orne: Hmm.
Sexton: He acted like *I* was awful too.
Orne: Mmhmm.
Sexton: When I wasn't being the least bit awful.
Orne: Mmhmm.
Sexton: Maybe I want you to tell me I'm not awful.
Orne: What do you mean? By being sexy?
Sexton: Awful?
Orne: Mmm, yeah.
Sexton: But I didn't describe it as though I thought it were awful.
Orne: No.
Sexton: Did I?
Orne: Yeah, but you were very careful to say so at times you were talk-
        ing about nice, healthy, conventional sex.

Sexton's father, who made crude sexual comments about her when he was drunk, is linked to Orne in these comments. Orne was careful to help Sexton identify her father's sexualization of her and to consider its ugly effects. Sexton brings the matter into the transference when she says that maybe she wants Orne to tell her she is not being awful, and Orne agrees that she was indeed describing "healthy conventional sex." But Sexton seemed to want and need more: an affirmation of her value as a human being who is sexy, talented, creative, loving, and loved.

Father-daughter convention as it was represented in Sexton's poems was never what we might consider "healthy." Nor can we find in Sexton's work an image of a father who is the object of his developing daughter's desire. Instead, in poem after poem, it is the father who sexualizes the daughter, rather than the reverse. "The Moss of

His Skin," for example, has been called "purely mythic"; it is perhaps most so in its rendering of Sexton's own particular version of the Oedipus myth, in which a daughter must surrender her life if she is to feel herself held in her father's arms.* Sexton wrote many versions of this story, but none in which the daughter seeks out her father as a love object through which she develops her own incipient sexuality. Instead, we find fathers who lasciviously poke, prod, and penetrate their daughters, who are ambivalent about accepting sexual attention as the only form of love offered to them. The daughters, eager as they are for fatherly love, do not seem to want it in the form of sex.

March 5, 1963

If sex with Kayo had provided a brief lift for Sexton, two days later she reported that she had decided to take off for Florida with her friend Rita to seek out her beloved sunshine and perhaps even more. She had a secret wish to find an old lover in Miami, although she had not really planned to meet him and did not even know if he still lived there. Right before the trip, after promising Kayo that she would not contact the old lover, she went for her session with Orne, leaving Rita in the waiting room with her bags. She spoke to Orne about how sex was very much on her mind, and she said, "Help me!" as she voiced her fear that she might become "manic" and find a new lover in Florida:

> *Sexton:* [Sex] is such an easy thing to deny myself. Why can't I?
> *Orne:* Omnipotent.
> *Sexton:* In case I get in that mood, I'll want that number.
> *Orne:* A major part of your neurosis is that it is so hard to deny yourself.
> *Sexton:* You know you talk about sin and all the bad things you do in the world. But what about the good things? Don't they ever count up? No one ever asks you about that if you're counting up things. Did you ever sleep with anyone? Well, alright, so that's not a good thing to do—sleep with anyone. I mean aside from my husband. Of course for me sleeping with

---

* Diana George's *Oedipus Anne* (1987) explores the Oedipus myth in Sexton's poetry as a representation of the daughter's desire for her father.

anyone is bad. What about the nice things you did? I mean the people you were kind to, the people you helped?

Orne: It's not the problem. The problem is freedom is only possible if you can trust yourself.

Orne's response leaves Sexton room to explore how trusting herself, freedom, and abstaining from sex might all be related. His willingness to hear about her infidelities without judgment had always been helpful, but here it seemed especially so, because it allowed Sexton room to consider why she wanted to have an affair and how she might avoid it. Telling him that she wanted to be "18 again," she expressed the difficulty of being at a resort and meeting men who wanted to buy her dinner. In a bold and very playful tone, Orne soon volunteered himself as one of these men to assist her in developing her resistance strategies.

Once Sexton and Orne entered into playful banter about how she might behave if she were to maintain her self-respect and not enter into a dangerous flirtation, both of them seem to enjoy the conversation even more:

Sexton: You meet someone and they buy you drinks, they buy you dinner, you spend the evening with them, you neck with them, and how can you put up with their anger? Obviously you can't allow them to buy you drinks and buy you dinner…. I'll just be awful like that.

Orne: It costs something. What's the difference? Who are you kidding?

Sexton: I want to go back to being 18 and out on a date. If you met a girl and bought her drinks and dinner you'd definitely sleep with her.

Orne: Seriously, if I met somebody it would depend on the situation. If I were at a hotel in Miami and I picked up somebody and had a few drinks with her and took her to dinner I would be certainly anticipating that this would lead somewhere. Now I'll admit if this were a kid, a real young girl, I probably wouldn't….

Sexton: [*laughing*] But what if she says, "I can't. I'm afraid I'll get pregnant?"

Orne: That's obviously not the reason.

Sexton: Yes it is too. That's the only reason that I can think of. That's the real reason.

Orne: You've got to live with yourself.

Sexton: I don't mind. When I'm like that I just don't even count it.

Orne: That means you will never allow yourself to put the pieces together. You have to be responsible when you're Anne for what you're doing when you're not Anne. It's not a moral question. It's about being able to become a whole person. If you didn't have all of the businesses you have about sex, this probably wouldn't … but let me just finish what I am saying. If I met someone and I enjoyed drinks and dinner and I felt attracted, it's quite clear she's working out something, god knows what. She isn't … You know. When I say "something," there's something going on with her. The question is what does she lead me to expect. Now you can't have your cake and eat it too. If you want him flirting with you and … that's looking for trouble.

Orne seems utterly engaged in his fantasy of meeting another woman in Florida, so much so that he initially makes her a "young woman," which he then needs to retract. Sexton laughs heartily at this, enjoying the game very much. Every time I listen to the exchange, I expect Orne to say that he is married, and therefore his attitude would be different were he to meet a woman in a bar. Instead he sets himself up as the kind of man who is willing to entertain the fantasy of seducing a woman who is "trying to work something out." It is hard not to interpret it as if he attributes the responsibility for transgression to the troubled woman, rather than the adventuring man. Whatever his motivations, his own desire to seduce a "much younger woman" is palpable, and perhaps liberating to Sexton, who saw sexual desire as complicated at best.

Sexton next provides many examples of what she might say to let a man know that she is not interested in sex, most of which Orne dismisses as come-ons. She asks if she can avoid sex by telling the man she is flirting with that she can't because she does not want to get pregnant, which Orne dismisses as irrelevant. Then she says maybe she should wear a sign, which he says is an invitation. Finally she decides she could show pictures of her charming husband and adorable children. Orne joins her in the game by playing the other man's role:

Orne: If you're so enchanted, why aren't you with him?
Sexton: Because, I came down here for five days in the sun!
Orne: I guess I might think of five days and five nights.
Sexton: [*laughing*] I hope I don't meet your kind!

This role-play is very rare in Sexton's treatment, and it seems to delight both Sexton and Orne. Going back and forth, they appear to be trying to work out a new way for Sexton to be with men by illustrating the limitations of the old way. But they are also enjoying the playful quality of the interaction, almost like old friends. Sexton's laughter signals her enjoyment, and she makes a statement: "I hope I don't meet your kind!" Her diction is most interesting to readers who know that she began every public reading with her signature poem, "Her Kind," in which Sexton plays with the image of a housewife as a "possessed witch." The speaker tells her listeners that "a woman like that is not a woman, quite," "a woman like that is misunderstood," and "a woman like that is not ashamed to die," even as she transforms herself in three stanzas from a lonely housewife into a witch carried off to be burned at the stake. The speaker is not a helpless victim, however; she is a powerful being, "dreaming evil." She is most importantly a "survivor," "braver at night," a woman who dares to do things other women shun. If Sexton used this poem as a celebration of herself as a writer of poetry, in her conversation with Orne she associates "her kind" with someone who is good with words as well, someone with whom she can make meanings and produce laughter. Sexton and Orne are "kin" in the banter above: healthy, playful, respectful, and thoughtful adults, working together on a problem that has plagued couples in monogamous relationships for centuries.

Oddly enough, Orne stayed with the phrase "her kind" as Sexton continued to fantasize about meeting other men. He was convinced that if a certain "kind" of woman were to appear, Sexton could become more than willing to try to win her husband. Orne told Sexton that he was talking about "a certain kind of other woman, or women that you can project this into. We talked about this with Johnny and Gloria." Sexton agreed that Orne was correct that she might like to overthrow a "certain kind of woman," but she was dubious that she would be able to stop herself if the opportunity arose. She even asked Orne if it was worth their time to discuss it. Orne, adamant and optimistic, stated what he saw as the value of their work together:

> *Orne:* It will make you aware of what's going on. See, I've got a lot more faith in you than you do. I think you can learn. I think you can learn by paying attention to what he does. You have great trouble paying attention to signals people send out and then you act on the basis of "I don't know what I'm doing."

Sexton commented that she did not think Orne appreciated the extent to which she could "really feel guilty about these things," and Orne said, no, he understood; otherwise he would have a hard time understanding why she did not enjoy sex more often with Kayo. Sexton then returned to the Oedipal theme:

> *Sexton:* I think it is because he is my father and I am his child. Maybe I feel he doesn't want me.
>
> *Orne:* These are all maybes, but it just doesn't add up.
>
> *Sexton:* I have two personalities. One loves it. The other …
>
> *Orne:* The other?
>
> *Sexton:* You know for a woman, it's a terrible opening, defenselessness, to be sexy. You have to take off about 25 clothes to be sexy. That's the feeling. And it's hard. But once they're all off, then it's easier to get it. But then, if I forget about it, well more and more layers. And I almost have a fear of it controlling me. Sex. I can't get it off my mind.
>
> *Orne:* Of it controlling you … and it's that you can't walk down the street.
>
> *Sexton:* It's hard for me to see the connection.
>
> *Orne:* Mmm.
>
> *Sexton:* Why am I afraid of that plane?
>
> *Orne:* Big and powerful and phallic.
>
> *Sexton:* Phallic! Ha!

Orne seems to steer Sexton back to a Freudian interpretation of her sexuality here, while Sexton attempts to draw his attention to what it means to be a woman in her time. For a woman, she argues, being sexual necessitates a removal of many layers that are required for daily interactions in the social world. Once these layers have been removed, she seems to say, one cannot simply walk around the grocery store feeling "that way." Orne suggests that a woman like that feels like a streetwalker, a prostitute, which was a common interpretation of a sexily dressed woman at the time. Sexton does not follow his analogy, perhaps because her fear of feeling sexy in public was not about being attractive to strangers. As we know, most of Sexton's anxiety about her sexuality seemed to originate and reverberate in relation to the people she knew, the ones who lived with her in her memories of her childhood home.

For a woman living in the suburbs in 1964, it was indeed not appropriate to embody one's sexuality on a daily basis. For Sexton as for other women in her era, sexuality was more likely something to be ashamed of. And yet, with Orne's encouragement, she seems to embrace her sexual side in these sessions without needing to act it out as a transgression. From her associations, we might hypothesize that there were several narratives at work: the woman as domestic, rather than sexual; the daughter, sexualized by her father, who guiltily wants love, just not "that kind"; and finally the poet, who can reshape the cultural meanings to transgress boundaries while still being herself. In the next session, Sexton was to show how very helpful the role-play with Orne had been, for it led her to embrace her own body as sexy without needing a man to do it for her.

March 12, 1964

Sexton returned from Florida in a sunny mood, saying she had "eaten loads," sunned herself every day, drunk martinis at lunch, and purchased not one but three bikinis, her first ones ever. While she was away, she called Kayo each night, purportedly to "reassure him," although Orne thought it was also because she needed her husband. Proud that she had not flirted at all, Sexton seemed to feel that her "Elizabeth self" had a purpose other than sex: just to have fun. Worried that she was becoming shallow, Sexton hypothesized that perhaps she was becoming frivolous. "If so," Orne commented, "then it is about time!"

Two elements of this session add to our picture of the discussions of parents, play, and sexuality that have animated this chapter. First,

Sexton arrived at the session with 10 photos of herself in plastic telescope cases. She showed them to Orne, who seemed delighted to receive them.

> *Sexton:* They cost me $10 but I got $10 worth of laughs.
> *Orne:* It's great that they put them up this way.
> *Sexton:* They're all me!
> *Orne:* I gathered that.
> *Sexton:* Don't I look happy?
> *Orne:* Uh huh. [*clanging in the background as he looks at the pictures*]

When asked which he thought was Kayo's favorite, Orne correctly chose the one with her lying down, wearing the bikini and a black hat. Orne said he was cheating as he guessed that one, because that happened to be a very beautiful picture. Clearly flattered and even thrilled by his praise, Sexton demurred, "Oh, I don't know." She claimed to be surprised because she was not posing in the bathing suit, but Orne said that it was hard to "convey a feeling" when one is striking a pose. Sexton agreed, "Right. It doesn't look real."

After this conversation, Sexton reported that her friend Rita had told her that she was "so much better than last time" they had gone to Florida, three or four years before. Orne agreed, and the warmth between them was palpable. When Orne pressed her, Sexton revealed that she went to Florida because she had been having nightmares about Orne leaving. She recalled a dream in which she had stumbled upon Orne in a different office, drinking. She commented, "Association: my father." Her role in the new office was to show people around the new abode, which she related to the fact that her parents were always moving when she was a child and she would often have to show people around. In the dream, the office was empty, and she lay on the floor crying, while the Dr. Orne in the dream said, "I'm sorry. I'm sorry."

The final words in the dream, "I'm sorry. I'm sorry!" are heartbreaking. We can hear Sexton's understanding that Orne is not trying to hurt her as well as the deep pain she is feeling about losing him. Although he might have explored her feelings about his departure, Orne seemed to think he had a good opportunity to help her by discussing his replacement, and he steered her toward a conversation about a possible therapist. She suggested that perhaps Erik Erikson would take her case, because she had been reading *Young Man Luther* and she was fascinated by his theory of creativity. Orne responded that he had great respect for Erikson but he feared that Erikson might be "too impressed by the writing." Orne's fear that Erikson might be seduced by Sexton's creative side, familiar to us and to Sexton and Orne, led him to dismiss her suggestion, and she did not pursue it again. He proposed another person, who he said was Erikson's "intellectual peer" and "also an analyst who is not rigorous, rigid."

As they discussed this person, who did not end up being Sexton's choice in the long run, it is hard to forget that Sexton might have been offered an incredible opportunity were she to work with Erikson. This feeling of opportunities lost, in great contrast to what had transpired in these March sessions, would unfortunately become more pronounced in the years to come, when the therapist that Sexton did choose, Frederick Duhl, entered into a sexual relationship with her. But what she and Orne had gained in these sessions was equally evident. As Kayo told Sexton, it seemed she had in some way "gotten over this idea that the body is bad," at least for the time being. She had also found a way to use both Kayo and Orne as her approving parents, each admiring her in her bikini: Kayo, like her father, in a clearly sexual way, and Orne, like a mother, loving how she looked when she was not posing, when she was real. Together, these two approving figures completed a longed-for picture in Sexton's mental landscape, although one of the figures was soon, like her own parents, to fade from sight.

7

"THE DISCOVERY OF
A HUMAN BEING"

April 21–28, 1964

The last four tapes in the Schlesinger archive are the only surviving recordings from April 1964: April 21–28. We might think of these as termination sessions, as Sexton was moving close to the time when Orne would be leaving Boston to assume his role as director of a research institute in Philadelphia. Sexton was naturally unhappy that Orne was leaving, although she wondered if his departure was fortunate in the sense that she would never be able to leave him. As is generally the case with termination, Sexton and Orne revisited the key themes of her therapy in these sessions. She discussed her fears of being left by Orne without a self, her "twinship" with her crazy Nana, her attachment to Orne, which felt familial in every sense of the term, her ongoing efforts to be a successful wife and mother, and importantly, her desire to write and publish "great" poetry. As they explored issues that were central to their work together, Sexton and Orne laughed a lot, seeming closer partners than ever. Their laughter conveyed the strength of their relationship, showing Sexton's "best self," as she told Orne. At times, Sexton seemed almost celebratory as she evaluated what she and Orne had managed to accomplish together. She eventually concluded that their work together amounted to "the discovery of a human being!" In a sense, this chapter is a celebration of the parameters of that discovery.

Sexton and Orne discussed his departure in terms that appear frequently in the termination literature. These have to do primarily with aspects of the resolution of the transference.* Sexton would, in Orne's words, need to become "more like a friend" to him, and indeed she sounds like one at times in these sessions. But they also discussed a more recent termination theory derived from Winnicott and his followers that focused instead on the resumption of a blocked developmental process.† Sexton described herself as now about "seven years old" developmentally, and she credited those seven years' growth to her work with Orne. How was she to continue to mature without him? Yet she also displayed in these sessions what she had learned with him: that she was capable of analyzing herself, a sign of a healthy patient who is terminating a treatment. At the same time, Sexton also sounded as if she might have been intoxicated in at least two of these sessions, suggesting that the stress of separation from Orne was placing an overload on her ability to cope. In the midst of these pressures, she wrote a poem based in their conversations of late April, "The Wedding Night," which appeared in her Pulitzer Prize-winning *Live or Die* (1966). Once again, poetry would provide a vehicle for Sexton to represent her attachment to Orne and to use their work together to fuel her own creative and increasingly lucrative career.

April 21, 1964: Unraveling

By the end of April 1964, Sexton was attending two appointments per week with her new therapist, Dr. Frederick Duhl, and continuing to see Orne twice a week. She was also preparing for a four-week trip abroad from mid-May to mid-June, which would include an African safari. Kayo had wanted to go on a safari for a long time, and Sexton's offer to use the remaining portion of her Ford

---

* Firestein (1974) offers an early and comprehensive overview of the literature.
† Alexandra Harrison (2009) argues that "a feature distinguishing child analysis from adult analysis in the literature is Anna Freud's emphasis on the goal of restoring the child to the path of progressive development (Freud, 1966, 1970). This goal is consistent with the child analyst's developmental perspective, but some ask, 'Is child analysis so different from adult analysis? Is the concept of transference neurosis inapplicable to children? Are the theories that help us evaluate progress and success in an analytic treatment so different in children from adults?'" (p. 176).

Foundation Grant to cover the expense of the trip was a significant gesture. It indicated that her marriage was improving, perhaps
because she was making an effort to take into account Kayo's point
of view. The trip was to begin in mid-May, which would take her
away from Orne for four weeks when they had only three more
months together.

In the first of these April 1964 sessions, Tuesday evening April
21, Sexton entered the office sounding drunk. Lamenting that she
and Orne had so little time left, she slurred her speech, opining that
life was all about loss. Orne was to attend an academic conference
in early May, after which she and Kayo were going to Europe. She
complained, "People always leaving, that is life." Orne did not comment on her slurred speech, seizing the opportunity to prescribe a
way of dealing with people leaving as a form of transition, rather than
loss. He emphasized the role of forming mental representations of our
interactions with others as essential to holding on to oneself:

> *Orne*: I can own the people who have left me.
> *Sexton*: You can own the self you are. People leave me and there
> isn't any me left. Lucky you. At least you can *take yourself away
> and be yourself.*
> *Orne*: Don't you realize that it's the same thing?
> *Sexton*: No.
> *Orne*: Who you are depends on your memory.
> *Sexton*: I don't believe you really. I don't think who you are
> depends upon your memory.
> *Orne*: That's an empirical fact.
> *Sexton*: I think you know who you are. You don't need to remem-
> ber someone else to know who you are.
> *Orne*: That's the way you get your identity.

Orne's theory of identity formation here is somewhat difficult to
follow. He argued that identities are shaped by memories of human
relationships, an idea that Sexton could not understand. Sexton's
assertion that selves simply exist a priori sounds remarkably like the
position Orne had voiced months before. Sexton argues that Orne has
an essential core self; he "knows who he is." Orne, however, almost
like an object relations theorist, reminded Sexton that selves are

created through relationships with others. We take others into us and "own" them as a way of becoming who we are.

Orne's statement about taking in others to form an identity seems a bit surprising for him, as he had often spoken to Sexton as if she already possessed a core inner self that she was unable to find. To a listener who has carefully followed years of Sexton's treatment, it would seem that his theory of the self was shifting. Today, of course, we have more precise terms to identify the role of relationships in shaping selves. We might argue that a particular *kind* of relationship produces a strong sense of identity, whereas other kinds do not:

> Growth occurs not in just any relationship or engagement but in interactions of mutual empathy and mutual empowerment. It happens when both parties are aware of vulnerability as part of the human condition, approach the interaction expecting growth, and feel a responsibility to augment the growth of the other. If growth-in-connection takes place, there are positive outcomes: empowered action, enthusiasm, increased self-esteem, new knowledge, and a wish for more connection. (Turkel, 2004, pp. 42–43)

Turkel's summary of relational theories of development privileges "growth in connection" over uncovering unconscious conflicts or differentiating reality from a patient's transference. The "empowered action, enthusiasm, increased self-esteem, new knowledge and a wish for more connection" that she describes do indeed characterize much of Sexton's work with Orne in her final months of therapy. In fact, although he had begun with a theory in which the self, or the ego, would be strengthened and in better contact with reality once the distortions of transference were cleared away, the approach to self taken by Orne in this session attests to his growing understanding of the value of the relationship in constructing identities.

It might seem as if terms like *mutual empathy* and *mutual empowerment* are too strong to describe what Orne may have felt with Sexton. And yet, if we look at the eight-year period in which they worked together, we can see that it was a period in which each of them had achieved recognition in their respective fields, recognition that was, for each, surely to grow in the years to come. We know that Sexton's "growth" was clearly a direct result of her work with Orne, and she repeatedly insisted that he admit that they together created the poet Anne Sexton. But it also seems more than possible that she contributed to his confidence in his own work as well. He did not say as much while she was alive, but he was to confirm their productive collaboration when her biography was published, long after her death.*

As if to illustrate the contrast between her current empowering relationship with Orne and the childhood relationships that inhibited her growth in the past, Sexton went into trance and stepped back into a painful scene from her childhood for most of the remainder of the first recorded April session. She seemed to be inviting Orne to appreciate that her earliest relationships fostered isolation rather than growth and connection. Sexton said she was feeling warm, and moved to the corner, where she cowered, almost out of contact, attempting to choke herself with her necklace. For almost a half hour, Orne urged her to voice her feelings rather than act them out:

> *Sexton:* [*crying*] I don't know what I am going to do. I am going to lose you. That's what's happening. It doesn't matter what I do.
> *Orne:* You don't have to deprive yourself.
> *Sexton:* I don't want to.... There won't be anybody. There won't be any hand.
> *Orne:* Don't pull away. Don't fight me! Let's stay on the same side. You are pushing me away. That's what made you dizzy, Anne. There's no need.

Sexton drew Orne's attention to his hand, which he must have offered her to coax her out of her trance. This was a kind of regression in the treatment, for he had not been holding her hand much since their December discussions of his withdrawal from her in 1962. Eventually, Orne was able to coax Sexton back to her chair, informing her in a soft, gentle voice of what had happened while she was in the trance-like state. In the tone of a child, she asked him where her necklace was, and he responded that he had unclasped it while she was in the corner, because she was choking herself with it. She

---

* Orne's foreword to the Middlebrook biography calls his work with Sexton "a true collaboration" (p. xvi).

attempted to retrieve it, but Orne urged her to stay seated until she was awake.

Orne awakened her from the trance as a hypnotist might awaken a hypnotized person. He counted down from 10 and clapped his hands. Slowly, she came back to consciousness, and Orne instructed her to stop pushing him away, denying him, and not letting him help her. He insisted, "We've got to be friends!" Orne interpreted that she had been frightened and tried to shut him out, which was an ineffective approach to the problem. He said, "I am not your mother!" Sexton agreed, but suggested that perhaps "going crazy" was the only way for her to deal with his departure, a theory Orne firmly rejected. He urged her to see that he was not her mother, who had locked Sexton in her room as a toddler, leaving her to cry out in desperation. Thus, their current situation did not warrant the response she had developed as a child, which was to unravel, to "go crazy." Seeming to agree, she left the office on time.

April 23, 1964

Sexton's return to the feelings that she once had in the closet seems quite predictable, given the looming termination of the therapy. Patients typically traverse the terrain of their entire therapy when they terminate, and this was an important part of Sexton's final sessions. But her ability to manage the above scene together with Orne was a remarkable accomplishment, and in the next session, she sounded much more optimistic. She seemed buoyed by the fact that she had allowed Orne to be with her even when she felt so alone. She said that he had been "like a friend" in her hour of distress, and the effect was transformative. The fact that Sexton could allow herself to be helped by Orne, to feel alone but then express that feeling and share it with him, apparently enabled her to articulate a new experience of herself, of being with another who loved her. She defined this important moment as a shared experience. Considered in terms of the resolution of the transference, once a cornerstone of termination theory, Sexton acted out her original transference to Orne as a bad parent who left her alone to sob in the closet in her room. Then, she showed her ability to move beyond that transference by inviting Orne to participate as a friend who might share her experience with her. This was a "corrective emotional experience" for Sexton, who showed signs of being able to heal the wounds of the past as she made a meaningful connection in the present moment.

Sexton began the Thursday session complaining about her appointment with Dr. Duhl the day before. Whatever she told him, she said, he reminded her of what the reality was. If, for example, she told him about her mother's treatment of her when she was a child, Duhl would explain why her mother might have acted that way. To her frustration, Duhl did not stay with her feelings, as Orne did. Sexton summarized what Dr. Orne did that Duhl did not:

Sexton: I guess it's terribly important to me that you understand me as I go. That I, make contact with, you know, the feeling.

Orne: Mmhmmm.

Sexton: That you know what I am feeling without telling me the reality makes some reality out of that feeling. Instead of an inside experience it becomes a shared experience.

Orne: Exactly.

Sexton: He's not going to share any experience with me. He's sitting there telling me reality. I was just telling him how I felt and immediately he's countering with how it must have been rationally. And I told him this is difficult!

Orne: There's one thing you said before. It's not an inside experience it's a shared experience. I happen to think it's been crucial for you to have shared experiences, because this is something you never had. It's also crucial for you to gain some insight.

Sexton: By someone telling me.

Orne: Both the same. You can share with yourself according to your logic, which you can't do.

Sexton: You can't share the feeling of being alone. I mean, if you interrupt, then it's just interrupted, that's all.

Orne: Mmm. And yet you were pretty good at it last time.

Sexton: Well, there's no way of changing it. That then becomes an experience, you see. I mean it's just as real, unquestionably, as being in the closet alone, as having a friend, who is talking to you. It no longer is that same experience exactly.

Orne: That's what's known as therapy.

Sexton: [*sounding satisfied*] That's therapy.

There is a singsong quality to this exchange, as Sexton and Orne go back and forth in a word dance, developing a vision of what they have managed to accomplish together. Sexton said it first, and Orne echoed it; they have transformed "inside experiences" into "shared experiences." He gave her credit for participating in this process in the previous session, which Sexton affirmed. Sexton then moved one step beyond that formulation to argue that it is not that they simply share experiences; they transform them by making new ones. They "interrupt" the old feeling and make a "new experience." Yes, Orne agrees, it was a whole new thing. He proudly stated, "That's therapy!" Sexton echoed, "That's therapy!" and they seemed to share a deep sense of mutual understanding.

Sexton's theory of the "shared experience" that becomes "new experience" had been described as "generative empathy" by Roy Schafer (1959) about five years before this session took place. Schafer explained that "generative empathy may be defined as the inner experience of sharing in and comprehending the momentary psychological state of another person." His paper presents an explanation of how empathic sharing can produce a change in the patient, which he calls the "transformation of the ego" (pp. 343–344). Drawing from Theodore Reik, Schafer explains that people transform themselves by taking others into them: "The observation of another is here diverted into observation ... of a part of the ego, transformed by taking some object into itself'" (p. 343). Perhaps this was what Orne had in mind in his comments to Sexton. While many theorists offered their own versions of this object relations process around this time (perhaps most notably Winnicott and Kohut), the advent of relational, intersubjective, and developmental approaches to therapy has expanded our ideas of how empathic sharing might lead to self-transformation. If we search for these terms in the psychoanalytic archives, we can find few references to "shared experiences" before 1980, but hundreds in the present day.

Perhaps our fullest understanding of how shared experiences become new experiences, and thus lead to personal growth, appear in applications of dynamic systems theory to formulations of therapeutic change:

Dynamic systems theory explains the analytic process in the most general sense as the analyst's scaffolding the patient's movement towards greater complexity and coherence, through the making of new meaning that is more adaptive than the patient's old meaning.... In contrast with theoretical models that explain new meaning as resulting from the resolution of unconscious conflict, *dyadic expansion* considers new meaning as being co-created by patient and analyst, using the repertoire of meanings and meaning-making processes contributed by both—including conflict resolution and other analytic forms of making meaning—in a "bit-by-bit" interactive process. (Harrison, 2009, p. 178, emphasis in original)

Harrison's summary of the way in which individuals gain complexity through therapeutic exchanges describes a "making of new meaning that is more adaptive than the patient's old meaning." Sexton's tendency to withdraw from feelings of anger or abandonment by becoming lost in a trance or abject depression was a maladaptive response to her earliest childhood experiences of being left to manage her feelings on her own. With Orne, she learned to develop a new way of relating to herself by expressing her emotions to him. The new "repertoire of meanings and meaning-making processes" was not isolated to her interpersonal relationships. It also included the growth of her creative career, which had also increased "bit by bit," or book by book, over the preceding years.

In fact, Sexton linked the creative processes of poetry and therapy in the next part of this second recorded April 23 session. She had written to her friend Anne Wilder about her personal growth in therapy as a "creative process," anticipating in many ways a theory of therapeutic change that would be fully developed long after her death. Orne commented that much of what Sexton experienced in therapy was what she "never had growing up." Sexton said that for Orne to have realized this at such an early point in the therapy attested to his gift "as an artist," but he demurred, "I'm not sure. But that's not the issue." Sexton went on to explain that she had been writing to her psychiatrist-friend Anne Wilder about her progress in therapy:

> *Sexton:* I told her I just started to grow in therapy: I'm now about seven years old! [Anne Wilder's] got this idea that psychiatry isn't creative.... But I said I am seven years old! You could call that the

discovery of a human being. How is that for a creative process? Because surely this is a creative process.... There's a great element of trust in our relationship, and me recognizing my needs.

Orne: That's the most impressive part.

Sexton: Well, you know, if you get something back and you've got something to give, it's really rather delightful.

Orne: That's the most remarkable part.

Sexton: So that's what I meant about the discovery of a human being, or whatever you want to call it. And that's a pretty creative process.

Sexton repeated "the discovery of a human being" twice in this short exchange, insisting that it is a creative process. Once again asserting the coconstruction of the self that she and Orne made together (having something to give and getting back in return), Sexton sought his recognition and confirmation of her theory. Orne agreed that therapy is a creative process, and marveled at Sexton's new ability to take another person's needs into account. For him, it seems, her acknowledgment of the needs of the other was integral to her development. In their exchange, she sounded as if she too felt a kind of urgency about labeling psychotherapy as a creative process and crediting Orne with having helped her. At the same time, however, she moved toward crediting herself with having had a particular aptitude, not only for poetry, but for shaping her own subjectivity:

Sexton: [Being a poet] isn't all of me, you know. That's just what I do.

Orne: It's impressive to hear you say that. Someday you'll even believe it.

Sexton: I am talking about the you and me. The me here.

Orne: Mmhmmm.

Sexton: The only trouble is that if I am a me here I am a much better me here than I am anywhere else. Who's me? I know it better in here. That's why I don't have so much tolerance for not seeing you for stretches of time. I start losing who me is.

Orne: Of course.

Sexton: Well I'm gonna lose you entirely. How do I keep me?

Orne: You won't lose me entirely.

Sexton: Except for occasional visits when we'll pretend it's okay. Right back in the closet.

> *Orne:* ... You're going to have to own, you know, take into you parts of
> me. And if my aspirations for you were basically *my* needs,
> you'd be in trouble and it would be a twin relationship.

Orne argued that if she could "take into [herself] parts of [him]," she would be able to keep the self she had been developing in dialogue with him as her own. Her ability to do so was tenuous, she said, and yet she could verbalize what she wanted, which seemed to bring her closer to the ability to make it happen. Yet Sexton's fear of losing her best self was palpable and plaintive. She realized that it takes two people to make a system, and that Orne could not simply be replaced, even by the most qualified therapist. Orne urged her to "own" him, but she knew that she could only expand in dialogue with him, not by swallowing him or remembering him, but by interacting with him in an unpredictable moment-to-moment interactive process as, for example, infant researchers describe.

In eight years of talking together two and three times a week, Orne had helped Sexton to discover a self that she could actually like. In labeling the process "the discovery of a human being," she recognized what developmental theory has strongly argued: that constructive dialogue creates an expanded version of a human identity, making the individual feel larger than her previous self. But Sexton also knew, in a way that Orne may not have wanted to see, that her ability to self-regulate was not nearly as developed as her capacity to create a self in dialogue with another:

> The individual's affective states, implicit knowing about the world, ways of being in the world, sense of agency and such are dyadic creations, which emerge from messy and unpredictable social exchanges. Of course, they are not only dyadic creations, because the products of these processes also require self-organizing capacities. (Tronick, 2007, p. 64)

Considered in the terms of Tronick's analysis of dynamic systems theory and infant research, we might conclude that Sexton's self-organizing capacities (as witnessed by her reliance on alcohol to both stimulate and soothe and on sleeping pills to calm herself) were much more limited than the "dyadic creations" she had forged with Orne.

She knew this, and also understood that simply remembering Orne would not solve the problem.

Perhaps to illustrate the origins of Sexton's problems with self-organization, the conversation turned to the topic of IQ. Sexton expressed her wish that Orne would think that her IQ was "really big." She reminded him that he had said she could not get through Harvard, an opinion her best friend Maxine did not share. Orne protested that he had formed that opinion long ago, and it might have changed. Sexton disagreed, stating that they had discussed it again quite recently. As if to protect him, Sexton changed the subject to Kayo's IQ. Orne immediately agreed that Kayo was very smart and would have been a good Harvard student. Sexton agreed, and expressed a wish that Kayo would act on his desire to go to medical school, which he felt was impossible because of his age. Orne replied that she could tell Kayo that he had recently "managed to get a 35-year-old man into five medical schools." His commentary sounded like one friend talking to another about schools, as if they were two experts consulting on the cases of potential applicants. He did not seem to recognize that Sexton herself was implicated in their conversation.

Much of this session's dialogue about Sexton's abilities and her identity revolved around the theme of "twinship." She told Orne early in the session Duhl's interpretation said that she and Nana had a twinship relation damaging to Sexton's self-esteem, but asserted that she and Orne had a much healthier bond: [*laughing*] "I said we share one thing. We both want to be great." He denied his own investment in her creative work by saying that it would be a "real twinship" if he pursued his own agenda through what she became through their work together. When she talked about writing to Anne Wilder about "the discovery of a human being," Sexton called her relationship with Wilder, who shared her first name, another twinship. Then, later in the session, Orne used the same term to discuss Sexton's mother. We might wonder whether either Orne or Duhl had read Erik Erikson's (1956) exploration of the link between twinship fantasies and identity:

> It is as if our patients surrendered their own identity to that of a brother
> or sister in the hope of regaining a bigger and better one by some act of

merging. For periods they succeed; the letdown which must follow the breakup of the artificial twinship is only the more traumatic. Rage and paralysis follow the sudden insight that there is enough identity only for one, and that the other seems to have made off with it. (p. 92)

Kohut would present a more positive model of twinship transference as a stage in development of healthy narcissism in the years to follow, but Erikson's formulation aptly captures Sexton's sense of her and Nana's mirroring relationship when she was young. Mental illness interrupted that relationship as Nana was sent to a mental institution soon after the incident in which she cried, "You are not Anne," and tried to choke her niece. As their conversation about IQ turned back to Sexton herself, Orne argued that her mother's need to have top billing and her aunt's mental breakdown each contributed to what Sexton called "acting dumb" and "wanting nothing for herself" as a young child:

Orne: You were actively trying to be dumb.

Sexton: If I had such a big investment, how did I let you convince me to do something so fast? If I hadn't really wanted to do a lot how could I have allowed you to convince me?

Orne: It wasn't that fast.

Sexton: First year of therapy. First poem was at Christmas time and I started seeing you in the summer.

Orne: And I saw you for two-hour periods.

Sexton: Yeah. [*both laugh*] I didn't know it, Dr. Orne! It was wasted on me.

Orne: It doesn't matter. The point is that I had to get important....

Sexton: You did get important. Two hours is a long time.

Orne: Yeah.

Sexton: Yup.

Orne: But I was the first person you'd ever known who genuinely cared about you doing something. And where you found that you wouldn't be rejected for it.

Sexton: But you had to make a very positive statement.

Orne: Yes. Because when I pointed out that you had a high IQ, your mother pointed out to you that she had the highest IQ at Wellesley and it didn't mean a goddamn thing. That statement by your mother typified your relationship like nothing else ever did. I can't think of a more harmful, destructive, more paralyzing thing that she could have done. Meaning it well. She thought she was supporting you.

Sexton: She was pretty sure I'd score badly.

Orne: She was wrong.

Sexton: How confused she must have been as my poetry started to get better and meanwhile she was dying. See how awful it is, that terrible parallel.

Orne: I know.

Sexton: Still it was worth it. To kill her. It's inevitable.

Orne: Yes that you would have fantasies of that sure. Talk about a twin relationship with Nana, you had one with your mother.

Sexton: Like what?

Orne: Like dancing the jig. She had to be the dominant twin.

Sexton's assessment of her mother here mingles Oedipal fantasy with real events. In fantasy, as Orne points out, a daughter might want to kill her mother in order to surpass her. In reality, however, Sexton's mother competed directly with her daughter, "damaging" and "paralyzing" her (in Orne's words). When Sexton proved her mother wrong, the timing was terrible, for her mother was already dying. To Sexton, it seemed as if she had killed her mother, which Orne reminds her is perhaps every daughter's fantasy. In reality, she did not kill her mother, cancer did. But the fact is that on some level Sexton felt guilty about her success, and perhaps this guilt fueled the anxiety she felt each time she was to give a public reading. She never made this connection, but she and Orne seemed poised to do so in the above exchange. But they also seemed to need to affirm Orne as a kind of author of her creative potential. Given the chance, he did not say, "Yes, you were ready to take off as a poet." Instead, he reminded her of his hard work to convince her of who she could become. Sexton could only agree, lamenting that she wished she had known what a gift it was to give a patient two-hour appointments ("If I'd only known!").

The session ended with Sexton explaining that at Orne's suggestion she had given Duhl her short story "Dancing the Jig," and she also wanted to show him her poem "The House," which would

explain to Duhl what it was like, "the feeling when she was growing up," the house with "the frozen people." Orne said he knew the
poem, but argued that this would be the same as having him tell Duhl
Sexton's most difficult memories (such as her fear that she was sexually abused by her father or Nana or both), which she had asked Orne
about earlier in the hour. Orne said he could not tell Duhl her story,
nor could her poems. She needed to learn to trust in her own ability to speak directly, he argued, rather than letting her doctor or her
poetry speak for her. While Sexton argued that the poems "express
things more honestly than fact," Orne contended that "what they do
is give a vignette of it." He disagreed that poetry spoke the truth of
the unconscious, but Sexton remained firm in her belief that feelings
could best be captured in poems, which had a more direct route to the
unconscious than any rational conversation, however intimate. As if
in illustration of her philosophy, she would compose a powerful and
evocative poem during the next few days about the subjects they had
been exploring in these sessions.

April 25, 1964

Sitting in her car before the next session, Sexton began to compose
"The Wedding Night," a poem about the themes of loss, self-transformation, and the passage of time. She discussed the imagery of the
poem with Orne during the hour, and they ended the appointment
talking about a Heinrich Heine poem that Orne remembered. When
he recited the final lines to her, she laughingly told him that she found
him very funny. Framed by the notion that creativity can somehow
transform loss and mortality, the session focused on Sexton's trip to
the Charles River the night before, a trip in which she had thought
about suicide, tried to call Orne, and ended up reaching Duhl. She
had an inexplicable "beautiful" feeling that moved her tremendously
as she sat looking at the river, and she wanted to explain it to her doctor, for it summoned her as if death itself were calling. She phoned
Orne from a booth but he was not in; she then tried Duhl, who spoke
with her until her dime ran out. Sexton told Orne that she had hoped
for more from Duhl, that perhaps he would have called her back, or
at least asked her to phone him when she got home. Because Duhl

"didn't do very well with this test," she had thought, "I might as well go kill myself," but instead she drove around, called Kayo, and eventually returned home.

Sexton wanted Orne to help her figure out what she was trying to accomplish when she drove to the river. She finally hypothesized, "I guess very much that I do want to matter, and sometimes you convinced me that I mattered to you. I'm not going to matter to him. He let the dime run out.... I guess I just wanted more of him than I got." She speculated that she was also feeling an urgency to get closer to Kayo, which seemed impossible but essential as Orne's departure loomed. Orne suggested that she did not reach him purposely; she wanted to see if Duhl could be there for her, if he could be someone who could understand what was most important to her. Sexton said she thought it went back to the idea of "shared experience." Orne did not think that she should share her suicidal feelings with Kayo, but he did believe that she needed to give Duhl more of a chance to share them with him.

Orne wanted to know why Sexton chose not to go into the river. She explained that the feeling by the river had something to do with perfection, which she associated with suicide:

> *Sexton:* I'm so fascinated with Sylvia's death. There's so much. It really needs to be analyzed. The idea of dying perfect, certainly not mutilated.
>
> *Orne:* Mmm.
>
> *Sexton:* There was something very perfect. It was getting dark, just a little light in the sky. But I kept hearing this voice say, "Come on, you've got to go call Dr. Orne." You hadn't left for good yet; you'd be there the next day. And the very effort to do that was healthy whether you were there or not.

We can see that Sexton's urge to kill herself relates to feeling utterly alone with her most intimate feelings. It also seems to relate to the fantasy of being captured in time in a perfect image of herself, as Sylvia Plath's suicide seemed to illustrate for her. When Sexton stood at the river, feeling its beauty, she knew that calling Orne would help her to experience the feeling without killing herself. But when she reached Duhl instead, she only partially completed the task. Her knowledge of the value of shared experience did not lead her to the conclusion that she was seeking a mirror for her feelings in her listener, but it was quite clearly what she was seeking in her phone calls.

Two months before, Sexton had written "Wanting to Die," one of her best known poems, which explicitly addresses the speaker's feelings about suicide. It begins with a response, presumably to her doctor, who had asked her to say more about her suicidal wishes:

> Since you ask, most days I cannot remember.
> I walk in my clothing, unmarked by that voyage.
> Then the most unnameable lust returns.

The desire to kill oneself is a "most unnameable lust," a yearning that cannot be articulated. In the next 10 stanzas the speaker attempts to name the "special language" of suicide. She talks about death as "the enemy" that she has twice "eaten." The speaker tells us that "suicides have already betrayed the body" by ingesting "a drug so sweet." As the poem progresses, the drug seems to have transformative power. It can make the presumably female speaker male:

> To thrust all that life under your tongue!—
> that, all by itself, becomes a passion.
> Death's a sad bone; bruised, you'd say,
> and yet she waits for me, year and year,
> to so delicately undo an old wound,
> to empty my breath from its bad prison.

The speaker's phallic imagination constructs death as female, in a gender reversal in which the living person controls death itself by "thrusting" it under her tongue. Taking a pill, which might seem like a passive gesture to annihilate one's self, is described instead as the power to penetrate. The listener, who might be imagined to be male, calls death "a sad bone," in another reference to its phallic quality. The adjective "sad" restores the phallic power to its earthly, embodied, and mortal home. The speaker does not agree, showing death as a woman ("she waits for me year and year"), who can undo "an old wound" that might be seen as femininity itself. Is the hole in herself the "bad wound"? If so, femininity is a "bad prison." Given Sexton's speculations about sexual abuse, including in the previous session, it would also make sense that the wound represents the soul murder of a child who was subjected to parental abuses and neglect that haunt her to the present (Shengold, 1974).

The relationship with death as the ideal liberating lover becomes a relationship with words in the final lines of the poem in which the unsuccessful suicide leaves books open and words unsaid:

> leaving the page of a book carelessly open,
> something unsaid, the phone off the hook
> and the love, whatever it was, an infection.

The "infection" of suicidal ideation lingers as the final image of this poem, but its allure cannot be erased. It is an unfinished conversation, an unconsummated love, a phone off the hook. But it is not idle chatter. Instead, it is delivered to us as audience as a way of finishing a conversation that leaves the speaker very much alive. The audience, to extend Sexton's metaphor, is brought to life by her embodiment of death; she has "eaten it," taken it into herself, and delivered it up to us. By reading the poem we pick up the phone and continue the conversation. If Sylvia Plath is a "blonde thing" at the end of Sexton's homage to her a year before in "Sylvia's Death," the speaker in "Wanting to Die" is a genuine living person. The power of the poem lies in the use of gerund; it is an action in process that is captured in the title, a state of being rather than an object that was, but no longer remains human.

Sexton used terms of death, loss, embodiment, and femininity as she described to Orne how she had tried to reach him from the pay phone, finding instead his answering service, which informed her that Orne was out for the evening. She next called Duhl, with whom she spoke until her dime ran out. Orne listened, but he clearly was most interested in how her feelings by the river formed a link between perfection and virginity, which she had said related to her fascination with Sylvia's death:

> *Sexton:* I was just now writing about it. The body shouldn't be mutilated.
>
> *Orne:* Were you thinking there was something virginal about that
>   death?

Sexton: I write a lot about virgins. It's certainly a subject I'm obsessed
with. I am just now writing about magnolias. I was in the car
writing a poem about magnolias. I gave George the image
one time that magnolias are like gull beaks, he wrote a love
poem to me that is now quite famous, but I'm still going to
use the image. I guess that will give it away. But the poem
isn't famous to Kayo…. The image of magnolias is not being
opened; to lose your virginity is to be mutilated…. Virginity
is unopen, not yet spoiled. I think I've got it confused in
my mind. A woman's body seems to me more perfect than a
man's. I must have done that neatly at some age! … Sleeping
Beauty remained perfect.

Orne: She was a virgin wasn't she?

Sexton: Of course, she did eat an apple, a poisoned apple. I'm just asso-
ciating. Fairy tales are part of my whole mythology, more
important than myth. Up to the age of 13 or 14, they were
my friends. I am always saying to my daughters, "You never
have to worry about having friends if you have books."

Orne: Grim[m] friends I guess.

Sexton: I have read them now with a sense of shock; horrible things
happen. But that's the way the unconscious works anyhow.
Now all books are about how to go to the supermarket with
your mother instead of how to kill your mother and stuff her
in the oven!

Orne's pun on "grim" characterizes this exchange. It is at once serious and playful. He does not focus on the woman's body as perfect,
nor do they investigate her idea that she is somehow linked to Sleeping
Beauty, who ingested a poison apple only to lie in her youthful state
for 100 years. In 1966, in "Briar Rose," Sexton would return to this
theme, casting Sleeping Beauty as an incest survivor who awakens
to a terrifying image of her father "thick upon [her]/like some sleeping jellyfish." Sexton's poetic imagination would trace the end of a
woman's perfection to her father's violation of her in childhood. If
she could only "get back," the speaker muses, she might be whole
again. Clearly Sexton was working with similar symbols in this session, for she associated the loss of virginity with mutilation, and then

considered how "today's books" teach girls how to go grocery shopping with their mothers. As we know, Sexton feared grocery shopping more than most things; she felt conspicuous at the market, as if people could see that there was something wrong with her.

Perhaps in order to test his ability to share with her the feelings by the river, Sexton asked Orne if he knew the feeling she was talking about, and he replied that he did. To illustrate, he told her he was reminded of a Heine poem in which a despairing man is gazing into the ocean, plumbing its depths for meaning:

> *Orne:* Heine wrote a poem about it.
>
> *Sexton:* Say it to me so I can write a better one. [*both laugh*]
>
> *Orne:* I don't know the name, but at one point he looks at the ocean lying very deep, drawing him in like a magnet. It is very well done. I can't describe it. But at end the captain comes by and says, "Stop. Are you mad?"
>
> *Sexton:* [*laughing*] I think that's funny. God, you have a good sense of humor.
>
> *Orne:* It isn't my poem.
>
> *Sexton:* Well, I know, but saying it you are offering a free translation. Well, Dr. Orne, I hope that magnet doesn't draw me too hard.
>
> *Orne:* Just remember the poem.
>
> *Sexton:* That doesn't help me at all. I think the captain running the ship is the one that's mad.

The sharing of a poem and laughter suggests a significant interruption of Sexton's narrative about the river. Orne seems to want to introduce a different image into her psyche when she thinks about suicide, as well as the captain's word, "Stop!" Although she resists the actual poem, saying it does not help her at all, her affect suggests that she has indeed experienced a change in state, from melancholia to something like joy. Shared with Orne and even transformed by him, the feeling of the river seems to have left her, replaced by the feeling of their mutual laughter over the ambiguity of "Are you mad?" and the joy of discussing poetry with a close companion. It reads as if death were a default lover, the ideal imaginary object of a person who has no real one. Offered the love of a real human being, Sexton lost interest in the anthropomorphic meaning she has attributed to the beckoning murky water. She also jokingly attributed madness to the "captain," her doctor, rather than herself; is he the one who is mad for missing the meaning that the water speaks?

It would appear that Sexton's proposal to write a better poem may have been meant quite literally. When we look at the Heine poem from *Pictures of Travel* (2009) we see significant similarities to Sexton's "The Wedding Night," which she dated as April 1964 in *Live or Die* (1966). Heine's poem, a love poem to death, is a fascinating gift from Orne to Sexton:

> And downward hasten I to thee,
> And with wide-spreading arms
> Throw myself down on thy heart.
> But just in time
> I was seized by the foot by the Captain,
> And torn from the side of the ship,
> While he cried, laughing bitterly:
> "Why, Doctor, are you mad?" (p. 249)

Heine's speaker (ironically a "doctor") is not just gazing into the sea; he has "thrown" himself down and is rescued by the captain. Death is described as a lover in this poem, from whom the speaker is rescued "just in time." The rescuing captain, afraid that the speaker is mad, seems not to realize the appeal of death as a beloved object. And yet Sexton, who thought the captain might be mad, clearly did.

"The Wedding Night," dated April 27–May 1, 1964, ends with "and before it was time," suggesting that Sexton did in fact try to improve upon Heine's poem. Replete with images of death, loss, sexuality, femininity, nature, and transformation, it represents many of the terms discussed in the session above. In her poem, the speaker describes "a short celebration" of magnolia trees bursting into blossom, a festival in the natural world, but one that happens abruptly, even violently, and ends far too soon. The poem accomplishes in metaphor what Sexton sought in her trip to the river, an articulation of ephemeral beauty that promises so much more and then disappears.

The speaker of "The Wedding Night" walks down Marlborough Street "the day you left me," observing the magnolia blossoms "before spring was ready." It is a time of promise. But the promise, like the events in the poem, is already past. Like the speaker, who at age 12 walked down the aisle "at Aunt Edna's wedding," the buds were once "sure-bodied," "tight and firm," and "none were clumsy." A relic from the past, the idea of untarnished virginity, clashes with the speaker's concern that "whatever it was that happened" was "unbelievable," and "pinned on." The images of unspoiled natural beauty are laced with two questions: Is it real? And why does it end? We can imagine that these two questions must have been very much on Sexton's mind as she approached the end of her therapy with Orne: Is this new me real? Why must this relationship, which has so nourished me, have to end?

The poem moves to depict a very specific moment, in the early spring, in Boston:

> There was this time in Boston
> Before spring was ready—a short celebration—
> And then it was over.
> I walked down Marlborough Street the day you left me
> Under branches as tedious as leather,
> Under branches as stiff as drivers' gloves.
> I said, (but only because you were gone)
> "Magnolia blossoms have a rather southern sound,
> so unlike Boston anyhow,"
> and whatever it was that happened, all that pink,
> and for so short a time,
> was unbelievable, was pinned on.

From the first lines of the poem the threat of an ending echoes in masculine images of departure and feminine images that depict abandonment. The branches of the tree are "tedious as leather," and "stiff as drivers' gloves"; the images convey the notion of someone driving away. The speaker finds the magnolia trees "southern" and "tedious," as if even the familiar Boston flowering that is before her once again belongs to another place. We might recall that during the week Sexton wrote this poem, it was very much on her mind that Orne was soon to drive south, on a journey down the Atlantic coast that many might find "tedious." The looming scene of departure clouds the speaker's memories of the past as well, and she speculates whether it was real it all, or instead "unbelievable, pinned on."

The speaker begins the poem telling us that she has already been left, and yet she is driven back into memories of the past. She recalls a time when the magnolias had sat once, each wearing a pink dress:

> Looking, of course, at the ceiling.
> For weeks the buds had been as sure-bodied
> As the twelve year old flower girl I was
> At Aunt Edna's wedding.
> Will they bend, I had asked,
> As I walked under them toward you,
> Bend two to a branch,
> Cheek, forehead, shoulder to the floor?
> I could see that none were clumsy.
> I could see that each was tight and firm.
> Not one of them had trickled blood—
> Waiting as polished as gull beaks,

The buds look at the sky, their "ceiling," evoking, an antsy 12-year-old staring up at the ceiling at a wedding. Although none of the buds on the tree "had trickled blood," there is a certainty in their "waiting," a knowing. The buds are feminine, with the masculine branches in sharp contrast. The speaker recalls asking the listener whether they "will bend," as if to assure herself that she is safe. Nonetheless, she knows the outcome. The speaker "walks towards you" under these branches in a kind of inexorable death walk as the magnolia passes from blossom to bloom to the inevitable falling of the flower from the tree.

In the final two stanzas, the speaker moves the poem into a fast symphony of flowering and almost simultaneous decay. Without her watching them, "someone (someone!) kicked each bud open." The image is violent, even as the perpetrator is unnamed. We have a sense that both the speaker and her listener know who that someone is. His action is meant to "disprove, to mock, to puncture" the virginal blossoms, and they appear to enjoy the process. "Moist, not flawed in fact," they engage in "such abandonment" and "entertainment/in their flaring up." This stanza makes their former, virginal state seem forced and overly prim. Here there is beauty in the letting go, and "they no longer huddled." The imagery is intensely sexual and intimate, while violent and apparently life altering.

The poem ends in a kind of meditation about what happened. The speaker recalls having visited the place repeatedly, much as Anne Sexton had visited the same office on Marlborough Street for many years. She attends a kind of vigil:

> I stood under them for nights, hesitating,
> And then drove away in my car.
> Yet one night in the April night
> Someone (someone!) kicked each bud open—
> To disprove, to mock, to puncture!
> The next day they were all hot-colored,
> Moist, not flawed in fact.
> Then they no longer huddled.
> They forgot how to hide.
> Tense as they had been,
> They were flags, gaudy, chafing in the wind.
> There was such abandonment in all that!
> Such entertainment
> In their flaring up.

The celebration of the opening of the buds is "abandonment" and "entertainment." But the sense of freedom is mixed with the double meaning of abandonment. Because of him ("someone!"), these hidden beauties no longer hide. They do not choose to open on their own but are disproved, mocked, and punctured. This personalized metaphor evokes a verbal rebuke as well as a physical penetration. And yet, the formerly "tense" buds are not any longer; they "chafe" in the wind, reminding us of the intrusive force in a cascade of sexual imagery. To lose one's virginity might carry with it a sense of freedom, but it is also a violation—even, we might guess, a rape. And if it is also a metaphor for therapy and its ending, as seems quite likely, we can only surmise that the premature termination could feel like a violation to the poet who crafts these images.

Once the opening of the blossoms has been registered, the speaker moves to a more melancholy position. She has trouble distinguishing the natural phenomenon from the social experience of "losing you" and the natural development of "losing them."

After that, well—
Like faces in a parade,
I could not tell the difference between losing you
And losing them.
They dropped separately after the celebration,
Handpicked,
One after the other like artichoke leaves.
After that I walked to my car awkwardly
Over the painful bare remains on the brick sidewalk,
Knowing that someone had, in one night,
Passed roughly through,
And before it was time.

The passage of a human being through the speaker's life, like the movement of the buds into flower and then on to decay, is "rough" for the speaker and untimely. She holds a certain "knowing" about the process, but it feels rushed and harsh. She is confused; did she lose a person or a flowering stage of life, another or a part of herself? The images merge and separate, but the "bare remains" leave her "awkward," as if she cannot walk properly (perhaps because she just lost her virginity)! The speaker has lost another kind of virginity, as if she fears that that her transition in the life cycle represents a deflowering that may be her last moment of ecstatic abandon and beauty.

Sexton did not discuss this poem with Orne, although she wrote it on the very weekend that he went away to his conference. This departure was a prelude to "losing [him]" definitively in August, and her poem offered her a vehicle to articulate its complex conscious and unconscious meanings. But before he left, she was, in their final session, to traverse the entire period of the treatment, like the season of the magnolias, in one brief hour. Not surprisingly, the familiar topics of incest, creativity, mental illness, weddings, losses, deaths, poetry, and betrayal were all on her mind.

April 28, 1964

On the afternoon of April 28, 1964, Sexton and Orne recorded the last session that is collected in the Schlesinger archives. Early in that hour, Orne reminded Sexton that he would soon be leaving Boston for his professional meeting, and Sexton begged: "Don't go!"

> *Orne:* I won't be gone a whole week, but I am not sure. To tell you the truth if I had my preference I wouldn't go to this meeting.
> *Sexton:* Well, come home early. Call me up. Make an appointment.
> *Orne:* If I come home early, I will call.
> *Sexton:* Oh, I don't know, Dr. Orne. I was looking over some old letters I wrote you today. Something we said reminded me. The letters were really amazing. First of all, I must be pretty well, because I see such sickness. I felt I was being jerky lots of times but I realize I wasn't being jerky. Well, I was kind of jerky, but I was really sick, begging you to believe. I had all these little rules. It's all so sick, it's really more than young. I don't even know if you remember. I don't know if you were the same person either. Were you that mature then? Could you see it as really quite strange?

Sexton's reaction to Orne's departure speaks volumes of the relationship they had developed in eight years. She is genuinely upset, just as she has been upset about being abandoned throughout their time together. Knowing that he would leave Boston in the fall, she begs him not to go to the psychiatric meeting. But when she heard that Orne intends to call her if he returned early and that he was not really that keen on going, she turned to analyze herself, as if registering her ability to work on her own. Reflecting on a previous, "sick" self, she invites him to assent that she has indeed changed, and she wondered whether he too has changed. In dialogue with Orne and with her previous self, a self documented in her own handwriting, Sexton engaged in a process hardly possible when they began their work together. Her ability to analyze her past behavior without labeling herself as "jerky" suggests a newfound compassion for her younger and sicker self. It also suggests a capacity to think beyond a world of black and white, sick and well, doctor and patient, to a world in which she can stand outside herself to reflect on her own behavior. She remarks that her "little rules" were "really quite strange," indicating that she had developed a different sense of human relationships than she once had. Then she offered Orne an opportunity to say that he had grown too, that together they have come a long way toward "maturity."

This triangle, of Sexton, her doctor, and her texts, that "told the truth" existed since the first years of her therapy. But her ability to use her text to understand her personal growth was new. Although we can see signs of Sexton's empathic and self-reflective capacity increasingly throughout the treatment (particularly, as I have noted, in December 1963), this session signified an enormous developmental accomplishment for Sexton. It was proof of what she and Orne managed to "discover" together, progress they would review in the final session, a session that quite curiously focused largely on Orne's mother, Dr. Brunner-Orne, who had initially served as Sexton's therapist before she was replaced by her son. Sexton's feelings about Orne and his mother had not been voiced during the entire treatment, and it surprised Orne that Sexton brought it up at this late hour. And yet it seems only fitting that this final recorded session documents what was indeed a very problematic triangle, a triangle that in many ways replicated the power structures in Sexton's own family.

Sounding drunk once again in this Tuesday evening session, Sexton began to voice her feelings about Orne's mother, who had seen her most recently when she was hospitalized in November, and who had refused to give Sexton her sleeping pills. Slurring her words, Sexton railed on about how Brunner was disrespectful to her, that she had treated Sexton like a baby and did not recognize how much she had grown since she began seeing Orne. She was especially insulted when Brunner suggested that Sexton might be lucky enough to read her poetry at a meeting Brunner chaired. Sexton laughed as she told Orne that Brunner had no idea whom she was talking to. Orne said that Sexton needed to realize that Brunner's treatment of her had more to do with him than her. Together, they discussed what they might mean to Brunner, especially in their position as "siblings" and achievers. For Sexton, having Orne as a sibling when he often felt like her parent made life very complicated.

Sexton associated to "Menstruation at Forty," the poem she had written in the hospital in November. She told Orne about the poem, quoting its final lines: "I would have possessed you before all women/ calling your name, calling you mine." Describing the dramatic situation of the poem, she identified it as the direct representation of herself at the time: turning 35, menstruating, thinking she would not have a son. She feared what she would do if she had a son, it would be so Oedipal. She said, "A baby, who wants a baby!" Orne said they both knew who wanted a baby, and they both laughed. Sexton said, "Me! Every month." But then she continued that there was much more to the poem; she remembered Orne had told her that David or Susan might have been his name if he had not been named Martin. Sexton suggests in this reference that she might have been his mother, and the conversation turned back to Brunner. Orne said that "she resented you taking my time." Sexton said, "Mmm. She told me that. So how could she really like me?"

As Orne tried to say, "No, that's not true," Sexton reminded Orne of something that she had never told him before, leading him to burst into laughter:

> *Sexton:* She's funny. She tells you the funniest things. She's so realistic. "Well, now, Martin is married to this nice girl, and you really shouldn't mind. She looks something like you!"
>
> *Orne:* [*roaring with laughter*]
>
> *Sexton:* That's just like Dr. Brunner: "She's tall, dark, thin. She looks a lot like you."
>
> *Orne:* That's great. Her unconscious was working overtime.

Sexton and Orne had never discussed the implications of her having seen Brunner first, nor that Brunner still saw her when she returned to Westwood. Nor did they discuss that Brunner had treated Sexton's father for his alcoholism years before, and her aunt as well. Orne was to bring this up later in the session, but the incestuous implications were there. It was as if Sexton were Orne's daughter in the transference, his sister via Brunner, his mother in her poem, even his wife in Brunner's mind! The multiple identifications might be seen as confusing, even wrong. But for Sexton they seemed to enable her to consider herself in multiple roles, a way of thinking that helped her to escape rigid definitions.

Sexton discussed the implications of Brunner's comparison, deciding that there was something wrong with Brunner's implication, and asking Orne to help her figure it out. She began by repeating what she had said:

Sexton: Dr. Brunner said, "She's tall and dark, she's very like you." As if this going to make me feel better, as if you couldn't marry me, you marry someone like me. The whole flavor of it is wrong. I don't have to feel this way about you getting married, do I?

Orne: That you would resent it you couldn't help, but that you would feel it was …

Sexton: In any way pertinent!

Orne: But uh.

Sexton: Of course if you'd married someone short and blond and fat I might have thought I wish I was short and blond and fat; maybe that what was what he'd really like. But I don't know. It's funny how much these things might influence you. I don't think that did. It was a little too late.

Orne: It's interesting that you couldn't bring it up before.

Sexton: I never would have…. I mean, I told you my anger and all that. I don't know why I mention this. It was as if she was giving me a private communication. I wanted her to talk to me!! Not that I didn't want her to communicate about me.

Orne: It's a very complex thing, Anne.

Sexton: I am sure being her son is a very complex thing!

Although it was quite brief, Sexton and Orne here touched on one of the most difficult issues they had faced together, the reality of his marriage, two years before, which he had concealed from Sexton for some time while trying to help her "get well by fiat." In the short exchange above, Sexton acknowledged both her wish to marry Orne and her awareness that this was a fantasy, a "complex" fantasy that related as much to her own parents as to Orne himself. It was further complicated by the fact that Orne's mother was the one who introduced the comparison. Remarkably, Orne suggested that his mother's statement meant more about his relationship to him than to her, that she had her own issues with him doing what he was doing. Sexton, only too willing to move the topic away from herself, concluded that "mothers have to be mothers." Orne said that his mother had moved on to new problems, but that she was bothered that he was leaving Boston.

Sexton asked, "She doesn't want you to go at all?" She associated to a nurse who had told Sexton that Orne's mother went in to wake him up every day, and she said that must make Orne mad. Then she commented that they should be talking about her anyway. Although Sexton agreed they should be talking about her, not him, an agitated Orne became involved in figuring out which nurse this was. He was wrong, naming a head nurse who turned out to be one of his biggest fans. Sexton said that the nurse he believed was critical of him actually thought he was fantastic at "establishing a transference with a patient." They concurred that the nurse ran the ward well, and was respectful toward the patients.

Sexton then returned to her irritation with Dr. Brunner for refusing to give her medicine when she was in Westwood:

> *Sexton:* Some things are over, and I would never go back to her for any reason … leave her to all the alcoholics, leave her to me as I was years ago … never mind it's over…. But I'll never with great sentiment forget that time I was going to kill myself and she pulled all the drawers out of her desk and said, "Life has many drawers, don't give up!" That has great sentimental meaning to me…. This is a difficult subject; it's all entangled. Stop saying she's entangled and you're not!
>
> *Orne:* I'm sure it is…. Why did you bring it up?
>
> *Sexton:* The people I used to be.

Orne himself seemed absorbed by Sexton's preoccupation with his mother. He offered:

> *Orne:* It's a pity that we're related.
>
> *Sexton:* No, it's interesting that you're related. I'm glad that you're not so related. I'm glad you're married.
>
> *Orne:* You were worried about that.
>
> *Sexton:* You weren't married. There was your mother. Your office is next door. You're leaving me, that's sad. I'm not going to go suffer with her about it.

Sexton summarized her anxieties about Orne before he was married. She had worried that he was too attached to his mother. She had wondered if he was gay, or a mama's boy, or somehow stunted in his development. These possibilities, particularly the idea that he might be too attached to his mother, bothered her. Naturally, the topic turned to Sexton's mother. Orne said that there were indeed similarities between the two. He said it was a pity her mother had not lived longer, so that Sexton would not have felt that her success killed her mother. Sexton commented:

Sexton: That's the expense of her death.

Orne: This is where we differ. You had nothing to do with her death. You push me for personal things at times. You ask whether I felt things at times, whether I know what it feels like. I can tell you it has nothing to do with her.

Sexton: What do you mean?

Orne: Just that it is necessary to grow.

Sexton: What do you mean?

Orne: Just that.

Sexton: What personal things?

Orne: You correctly perceived that at one time I had a conflict about wanting to be better than she is, but it really isn't a problem for me … now I don't have to compete with her.

Sexton: And what about her feeling?

Orne: I think she still has to compete to a certain extent.

Sexton: How can she?

Orne: She's in a very difficult bind. We all want our sons to be the best and at the same time, you know, it's a difficult situation but that she has to resolve as best she can; it isn't my problem.

Sexton: What a strange Oedipal situation you and I are in! Our mother is the same one.

Orne: Mmhmm.

Sexton: I love you like a brother! [*both laugh*]

Orne: It is complicated.

Sexton: You don't have a sister. But now you have one—me! I am really so much a daughter I don't know how I could be a sister. This is very upsetting. Shit on the whole thing. I don't like talking about such rejecting situations.

Orne: I don't know that you were rejected.

Sexton: I guess I think so. You know it really is a whole human being you know. Even a sick one. Any old one you want. There are about six of me, you can pick one.

Orne: Huh. We have to stop in a bit.

Sexton's conclusion, that she is "really a whole human being," is nothing short of remarkable. Based on their conversation, she summoned a few identities simultaneously. She was Orne's daughter at times, his sister at times. She was Brunner's daughter and a fellow mother. She was her mother's daughter. She was a poet who had achieved as much in her realm as Orne had in his; they were both successful and driven. These multiple selves, all owned by Sexton in her final statement here, might surely be named the achievement of her therapy. It is an achievement that seems to be celebrated, if only for a fleeting moment, in "The Wedding Night," which she wrote after this session: "There was such abandonment in all that!/Such entertainment/In their flaring up." And yet, as the poem attests, it all seemed too fast, ending far too soon, "before it was time."

Flash Forward—An Epilogue

July 1964–February 1965

Writing about the therapy of one of America's most illustrious women poets is a journey into the life, the work, the family, and most importantly, the archives in which her papers, letters, and tapes are held. Most of my archival research took place in the Schlesinger Library at Harvard University, where a number of very helpful research librarians assisted me in sorting out the files that accompanied the 300 therapy tapes. The files contain Diane Middlebrook's thick "transcription" of the tapes, in which she excerpted the bits of dialogue that were most important to her. A timeline of her research on Sexton is included with the transcripts, so that we can see excerpts from her interviews with important figures like Linda and Joy, Maxine Kumin, and Martin Orne (as well as many others). The file also contains letters from Sexton to Orne, a few notes from Orne to Sexton, and some poems, many of which she had given to Orne and he had kept in his own collection.

As I listened to the tapes, I sought correspondences between Sexton's tenacious effort to overcome her battle with mental illness and the workings of her poetic imagination. It became clear that she was working hard as a patient pursuing the complex task of therapy to speak freely and directly to another person while simultaneously dipping into the resources of her unconscious poetic imagination to express the sense of her life in historical and figurative terms. A witness to her private and familial world, I confronted painful contradictions of her existence. I felt strongly, for instance, that she loved her family fiercely but could observe how she failed them in major ways. And it was painful how much she loved but did not feel loved by her own parents.

With the voices of Martin Orne and Anne Sexton in my ears for hours, day after day, I slowly and laboriously transcribed the sessions I wanted to discuss: over 25 of them in their entirety. Attempting to be as faithful as possible to the reality of their work together, I felt inevitably drawn into the chaotic world in which she lived so much of the time. The process was painstaking, the content sometimes very painful to witness. As I was born in March 1965, a year after the tapes I study were recorded, at times I also felt that I had been invited to walk into my own prehistory in a particularly intimate way. I often found myself wondering how my life would have been different if a poet like Anne Sexton had not been brave enough to confront her demons and write beautiful poems about them as well. My doctoral thesis focused largely on Sexton. And I knew I was a better woman for having "known" her.

Inevitably, my empathic connections to Sexton or to Orne led me to oscillate between believing that one or the other was holding rigidly to personal fears and preferences. Sometimes I identified with Orne, the ever-reasonable psychiatrist, for Sexton could be so difficult to deal with: falling into trances when she was angry, refusing to listen to Orne when he said something she disliked, failing to leave his office when her session was over, even calling him from Europe in the wee hours of the morning. At other times, however, it became difficult for me not to feel angry at Orne. This was particularly true in December, when he seemed to refuse to admit that his departure would affect her, claiming that she always felt abandoned by those she loved. In many of these December sessions, Orne remained silent at moments that seemed to cry out for a response. I see now that my rage at him must somehow mimic Sexton's largely unexpressed anger. That makes it clear to me, although it will of course be clearer to my readers, that in this and in many other places there are many ways in which my own countertransferences to Orne and to Sexton have influenced my work.

Enlightening, moving, and vexing as the sessions can be to listen to, much more happened on the edges of my scholarly research experience to challenge my interpretations of the material on the tape than I could articulate in the preceding chapters. Most important were my e-mail and phone conversations with Linda Sexton, Anne's older daughter and literary executor. Linda communicated with me to answer questions and to approve of the excerpts I chose to use from the tapes. She never asked me to remove any part of any session from the record. But she did offer her version of a few of the stories I told, which at times differed markedly from her mother's. It was difficult to hear another side of Sexton's story, for it made me question the validity of what I believed I had heard. Knowing that this is how therapy works—that we tell our subjective version of what we experience—did not make me feel any better.

The most significant example of Linda's version of a story being different from her mother's is the one that Anne Sexton reported to Orne about Kayo having killed a prisoner of war in Korea, which I discussed at length in Chapter 2. Linda's letter to me about this incident illustrated the difference between her understanding of her father's story and the details Sexton related to Orne. Linda wrote:

> I think the main difference between what she represents here and what [my father] said to me was the "cast" of the story: When he told it to me, he told it as if it were unfolding—the darkness all around him as he struggled to cope with his captive and his fear. Fear of the night, fear of the war, fear of the new and never-before experienced burden that had just been thrust upon him.... And, there is the added detail which is left out here, that his best friend, Jerry, also aboard the Boxer (his aircraft carrier), had been killed on the bridge on the carrier that very day while thrusting my father to one side as a bomber came in and hit them. Jerry was killed in the aftermath of that attack. My father lived because of Jerry's action. My mother, till the day she died, had beside her bed a matching black china ashtray to the one my father had on his side, and she had told me that these were Jerry's ashtrays. She then related to me the main part of the story about Jerry's death.

After reading this letter and being plunged into an entirely different version of the story I recount in Chapter 2, I was faced with a dilemma. Should I tell my readers the "rest of the story," at least another important version of the story, as Linda and her father knew it? Should I put it in a footnote? Or should I remain true to the fact that therapy is always a one-sided enterprise, with patients necessarily constructing the world as they see it and seeking counsel on how to experience it less painfully?

The fact is, Sexton left out a piece of the story that made me feel much more empathic toward Kayo and much less so toward her. It made me question what I argue in the book overall, for it was quite obvious to me that Sexton probably left out the other details of the story to maximize sympathy for herself and the danger she was in, rather than for her husband, who had lost his best friend and was terrified when he killed the young Korean soldier (Sexton does mention his terror in the night, etc.). Although I decided not to change the chapter, I had to include the amended story here, because it strikes me as an important addition to our understanding of Sexton's tendency "to forget." Of course, her persistent forgetting must have involved many dynamic aspects, perhaps including an element of manipulation in presenting herself in a preferred way to Orne. Although the tapes were designed to work against her tendency to lose connection with important things said in the sessions, we can see that in this case they most certainly did not correct other kinds of distortions of memory. Thus it is clearer to me than ever that therapy itself is a kind of fiction, even as it exists to pursue the truth. This of course takes us back to the Schopenhauer quote that Sexton used as an epigraph in her first volume of poetry, and which I cite in my introduction.

As I was finishing my draft of the book, Adrian Jones, a wonderful young Sexton scholar, was at the Harry Ransom Humanities Research Center in Texas, reading Sexton manuscripts and fan letters. We corresponded quite a bit, as we are apparently the only two living scholars who have listened to the tapes. Adrian reminded me that there were a few additional tapes in the archive at the University of Texas, in a restricted box of materials that were to be released only at Linda Sexton's discretion. When I learned from Adrian that the box included four tapes that were recorded after Orne left Boston, dating from July 1964 to January 1965, I realized that I should make an effort to listen to them if possible. Sexton was seeing Dr. Frederick Duhl two to three times a week during this period, and from what I can determine, he entered into a sexual relationship with her as early as 1965. I wanted to know if any of the tapes mentioned Duhl, and also how Sexton and Orne related to each other once the regular therapy had ended. Was there a shift in the transference, for example?

After a few letters back and forth with Linda, she released the restricted box, including the tapes, to the public collection in Texas. That way I could have access to them to pursue the rest of the story of the final tapes, and future scholars could do so as well. She was no longer concerned that her father would listen to the tapes or read the materials that had been placed on restriction because he was too ill. And she seemed ready to make the missing chapters of her mother's story available to a public audience.

Thus, when I had nearly completed this manuscript, I headed to the Henry Ransom Humanities Research Library in Austin, where I met a dedicated and extremely knowledgeable team of research librarians who were in the process of cataloguing the newly released Sexton files. The collection in Austin contains numerous folders, including manuscripts of Sexton's earliest poems, which were clearly written to Orne. It also contains a file entitled "MEN," which represents mostly a file of letters to Sexton from Frederick Duhl, and from Duhl to Sexton. A few other fascinating artifacts are in the file, including an article cut from the newspaper about a therapist who was being sued for encouraging his patient to break up with her husband in order to pursue a relationship with him (her therapist). There are also articles and poems written by Duhl and mailed to Sexton, as well as a poignant and heartbreaking letter from Sexton to Martin Orne in 1969, in which she detailed the incipient "break-up" with her therapist (which Duhl initiated).

Even more than Duhl's inappropriate letters and poems, the therapy tapes that had been in the restricted collection held surprises. Of the four in the files, only the one dated July 30, 1964, was from the time before Orne had moved to Philadelphia. This session began with Sexton claiming that Kayo and the girls were concerned about her, that Kayo thought she might need to go to the hospital. She told Orne that

Storrow Drive, the river road she took to see him, had been renamed Sorrow Drive in her mind because of the terrible memories it brought her. During the session, apparently because Kayo was so concerned, Orne called a doctor at Massachusetts General to have her admitted that day, although she does not demonstrate a high level of distress on the tape itself. The tape records Orne calling the doctor, discussing Sexton's illness, and setting up her admission. Sexton wondered what she should wear to the hospital, claiming that she had only a bathing suit and bathrobe or very dressy clothes, "no in between." After they had organized the admission to Massachusetts General's psychiatric unit, Sexton proceeded to discuss details of her play *Mercy Street*, which Maxine Kumin told her would shock Boston audiences. Orne offered suggestions for setting up the scene of sexual abuse, and Sexton seemed to appreciate his input. It sounded to me as if she would not have needed to go into the hospital if Orne had not been leaving Boston and was in a position to continue this conversation with her.

The next three tapes were recorded after Orne had left Boston: October 24, 1964, January 25, 1965, and February 20, 1965. These provide fascinating material in relation to two topics: Orne's difficulty acknowledging that he was no longer living in Boston and acting as Sexton's therapist, and Duhl's already apparent tendency to bend the boundaries of the doctor-patient relationship. Much of the material on the tapes reveals Sexton's difficulties saying goodbye to Orne and attaching to Duhl. Orne encouraged her to start to trust Duhl, while Sexton claimed she could not. With Duhl's encouragement, Sexton speculated that perhaps she needed to stop seeing Orne. And yet she felt that she could not. For his part, Orne seemed invested in continuing to treat Sexton, and was unswayed by Sexton's fear that having two therapists could somehow be making her worse. He also steered clear of what Duhl told Sexton about their new relationship, attempting to stay out of the middle of what was a sticky situation.

Readers of the preceding chapters will imagine my surprise when I listened to the beginning of the first tape recorded after Orne had left Boston, recorded in October 1964:

> *Orne:* Today is Saturday the 24th of October, 1964.
> *Sexton:* What are you keeping all these tapes for?

Orne: Uh, I don't really know.

Sexton: Is anyone ever gonna listen to them and make something out
of them?

Orne: Well.

Sexton: What's the purpose?

Orne: I haven't really thought it through.

Sexton: You are just doing it with some patients.

Orne: Only if there is a specific indication for it.

Sexton: I know but we could tape right over. You wouldn't need to
keep them.

Orne: Mmhmm that's true.

Sexton: But you are keeping them so there's kind of a reason.

Orne: Uh. I don't know. I guess I have had the feeling that there would
be times when it would be useful. [*unwrapping cigarettes*] You
know, just to the extent … that uh…. Not anything else.
I certainly don't intend to uh you know give them to anyone else or that sort of thing. Uh. I don't know. Uh. I guess
it's just part of the same tendency that I tend to collect all
kinds of uh data which may be much more than needed to
be saved.

Sexton: I understand. It's a creative thing.

Orne: Well, I don't know what it is. I kind of have the feeling sometimes maybe that 10 years hence that I'll wish that I could go
back and really know what happened then.

Sexton: That's right. I understand. It's a little bit of the reason I write
poems. But I won't get into that. The keeping of something.
In case you misplace it. Then you can go back and really
check. So I can go back later.

Orne: Exactly.

The tone of Sexton's voice was politely curious but adamant as she
attempted to get to the bottom of Orne's use of the tapes. As he stut-
tered in reply, it is evident that Orne was not at all prepared to answer
her question. When he did, she seemed satisfied that he intended the
tapes for future information or research, the nature of which was not
certain. Sexton, sounding pleased, compared Orne's work as a scientific investigator to hers as a poet. She sounded relieved that he would

want to think about her in 10 years, and was honored that his research might include their work together.

For me, this exchange rings with irony, on multiple levels. First, Sexton seemed more curious about the tapes than she had when she was working with Orne on a regular basis. Back then, she had told him to use the tapes as he saw fit. But once the therapy was over, for all practical purposes, and she had a new therapist, she wanted to know why Orne might hold onto a relic of theirs. Perhaps she longed to be told that he wanted to remember their work together, but it also seems that she might have wanted to keep the tapes herself (she did not say so, however). It was difficult not to enter into hypothetical or even mystical thoughts as I listened to Sexton questioning Orne. Was she posing a question to be asked 25 years later, about Orne's releasing the tapes to her biographer? Was she answering it for herself? More hauntingly, when Orne told Sexton that he might want to look back 10 years from that day, I gasped aloud. The fact is that Sexton killed herself almost 10 years to that day, on October 4, 1974. Of course this is an uncanny coincidence, and yet it leads to important questions about how Sexton's therapy influenced her most important decisions.

For the remainder of the session, Sexton speculated about why it was difficult for her to attach to Duhl, and why she still wanted Orne to be her primary therapist. Orne claimed it was natural and that she should give it time. Sexton ruminated that one of the things that bothered her about Duhl was his apparent lack of "any limits." She cited as an example the fact that he had let her session run over by 30 minutes because she was crying. When she had questioned him about it, he replied that it was natural for her that sometimes her sessions would "slop over." Sexton told Orne that this exchange made her wonder what was so special about her. She could see that Duhl saw his other patients for less than an hour; why was he allowing her to go on for an hour and a half?

> *Sexton:* I am crying. He says, "You won't let me give you anything."
> I don't like it. And I said don't like it. That doesn't sound like me, does it? I don't know where the limits are! It's very confusing.

Orne told Sexton that she was indeed a bit different from other patients in that it sometimes took her until the end of an hour to get to the real content that she wanted to work on. It struck him as logical that Duhl might therefore want to go on for another half hour, once he'd gotten to the affect with Sexton. He told her that she was making up reasons not to like Duhl:

> *Orne:* Be careful about that. What you are really saying is, if I allow myself to accept this guy, accept his gifts—well it isn't really accepting his gifts. If I allow myself to accept that he cares about me, get into a situation where I care, I'm going to be hurt. This is what you're afraid of. I mean this is very much related to whether or not I am gone or not. Just what you said a minute ago. You'd just as soon start off with me as I was seven or eight years ago, knowing perfectly well I was a lot less sophisticated. Yet he is starting off in many ways where I started off seven years ago.

Sexton agreed that Orne might be correct, although she persisted in her questions about Duhl's boundaries. She could see that Orne had changed in the years they had worked together, and it made sense to allow Duhl to grow as well. And yet she thought it was odd that Duhl was willing to talk to Kayo about them getting a Swedish nanny and a bigger house, offering to come out to her house and see how small it was for himself, and arguing that she had previously gone into trance because "don't forget you went to a hypnotist."

Orne disagreed with Sexton on every point, reminding her that he too had talked to Kayo, that he had driven her home from an appointment while she was in trance, and that his use of hypnosis did not predate her tendency to go into a trance. If Sexton seemed to know that patients in therapy need boundaries to protect them, much as they might push against them, Orne had his own understanding of those rules. Most crucially, Orne kept the boundary of sexual abstinence and remained largely within the bounds of therapeutic relationship. He encouraged Sexton to attach herself more firmly to her husband in a loving way. But he also permitted many of Sexton's sessions to extend overtime, especially in the first years of the treatment. And he held her hand, drove her home, once pulled her out of a snow bank, and slapped her across the face to awaken her from a trance. But Orne did not seem to be able to imagine that Duhl's boundary crossings might include some things that he would not do. After Sexton's death, he expressed regret that he had not been more diligent in protesting Duhl's actions, commenting that he had been concerned about ruining Duhl's career.

On the January 23, 1965, tape, Sexton told Orne that Duhl wanted her to stop seeing him [Orne], and that he had offered to tell Orne himself if necessary. She said that Duhl asked her how often she thought about Orne, and that he argued that she would have to choose one therapist for herself. Sexton spoke as if she were uncertain about it herself, asking Orne if he really knew "what he [was] doing" by continuing to see her once a month. Orne did not seem convinced that they should discontinue their meetings, reminding her of the importance of assimilating what they had accomplished together:

> *Orne:* I think it is vital that you be able to work with Dr. Duhl and that probably my seeing you interferes with really knowing who your doctor is.
>
> *Sexton:* And I said that I had a fantasy that one day you'd come back and then I wouldn't know who my doctor is and he said well that is up to you.
>
> *Orne:* At the same time the important question remains that you are able to own your own development. You see, at the time I was leaving you had a period where you regressed psychologically which you had to get over.
>
> *Sexton:* I am not totally over it. I am not manic though. I wish I were....
>
> *Orne:* Have you talked about how angry you are at me?
>
> *Sexton:* ... I was talking about resenting you. And I brought up this tape and it was filled with all this unconscious material and he agreed with you that unconscious material can be used as a defense. And I wish I had not brought it up. I said it was all obviously sexual and he said it was a parent relationship.
>
> *Orne:* Does that make it less sexual?
>
> *Sexton:* And then I have a dream about you and he says it is about him.
>
> *Orne:* I guess you use it [your therapy with me] a great deal!

Orne disagreed with Duhl's comment about Sexton's transference, suggesting in his Freudian way that parent–child relationships are not "less sexual" than others. Here, he uncharacteristically took exception to Duhl's interpretation, urging Sexton to acknowledge both the sexual and the angry feelings that were evident in her dream and in the session she was reporting to Orne. Duhl took Sexton's dream as a transferential one, interpreting himself to be its real object. It is difficult to hear Duhl's reference to himself without thinking that he was a very narcissistic therapist, although in another context it would seem an entirely appropriate comment. Sexton seemed to be caught in a battle of the therapists in her own mind, and she naturally attempted to recreate it in her sessions. But it is evident that both Orne and Duhl entered into a competition about their patient, a duel that was initiated not by Sexton but by the circumstances into which she had been placed.

The final tape in the archive, dated February 20, 1965, offers a poignant scene in which Sexton tells Orne that he had been her "Pygmalion," and that therefore she had not written since she had started seeing Duhl:

> *Sexton:* You were pleased if I wrote.
> *Orne:* Remember you telling me with this great fury I wasn't reading things, that I didn't like your writing. I was not interested in your writing.
> *Sexton:* You did in the beginning when it wasn't any good…. Well someone had to like it then.
> *Orne:* On the contrary. It seems important to understand what it means to you to have him like it.
> *Sexton:* You liked it in the beginning and I wrote every minute…. Maybe that's why I am not writing. You, my Pygmalion, [are] here.
> *Orne:* I think that not writing is a way of keeping that fantasy going.
> *Sexton:* You know the majority of that work was done for you. And me …

Here we hear a theme that echoed throughout the tapes. But never before had Sexton directly claimed that Orne was her Pygmalion. When Orne called that her "fantasy," he revealed why he was so reluctant to have Sexton attribute her poetry to him. He wanted her to be a person in her own right, rather than the creation of her psychiatrist. And yet, Sexton added that the work was done for both of them, asserting again her belief in their cocreative powers. Orne was intent on showing her that she could create something important in therapy with Duhl as well, and Sexton seemed to agree, if grudgingly. She was, after all, writing *Mercy Street* during this period.

Sexton told Orne that Duhl had arrived very late for an appointment, and that she had become frightened in the waiting room, feeling abandoned by him:

> *Sexton:* Hmmm. I was just scared. I thought maybe I was at the wrong [place]. You know how it is. Deserted. I had a dream that I was lost and I was going to the appointment with him and I was in all these strange places and he found me and he was a car dealer and I said there is no couch and he said don't worry about it. And he put his arms around me and just held me and I was very cold and I thought, "Is there anything going to change or am I always going to be frozen?"
>
> *Orne:* You seem sad about not getting angry.
>
> *Sexton:* It's not the same. Seems to me, he said, you [Orne] were playing the role of the good mother and he said he was the good father. And I said, "Maybe you are the good mother," and he didn't seem to like that.
>
> *Orne:* Maybe he doesn't feel comfortable in the role of the good mother.

Sexton's dream and her doctors' different interpretations of it might give readers the same shudders they do me. For Orne, the dream was about a woman who is frozen by her anger and wondering if she will ever be able to feel safe enough to express it. For Duhl, the dream is about the symbolic meaning of the characters in her mental landscape. Read as a plot of human beings interacting as equals, Sexton's yearning for her doctor to "put his arms around [her]" is met by Duhl's fantasy of being her father rather than her mother figure. But his fantasy, unfortunately, led him to attempt a relationship of equals in what was clearly an unequal, therapeutic arrangement. In the months to follow, Sexton would begin to pay her psychiatrist to have sex with her.

Knowing what came next, I was not entirely surprised to read a letter from Duhl to Sexton written only a few months after this last

session with Orne. Duhl's violation of the boundaries of his therapeutic relationship with Sexton may have influenced her decision to
divorce Kayo, and also might have been a factor in her untimely death
in 1974. The letters from Duhl to Sexton in the archive address her
as "my Stringbean," and are signed "as ever," "love, Fred," or "love,
Dr. Duhl." The first, written in August 16, 1965, responds to a letter
from Sexton in which she had "taken to her bed" while Duhl was on
vacation. Sexton told him that she had written to Orne many times
over the years, but he "did not really read [her] poems," had probably
not even read her letters. She said she was "very alone" with Orne, in
her "letters and in the therapy." Duhl responded to Sexton's letter by
assuring her that their four-week break would "slide by like the good
times which seem to elope to another state." He informed her that he
was reading her poems "slowly now for the feeling of You, as well as
for their poetic syntax." He invited her to come out to Cooperstown
to see him if she wished. Sounding alternately like a lover and an
aspiring writer, he appeared to be trying to impress his patient with
his literary style. He wrote that "here at the Glimmerglass Lake (c.f.
James Fenimore Cooper, *The Deerslayer*, et al.) the weather has been
delightful and surprising. Every doubt that the day will escape the
foggy humid morning seems to run into the reality of brilliant sunshine." In later letters, Duhl included his poems, some of which he
published in professional journals.

In June 1964, while Sexton was still seeing both Orne (intermit-
tently) and Duhl, she wrote "Little Girl, My Stringbean, My Lovely
Woman," a poem dedicated to her daughter Linda. The poem uses
imagery of a garden to chart her daughter's journey into adulthood, a
journey that gives the speaker-mother both pride and pain. The poem
is a letter to her daughter, which ends:

> What I want to say, Linda,
> is that there is nothing in your body that lies.
> All that is new is telling the truth.
> I'm here, that somebody else,
> an old tree in the background.
> Darling,
> stand still at your door,

sure of yourself, a white stone, a good stone—
as exceptional as laughter
you will strike fire,
that new thing!

Sexton's speaker's wish for her daughter might also have expressed a wish for herself. She had never been "sure" of herself, nor had she ever really felt that she was good. Difficult as it was to experience herself as "exceptional," she did indeed "strike fire" when she won the Pulitzer Prize for *Live or Die*, the volume in which this poem appears.

Years later, in 1969, Sexton wrote the most painful letter to Martin Orne that exists in the files. Although the two clearly exchanged other letters and visits after that time, the letter marks the end of an era in which Orne and his successor each saw Sexton, offering her very different kinds of therapy. Sexton told Orne that she and Duhl had spent a weekend in Washington together, after which Duhl learned that his wife had read all of Sexton's *Love Poems*, most of which were dedicated to Duhl, and that he was threatening to end the therapy. Lamenting her situation, Sexton exclaims:

> Dr. Orne, he spends the whole hour talking about his changes, his new approach to his wife (all from talking with a colleague) and I sit there hearing voices. It seems out of control. I feel like a leaf blowing across the lawn. I feel like a nobody in control of nothing. It's my life but I can't change what happens to it. Maybe that's what happened when Nana went crazy and Mother died. I have such anxiety. I can bear to lose him as a lover. It will be hard but I can bear that. But I can't bear to lose him as a therapist....

What Sexton lost when she lost Orne was a relationship that she would not have with another therapist, a relationship in which she felt safe enough to show the darkest parts of herself without shame and to try to heal them. In Orne, she had an interlocutor who, for all his limitations as a therapist, kept trying to hear her until she spoke no more.

For Further Reading

Beam, A. (2001). The mad poets society. *The Atlantic Monthly*, July/August.

Bergmann, M. S. (1997). Termination: The Achilles heel of psychoanalytic technique. *Psychoanalytic Psychology*, *14*, 163–174.

Berlin, R. M. (2008). *Poets on Prozac: Mental illness, treatment and the creative process*. Baltimore: John Hopkins University Press.

Bibring, E. (1954). Psychoanalysis and the dynamic psychotherapies. *Journal of the American Psychoanalytic Association*, *2*, 745–770.

Billow, R. M. (1999a). An intersubjective approach to entitlement. *Psychoanalytic Quarterly*, *68*, 441–461.

Billow, R. M. (1999b). Power and entitlement: Or, mine versus yours. *Contemporary Psychoanalysis*, *35*, 473–489.

Bixler, F. (Ed.). (1988). *Original essays on the poetry of Anne Sexton*. Conway, AR: University of Central Arkansas Press.

Bowlby, R. (1992). *Still crazy after all these years: Women, writing and psycho-analysis*. New York: Routledge.

Bullough, V. (1992). Sexton's daughter, biographer and psychiatrist. *Society*, *29*(2), 12–13.

Butler, J. (1997). *The psychic life of power: Theories in subjection*. Stanford, CA: Stanford University Press.

Chesler, P. (1972). *Women and madness*. New York: Avon Books.

Clark, H. (1999). Depression, shame, and reparation: The case of Anne Sexton. In J. Adamson & H. Clark (Eds.), *Scenes of shame: Psychoanalysis, shame and writing* (pp. 189–205). Albany, NY: State University of New York Press.

Colburn, S. E. (Ed.). (1988). *Anne Sexton: Telling the tale*. Ann Arbor, MI: University of Michigan Press.

Couch, A. S. (1999). Therapeutic functions of the real relationship in psychoanalysis. *Psychoanalytic Study of the Child, 54*, 130–168.

Davidson, P. (1994). *The fading smile: Poets in Boston, 1955–1960: From Robert Frost to Robert Lowell to Sylvia Plath*. New York: Knopf.

Dickey, J. (1988). First five books: Review of "To Bedlam and part way back," by Anne Sexton. In S. E. Colburn (Ed.), *Anne Sexton: Telling the tale* (pp. 63–64). Ann Arbor, MI: University of Michigan Press.

Foucault, M. (1990). *The history of sexuality: An introduction* (R. Hurley, Trans., Vol. 1). New York: Vintage.

Freud, S. (1893). On the psychical mechanism of hysterical phenomena. In J. Strachey (Ed. & Trans.), *The standard edition of the complete psychological works of Sigmund Freud* (Vol. 3, pp. 25–39). London: Hogarth Press.

Freud, S. (1916). Some character-types met with in psycho-analytic work. In J. Strachey (Ed. & Trans.), *The standard edition of the complete psychological works of Sigmund Freud* (Vol. 14, pp. 309–333). London: Hogarth Press.

Garfield, E. (1992). Psychiatrist and biographer differ over Anne Sexton's suicide: Was it preventable or inevitable? *Current Contents, 11*, 5–13.

Gay, P. (1995). *The Freud reader*. New York: W. W. Norton & Company.

Gedo, J. E. (1977). Notes on the psychoanalytic management of archaic transferences. *Journal of the American Psychoanalytic Association, 25*, 787–803.

Gill, J. (2004). Textual confessions: Narcissism in Anne Sexton's early poetry. *Twentieth Century Literature, 50*(1), 59–87.

Gill, J. (2007). Anne Sexton's poetics of the suburbs. In M. Jackson (Ed.), *Health, heredity and the modern home* (pp. 63–83). London: Routledge.

Goldstein, R. (1992). Psychiatric poetic license? Post-mortem disclosure of confidential information in the Anne Sexton case. *Contemporary Psychiatry, 22*(6), 341–347.

Hausman, K. (1991, September 6). Psychiatrist criticized over release of poet's psychotherapy tapes. *The Psychiatric News*.

Hoeveler, D. L., & Schuster, D. D. (Eds.). (2008). *Women's literary creativity and the female body*. New York: Palgrave Macmillan.

Horowitz, F. D. (1992). Confidentiality and privacy. *Society, 29*(2), 27–29.

Hunter, D. (Ed.). (1989). *Seduction and theory: Readings of gender, representation, and rhetoric*. Chicago: University of Illinois Press.

James, W. (1977). *The writings of William James: A comprehensive edition* (J. J. McDermott, Ed.). Chicago: University of Chicago Press.

Jong, E. (1991, August 17). Anne Sexton's river of words. *New York Times*.

Kamp, D. (2009). Rethinking the American dream. *Vanity Fair*, 78–83.

Kavaler-Adler, S. (1993). *The compulsion to create: A psychoanalytic study of women artists*. New York: Routledge.

Kavaler-Adler, S. (1996). Anne Sexton's treatment, part I. In *The creative mystique: From red shoes frenzy to love and creativity* (pp. 183–210). New York: Routledge.

Kavaler-Adler, S. (1996). Anne Sexton's treatment, part II, and addendum on her demon lover complex. In *The creative mystique: From red shoes frenzy to love and creativity* (pp. 211–239). New York: Routledge.

Kavaler-Adler, S. (2003). *Mourning, spirituality and psychic change*. New York: Brunner-Routledge.

Kevles, B. (1968). Through bedlam's door with Anne Sexton. *Look*, 39–44.

Kriegman, D. (2002). Interpreting and negotiating conflicts of interests in the analytic relationship. *Progress in Self Psychology*, *18*, 87–112.

Kroll, J. (1992). The silence of the tapes. *Society*, *29*(2), 18–20.

Kumin, M. (1975). How it is. *The New Yorker*, 38.

Kumin, M. (1999). Foreword: How it was: Maxine Kumin on Anne Sexton. In L. G. Sexton (Ed.), *Anne Sexton: The complete poems* (pp. xix–xxxiv). Boston: Houghton Mifflin.

Laub, D., & Felman, S. (1992). *Testimony: Crises of witnessing in literature, psychoanalysis, and history*. New York: Routledge.

Lewin, B. R. (1992). The Anne Sexton controversy. *Society*, *29*(2), 9–11.

Lewis, A. (1990). One person and two person psychologies and the method of psychoanalysis. *Psychoanalytic Psychology*, *7*, 475–485.

Lewis, J. M. (2000). Repairing the bond in important relationships: A dynamic for personality maturation. *American Journal of Psychiatry*, *157*, 1375–1378.

Liederman, E. (1993). From behind the bedlam. *San Francisco Review of Books*, 31–33.

Lucas, R. (2009). Gifts of love, gifts of poison: Anne Sexton and the poetry of intimate exchange. *Life Writing*, *6*(1), 45–59.

Malcolm, J. (2004). *In the Freud archives*. London: Granta.

Malcolm, J. (2004). *Psychoanalysis: The impossible profession*. London: Granta.

Matthews, G. (1987). *Just a housewife: The rise and fall of domesticity in America*. New York: Oxford University Press.

McClatchy, J. D. (1988). Anne Sexton: Somehow to endure. In D. Hume (Ed.), *Sexton: Selected criticism* (pp. 29–72). Chicago: University of Illinois Press.

McGowan, P. (2004). *Anne Sexton and middle generation poetry: The geography of grief*. Westport, CT: Praeger.

McHugh, K. A. (1999). *American domesticity: From how-to manual to Hollywood melodrama*. Oxford: Oxford University Press.

Merkin, D. (1994). The good daughter: Review of *Searching for mercy street: My journey back to my mother, Anne Sexton*, by Linda Gray Sexton. *The New Yorker*, 108–113.

Meyerowitz, J. (Ed.). (1994). *Not June Cleaver: Women and gender in postwar America, 1945–1960*. Philadelphia: Temple University Press.

Michailidou, A. (2004). Edna St. Vincent Millay and Anne Sexton: The disruption of domestic bliss. *Journal of American Studies*, *38*(1), 67–88.

Middlebrook, D. W. (1989). 1957: Anne Sexton's bedlam. In L. Wagner-Martin (Ed.), *Critical essays on Anne Sexton* (pp. 239–246). Boston: G. K. Hall.

Mitchell, J. (1998). Trauma, recognition, and the place of language. *Diacritics*, *28*(4), 121–133.

Morrow, L. (1991, September 23). Pains of the poet—and miracles. *Time*.

Onek, J. N. (1992). Legal issues in the Orne/Sexton case. *Journal of the American Academy of Psychoanalysis, 20*, 655–658.

Orne, M. T. (1991, July 23). The Sexton tapes. *New York Times*.

Orne, M. T. (1992). Foreword. In D. Middlebrook, *Anne Sexton: A biography* (pp. xiii–xviii). New York: Vintage.

Pellegrino, E. (1998). Secrets of the couch and the grave: The Anne Sexton case. In S. Lammers & A. Verhey (Eds.), *On moral medicine: Theological perspectives in medical ethics* (pp. 872–873). Grand Rapids, MI: William B. Eerdmans Publishing.

Pollard, C. (2006). Her kind: Anne Sexton, the Cold War and the idea of the housewife. *Critical Quarterly, 48*(3), 1–24.

Pollitt, K. (1991, August 18). The death is not the life. *New York Times*.

Pollitt, K. (1991, August 18). Review of *Anne Sexton: A biography*. *New York Times Book Review*, pp. 21–22.

Roazen, P. (1992). Privacy and therapy. *Society, 29*(2), 14–17.

Rose, J. (2003). Faking it up with the truth: Anne Sexton. In *On not being able to sleep: Psychoanalysis and the modern world* (pp. 17–25). Princeton, NJ: Princeton University Press.

Rosenbaum, M. (1994). The travails of Martin Orne: On privacy, public disclosure, and confidentiality in psychotherapy. *Journal of Contemporary Psychotherapy, 24*(3), 159–167.

Salvio, P. (2007). *Anne Sexton: Teacher of weird abundance*. New York: State University of New York Press.

Semrad, E. (1964). Assisting psychotic patients to recompensate. *Mental Hospitals, 15*(7), 361–366.

Sexton, A. (1965). Interview with Patricia Marx. *Hudson Review, 18*(4).

Sexton, A. (1968). Telephone interview with the students at Stephens College, April 13, 1964. In C. F. Madden (Ed.), *Talks with authors* (pp. 151–200). Carbondale, IL: Southern Illinois University Press.

Sexton, A. (1970). Interview with William Packard, "Craft interview with Anne Sexton." *New York Quarterly, 3*, 8–12.

Sexton, A. (1971). Interview with Barbara Kevles, "The art of poetry: Anne Sexton." *Paris Review, 52*, 159–191.

Sexton, A. (1976). Interview with Maxine Kumin, Elaine Showalter, and Carol Smith. *Women's Studies: An Interdisciplinary Journal, 4*.

Sexton, A. (1981). *The complete poems* (L. G. Sexton, Ed.). New York: Houghton Mifflin.

Sexton, A. (1991). *Anne Sexton: A self-portrait in letters* (L. G. Sexton, Ed.). New York: Houghton Mifflin.

Sexton, L. G. (1991, August 8). A daughter's story: I knew her best. *New York Times Book Review*, p. 20.

Sexton, L. G. (1994). Half in love: Surviving the legacy of suicide. In *Searching for mercy street: My journey back to my mother, Anne Sexton*. Boston: Little Brown & Co.

Sexton, L. G. (2009, April 3). Letter: "A tortured inheritance." *New York Times*.

Sexton, L. G., & Ames, L. (Eds.). (1977). *Anne Sexton: A self-portrait in letters*. Boston: Houghton-Mifflin.

Shopper, M. (1992). Breaching confidentiality. *Society*, *29*(2), 24–26.

Simpson, L. (1967). The new books: Review of *Live or die*, by Anne Sexton. *Harper's*, *235*, 90–91.

Sokolov, R. (1991). Shushing the dead and the dying. *Wall Street Journal*, p. 21.

Stanley, A. (1991, July). Poet told all: Therapist provides the record. *New York Times*, p. 15.

Trinidad, D. (2001). Anne Sexton: An actress in her own autobiographical play. *Crossroads: Poetry Society of America Journal*, *57*.

Tronick, E. (n.d.) Dark side of infant mental health. Unpublished manuscript.

Viorst, J. (1992). Listening at the keyhole: The Anne Sexton tapes. *Journal of the American Academy of Psychoanalysis*, *20*(4), 645–653.

Wagner-Martin, L. (Ed.). (1989). *Critical essays on Anne Sexton*. Boston: G. K. Hall.

Weissberg, J. H. (1992). Therapeutic responsibility in the case of Anne Sexton. *Journal of American Academy of Psychoanalysis*, *20*, 633–638.

Williams, I. (2007). Female voices, male listeners: Identifying gender in the poetry of Anne Sexton and Wanda Coleman. In D. L. Hoeveler & D. D. Schuster (Eds.), *Women's literary creativity and the female body* (pp. 175–192). New York: Palgrave Macmillan.

Winnicott, D. W. (1971). *Playing and reality*. London: Routledge, 2005.

References

Alpert, J. L. (1991). Retrospective treatment of incest victims Suggested analytic attitudes. *Psychoanalytic Review*, *78*, 425–435.

Beebe, B., & Lachmann, F. M. (1998). Co-constructing inner and relational processes: Self- and mutual regulation in infant research and adult treatment. *Psychoanalytic Psychology*, *15*, 480–516.

Benjamin, J. (1988). *The bonds of love: Psychoanalysis, feminism, and the problem of domination.* London: Pantheon.

Colburn, S. E. (Ed.). (1985). *No evil star: Anne Sexton: Selected essays, interviews and prose.* Ann Arbor, MI: University of Michigan Press.

Cooper, A. (1986). Discussion. *Contemporary Psychoanalysis*, *22*, 597–602.

Davies, J. M., & Frawley, M. G. (1992). Dissociative processes and transference-countertransference paradigms in the psychoanalytically oriented treatment of adult survivors of childhood sexual abuse. *Psychoanalytic Dialogues*, *2*, 5–36.

Dickey, J. (1988). Dialogues with themselves: Review of "All my pretty ones," by Anne Sexton. In S. E. Colburn (Ed.), *Anne Sexton: Telling the tale* (pp.). Ann Arbor, MI: University of Michigan Press.

Elliot, P. (1991). *From mastery to analysis: Theories of gender in psychoanalytic feminism.* Ithaca, NY: Cornell University Press.

Erikson, E. H. (1956). The problem of ego identity. *Journal of the American Psychoanalytic Association*, *4*, 56–121.

Erikson, E. H. (1962). Reality and actuality: An address. *Journal of the American Psychoanalytic Association*, *10*, 451–474.

Ferenczi, S. (1949). Confusion of the tongues between the adults and the child. *International Journal of Psychoanalysis*, *30*, 225–230.

Firestein, S. K. (1974). Termination of psychoanalysis of adults: A review of the literature. *Journal of the American Psychoanalytic Association, 22,* 873–894.

Fonagy, P., & Target, M. (2002). Early intervention and the development of self-regulation. *Psychoanalytic Inquiry, 22,* 307–335.

Ford, M. G., & Tompson, L. T. (1991, August 25). Letter. *New York Times.*

Freud, S. (1914). Remembering, repeating and working-through (Further recommendations on the technique of psycho analysis II). In J. Strachey (Ed. & Trans.), *The standard edition of the complete psychological works of Sigmund Freud* (Vol. 12, pp. 145–156). London: Hogarth Press.

Freud, S. (1915). Observations on transference-love (Further recommendations on the technique of psycho-analysis III). The standard edition of the complete psychological works of Sigmund Freud (Vol. XII: 1911–1913): The Case of Schreber, Papers on Technique and Other Works, 157–171.

Freud, S. (1920). *Beyond the pleasure principle.* In J. Strachey (Ed. & Trans.), *The standard edition of the complete psychological works of Sigmund Freud* (Vol. 18, pp. 1–143). London: Hogarth Press.

Freund, J. (1991, July 26). The poet's art mined the patient's anguish. *New York Times.*

Friedan, B. (1963). *The feminine mystique.* London: Penguin.

Gentile, J. (2001). Close but no cigar: The perversion of agency and the absence of thirdness. *Contemporary Psychoanalysis, 37,* 623–654.

George, D. H. (1987). *Oedipus Anne: The poetry of Anne Sexton.* Chicago: University of Illinois Press.

George, D. H. (1988). *Sexton: Selected criticism.* Chicago: University of Illinois Press.

Goldner, V. et al. (1990). Love and violence: Gender paradoxes in volatile attachments. *Family Process, 29*(4), 343–364.

Greenson, R. R. (1958). Variations in classical psycho-analytic technique: An introduction. *International Journal of Psychoanalysis, 39,* 200–201.

Grotstein, J. S. (1991). Nothingness, meaninglessness, chaos, and the "black hole" III. *Contemporary Psychoanalysis, 27,* 1–33.

Hall, C. K. B. (1989). *Anne Sexton.* Boston: Twayne Publishers.

Hare-Mustin, R. (1992). Cries and whispers: The psychotherapy of Anne Sexton. *Psychotherapy, 29*(3), 406–9.

Harris, A. (1996). The conceptual power of multiplicity. *Contemporary Psychoanalysis, 32,* 537–552.

Harrison, A. M. (2009). Setting up the doll house: A developmental perspective on termination. *Psychoanalytic Inquiry, 29,* 174–187.

Heine, H. (2009). *Pictures of travel.* London: General Books LLC.

Herman, J. L. (1992). *Trauma and recovery.* New York: Basic Books.

Herzog, J. M. (2004). Father hunger and narcissistic deformation. *Psychoanalytic Quarterly, 73,* 893–914.

Herzog, J. M. (2005). Triadic reality and the capacity to love. *Psychoanalytic Quarterly, 74,* 1029–1052.

Hirsch, I. (2002). Beyond interpretation: Analytic interaction in the interpersonal tradition. *Contemporary Psychoanalysis, 38,* 573–587.

Hoffman, I. Z. (1996). The intimate and ironic authority of the psychoanalyst's presence. *Psychoanalytic Quarterly, 65*, 102–136.

Hughes, S. (1991). The Sexton tapes. *The Pennsylvania Gazette, 20*, 39.

Jacobs, T. (2001). On misreading and misleading patients. *International Journal of Psychoanalysis, 82*, 653–669.

Jiménez, J. P. (2008). Theoretical plurality and pluralism in psychoanalytic practice. *International Journal of Psychoanalysis, 89*, 579–599.

Jones, A. (2010). Resistance, rejection, reparation: Anne Sexton and the poetry of therapy. Unpublished dissertation, University of Sidney, Australia.

Knox, J. (2007). The fear of love: The denial of self in relationship. *Journal of Analytic Psychology, 52*, 543–563.

Kohut, H. (1966). Forms and transformations of narcissism. *Journal of the American Psychoanalytic Association, 14*, 243–272.

Kohut, H. (1977). *The restoration of the self.* New York: International Universities Press.

Kohut, H., Tolpin, M., & Tolpin, P. (1996). *Heinz Kohut: The Chicago Institute lectures.* Hillsdale, NJ: Analytic Press.

Lacan, J. (1977). *The seminar, book XI: The four fundamental concepts of psychoanalysis* (A. Sheridan, Trans.). London: Hogarth Press.

Laub, D., & Auerhahn, N. (1993). Knowing and not knowing: Forms of traumatic memory. *International Journal of Psychoanalysis, 74*, 287–302.

Levine, H. (2002). Building bridges: The negotiation of paradox in psychoanalysis. *Psychoanalytic Dialogues, 12*, 305–315.

Little, M. (1990). *Psychotic anxieties and containment: A personal record of an analysis with Winnicott.* Northvale, NJ: Jason Aronson.

McClatchy, J. D. (Ed.). (1978). *Anne Sexton: The artist and her critics.* Bloomington, IN: Indiana University Press.

McLaughlin, J. T., & Johan, M. (1992). Enactments in psychoanalysis. *Journal of the American Psychoanalytic Association, 40*, 827–841.

Middlebrook, D. W. (1991). *Anne Sexton: A biography.* New York: Vintage.

Mitchell, S. A. (1984). Object relations theories and the developmental tilt. *Contemporary Psychoanalysis, 20*, 473–499.

Mitchell, S. A. (1986). The wings of Icarus. *Contemporary Psychoanalysis, 22*, 107–132.

Modell, A. (1984). Self preservation and the preservation of the self. *Annual of Psychoanalysis, 12*, 69–86.

Murray, J. M. (1964). Narcissism and the ego ideal. *Journal of the American Psychoanalytic Association, 12*, 471–511.

Ostriker, A. (1983). That story: Anne Sexton and her transformations. In *Writing like a woman* (pp. 59–85). Ann Arbor, MI: University of Michigan Press.

Ostriker, A. (1986). *Stealing the language: The emergence of women's poetry in America.* Boston: Beacon Press.

Ostriker, A. (1989). Anne Sexton and the seduction of the audience. In D. Hunter (Ed.), *Seduction and theory: Readings of gender, representation, and rhetoric* (pp. 154–169). Chicago: University of Illinois Press.

Poland, W. S. (2000). The analyst's witnessing and otherness. *Journal of the American Psychoanalytic Association, 48,* 17–34.

Press, C. M. (2005). Psychoanalysis, creativity, and hope. *Journal of the American Academy of Psychoanalysis, 33,* 119–136.

Riviere, J. (1929). Womanliness as a masquerade. *International Journal of Psychoanalysis, 10,* 303–313.

Schafer, R. (1959). Generative empathy in the treatment situation. *Psychoanalytic Quarterly, 28,* 342–373.

Segal, H. (2006). Reflections on truth, tradition, and the psychoanalytic tradition of truth. *American Imago, 63,* 283–292.

Seligman, S. (2003). The developmental perspective in relational psychoanalysis. *Contemporary Psychoanalysis, 39,* 477–508.

Shengold, L. (1974). Soul murder: A review. *International Journal of Psychoanalytic Psychotherapy, 3,* xx.

Simon, B. (1992). Incest—See under Oedipus complex. *Journal of the American Psychoanalytic Association, 40,* 955–988.

Skorczewski, D. (1996). What prison is this? Literary critics cover incest in Anne Sexton's "Briar rose." *Signs, 21*(2), 309–342.

Stern, D. B. (2009). Partners in thought: A clinical process theory of narrative. *Psychoanalytic Quarterly, 78,* 701–731.

Tronick, E. Z. (2003). Of course all relationships are unique: How co-creative processes generate unique mother-infant and patient-therapist relationships and change other relationships. *Psychoanalytic Inquiry, 23,* 473–489.

Tronick, E. (2007). *The neurobehavioral and social-emotional development of infants and children.* New York: W. W. Norton & Company.

Turkel, A. R. (2004). The hand that rocks the cradle rocks the boat. *Journal of American Academy of Psychoanalysis, 32,* 41–53.

Umberson, D., et al. (1998). Domestic violence, personal control, and gender. *Journal of Marriage and Family, 60*(2), 442–452.

Van der Kolk, B. A. (2002). Posttraumatic therapy in the age of neuroscience. *Psychoanalytic Dialogues, 12,* 381–392.

Van der Kolk, B. A., & Van der Hart, O. (1986). The intrusive past: The flexibility of memory and the engraving of trauma. *Am. Imago, 48,* 425–454.

Winnicott, D. W. (1965). *Through paediatrics to psycho-analysis.* London: Hogarth Press.

Index